5th July 06.

Dear Mr Blair,

I am writing to you about the Natwest 3 issue. I am Ellenor Darby, daughter of Giles Darby. I am ten years old and, as I write these words, I am thinking about July 17th, AKA the day my daddy goes away.

He should not be in this mess. Just because he knew the criminal who stole the money, you and your friend Mr Bush blamed him, David Birmingham and Gary Mulgrew for something they did <u>not</u> do.

I have heard that you are not helping them through this dark path. Why? Surely, you are part of guarding Britain, aren't you? Therefore, you have <u>NO EXCUSE</u> to ignore this. If you change your direction and guard these Britains, then I will think greatly of you. Not everybody might, but I will.

Please don't take this letter as immature, rude post. I am a mature ten year old and if you ignore this I will be upset. Not just because I put a lot of effort and courage into writing this, but because of future children who have accidentally landed in this mess with no way out.

Yours Sincerely,

Ellenor Darby.

T0307377

INSIDE ALLENWOOD

INSIDE ALLENWOOD

THE STORY OF A BRITISH BANKER IN A US PRISON

GILES DARBY

WITH GEORGE HARRISON

Quiller

Published in the UK in 2021
by Quiller, an imprint of Quiller Publishing Ltd

British Library Cataloguing-in-Publication Data
A catalogue record for this book is available from the British Library

ISBN 978 1 84689 3292

Printed in Great Britain by Bell and Bain Ltd, Glasgow

Quiller
An imprint of Quiller Publishing Ltd
Wykey House, Wykey, Shrewsbury, SY4 1JA
Tel: 01939 261616
Email: info@quillerbooks.com
Website: www.quillerpublishing.com

Dedication

For Deborah Jane who loved me and supported me throughout these events.
Thank you for everything. Rest in peace.

CONTENTS

GLOSSARY

Financial terminology (UK)

CSFB	Credit Suisse First Boston
FSA	Financial Services Authority
GNW	Greenwich NatWest
LJM	A private equity vehicle set up specifically by Fastow
RBS	Royal Bank of Scotland
SPV	Special Purpose Vehicle
Swap Sub	A package of volatile financial assets tied to Enron, part-owned by NatWest

Prison terminology (USA)

BOP	Bureau of Prisons
DOJ	Department of Justice
FDC	Federal Detention Centre
MCC	Metropolitan Correctional Centre
MDC	Metropolitan Detention Centre
MSU	Maximum Security Unit
SHU	Special Housing Unit ('the hole')

PROLOGUE

WHAT THE HELL HAPPENED?

I had always thought that extraordinary things happened only to extraordinary people. Then something extraordinary happened to me: not in a good way but in an awful, earth-shattering way, leaving my career in tatters and almost destroying the entire fabric of my life.

Perhaps I should have seen disaster coming. At the time, I did not lead an ordinary life, but rather a charmed one, which I thoroughly enjoyed. I was born in India, the son of a British diplomat, but spent my early years in Africa. Later on, by now a teenager in a small market town in Wiltshire, I had decided that I wanted to do something special with my life and, in my own way, that's exactly what I did. I left home at eighteen and was now in my late thirties, with a successful career in investment banking, a beautiful, loyal and supportive wife and five wonderful daughters. We lived in a large house in north London and were lucky enough to have a weekend cottage in the New Forest as well. Life couldn't have been any better.

My time was spent making deals and travelling the world, and I lived the good life while I was doing it: a life of chauffeur-driven cars, unlimited expense accounts, fabulous restaurants, first-class flights and nights in some of the world's best hotels. Each and every moment of my day was something to relish, wherever I was and whatever I was doing. I had my health, a lovely family and great friends – and I was earning more than most people could even imagine.

And then, suddenly, I wasn't: in a flash, that life was gone forever. Because of one ill-judged decision, I lost almost everything and, before I knew it, I was sitting in solitary confinement in a US prison. It was hard not to wonder: how the hell did that happen?

Even as I was arriving at the prison, it occurred to me that there were countless life choices I could have made, or different paths I could have taken, which would have led to anywhere else but here. Equally though, taking a different route at a couple of crossroads might have sent me somewhere even worse. Over the next year or so, I would have plenty of time to map all these out and reflect on them, as well as contemplate the one decision that had resulted in me ending up at Allenwood Federal Correctional Institution, Pennsylvania, USA.

Let's go back a bit. I had joined the National Westminster Bank, commonly known as the NatWest, straight from school, and worked at my local branch in Trowbridge, Wiltshire. Those were the days when everyone wore their smartest clothes to work, staff were referred to as Mister or Miss, and going to see the bank manager was like being summoned to the headmaster's office.

I may have started at the bottom of the employment pile, spending my first few months putting around five hundred statements a day into envelopes, but I was fiercely ambitious. A combination of luck and judgement over the next few years led me to a job at the NatWest Investment Bank, via the International Banking division. Once there, some smooth-talking and deal-making ability helped me rise through the ranks and, along the way, I became great friends with Gary Mulgrew and David Bermingham, who were later to become my co-defendants: collectively we became known as the NatWest Three.

Gary was a rugged Glaswegian, a high-flyer, earmarked to go to the very top of the bank. When Greenwich Capital Holdings, an American financial services company, was acquired by NatWest in 1996 and we became Greenwich NatWest (GNW), Gary was appointed the head of Structured Finance and Origination and I was appointed Managing Director of the Energy group.

In the late nineties banks were starting to work in emerging markets for the first time since the Latin American crises of the early eighties. We were no exception. When Russia, with its vast supply of natural resources, began to open up its markets after the collapse of the Soviet Union, we decided that it would be a tremendous growth area for our business, so we created a Russian energy team and set up shop in Moscow. They were heady days and we put together a number of trade-related deals, always taking care to safeguard the bank's position against any potential volatility on the part of our new Russian partners by financing hard assets. Before long, we had made a name for ourselves and we were asked to finance a transaction involving Russian diamonds. The Russian banker concerned, Sasha, came to London to broker a deal, but he spent more time arranging his wife's store cards and taking her shopping at Harrods and Liberty's than he did discussing with us the detailed financial structures that we wanted to set up.

Eventually, excited by the potential for further business down the line, but frustrated by Sasha's lack of focus, we abandoned some of our usual asset-dependent safeguards to get the deal done. We ended up making an unsecured loan of $10 million to Sasha's bank, hoping that this initial deal would lead to more lucrative work in the near future. It was the only unsecured Russian deal we ever did.

Unfortunately for us, a few months later in the August of 1998, the Russian government unexpectedly defaulted on its debt and stopped all trade-related financing payments – including our $10 million, which had effectively gone up in smoke. Reward and remuneration at GNW was based on one thing: profitability. I knew that such a loss would affect our whole business and could potentially cost me my job, so I had to make things right somehow.

I sat down with Mulgrew and his boss, the CEO, Chip Kruger, a man who was exceptionally smart, seriously driven and highly entrepreneurial. I informed Chip of the good news first: of all the deals we'd done in Russia, all but one had been fully secured against this kind of catastrophe. Then came the bad news: the one unsecured deal had cost us $10 million.

'You'd better go and get that money back then,' said Chip, as if it was that easy.

Sure enough, the next day I was on a plane to Moscow with Misha, our leading Russian banker. We met Sasha to discuss the default and ask how we could be repaid. After the normal pleasantries, and with Misha doing the translating, we got to the point.

'Sasha,' I said, 'we need to find a way to repay that ten million dollars. Is there a trade deal we can work the figures around?'

'Or what?'

Good question, I thought.

'Are you going to write me some letters?' he asked. 'Are you going to tear up my store cards, perhaps? Take me to court? Which court?'

Then, in the middle of translating, Misha began to laugh.

'What is it?' I was hoping he had found a glimmer of light, a way out of this mess that would allow me to keep my job.

'You Westerners are pussies, Giles,' he said.

'Why?'

'Because he says all you can do is write him some letters. There are people he owes money to who will bend him over the table and stick a red-hot poker up his ass if he doesn't figure out a way to repay them.'

I slumped back in my chair. So that was that: we weren't getting the money back. I would fly back to London empty-handed, and probably get the metaphorical bullet from GNW.

As I walked back into the office a couple of days later, feeling particularly morose, I was met by a smiling Gary.

'Well done, mate,' he said. 'You've done really well.'

'Why?' I asked. 'What's happened now?'

'Other banks have declared their losses from the Russian default – some are in the hundreds of millions. We've lost only ten million dollars. Turns out it's nothing in comparison, so Kruger is delighted. Oh, and he thinks the poker story is hilarious and that you're great for even trying!'

That was the world I lived in – and that was my life for many happy years. It was fast-paced and hectic, but I loved almost every minute of it. The big-money deals and rewards were intoxicating, and even when things went wrong, I often felt as if I was living in a movie. It still felt like that after things went south and I was sent to prison, only the film had changed. It had gone from *The Wolf of Wall Street* to *The Shawshank Redemption*, and everything had happened so traumatically that I was still struggling to process it on the day I arrived at Allenwood.

'Name?' The guard's harsh voice jolted me back into the present. As he looked from me to my attorney, and then down at his clipboard, I found myself thinking that his size would have made him a handy rugby player.

'Darby,' I said, trying my best to speak loudly and clearly over the low drone of the air-conditioning. It was early May 2008. My mouth was dry, and it was excruciatingly hot. After years in limbo, fighting our case at every turn, I seemed to have arrived in hell: and I was terrified.

The guard was not impressed with my response. 'Full name!' he snapped, raising his voice so loud that I recoiled at the sound.

I swallowed hard. 'Giles Robert Hugh Darby.' My accent sounded as out of place as it undoubtedly was. You don't find many West Country bankers in places like this – a prison in the middle of Pennsylvania, some three and a half thousand miles away from home.

My friend and attorney, Matt Hennessy, helpfully pounced on the moment of silence that followed. 'He's here to self-report,' he chipped in.

The guard consulted his papers for a moment and nodded. There was something sadistic now in the lazy smirk on his face. 'Offence?' he demanded, and in that moment I made the mistake of looking down at his clipboard, searching for clues about the kind of dangerous criminals with whom I would be sharing my new home. The guard caught me looking and burst into life, jerking his papers away from me as if I had tried to steal them.

'Don't look at my file!' he yelled, spraying a shower of spit as he spoke. 'Don't you fucking know what you're here for?'

'Wire fraud,' I said, knocked off kilter by his sudden aggression. I could feel my heart racing. 'Thirty-seven months.'

He scrawled a note on his clipboard, and then looked over at Matt. 'All right,' he grunted. 'Say your goodbyes.'

Matt and I had been on a two-year journey together. We had become good friends and it was hard to keep my emotions in check as we embraced. We shared a few warm words, but we both knew there was no point in delaying the inevitable. As it happened, there was barely even time for this brief farewell, before the short-tempered guard clipped on my cuffs and motioned for me to follow him into the prison. My sentence had officially begun.

I was led through to the reporting area, my last stop before entering the prison proper. Inside there was a small table heaped with a tangle of garish orange clothes in different sizes, although none of them looked to be in particularly good condition.

'What's the address for us to ship your clothes?' he asked.

'The UK?' I knew it was optimistic as soon as I said it.

'We don't ship overseas. What do you think we are, Darby? Amazon?'

I suspected that offering a couple of dollars to cover postage and packing wouldn't help, so I had no choice but to surrender my clothes forever. Of all the myriad injustices and losses that I endured, strangely this one still irritates. Not only did I have to sacrifice a good pair of jeans, I had also made the mistake of wearing one of my favourite American Eagle shirts. But there was nothing I could do about it, so begrudgingly I handed over the clothes, never to be seen again.

Before I could get dressed, I had to undergo the obligatory strip search – one of the things I had been dreading the most. In my mind was an incident on extradition day, two years earlier, when my co-defendants and I were first escorted onto American soil by armed US marshals. These days I can laugh about it, but it wasn't funny at the time.

Upon landing in the US and going through border controls, I had been taken to a side room to be searched. I was ordered to face the wall and strip, layer by layer, until I was standing in only my underpants. The marshal checked my clothes as I dropped them to the floor. At this point I was dreading the worst – the spine-chilling order to drop my pants and bend over – but the marshal simply told me to get dressed again. I couldn't help smiling with relief as I turned around and pulled on my shirt.

'What the fuck are you smiling at?' he shouted at me. 'Do you think this is funny?'

'Er, no sir,' I stammered. But the damage had already been done.

'Then why are you fucking smiling?' he repeated.

'You really want to know?'

'Yeah.'

'I thought you were going to stick your finger up my arse.'

Now the marshal was really riled, shouting point-blank into my face.

'Well, do you want me to stick my finger up your *ass?*'

Thoughts of latex gloves flashed through my mind: that loud snapping sound and the dentist-chair smell of cheap plastic.

'Um, no sir. I really don't.'

Evidently, he was no keener on the idea than I was. He shook his head and then snarled at me, 'Go put your clothes on!'

Thus I was reassured when my initial strip search at Allenwood turned out to be less eventful. After a quick once-over and a spread of the cheeks, I was given my all-orange outfit, right down to the dyed socks, boxers and shoes. I felt a wave of sheer relief as I stepped into the scratchy jumpsuit without having to endure so much as a prod. The tiniest of small mercies can make a big difference when you're on the inside.

New arrivals at most American federal correctional facilities get their first introduction to prison life in solitary confinement, also known as the Special Housing Unit (SHU) or the hole. The experience is designed to keep you in line by demonstrating exactly how miserable your life could be if you don't behave. Once you've done a few days or weeks in the hole, they put you in with the general population. But if you misbehave at any point, then you go straight back. It's a great way to teach people a lesson and, having experienced it, I can say it works extremely well. Only a masochist could possibly enjoy being in solitary. It's an utterly miserable experience.

As well as housing the newest inmates, the hole is also used as a punishment for poorly behaved or particularly violent prisoners, and as a refuge for those who have problems being in the general population, including paedophiles or sex offenders. All this meant that I would be spending my first night in the worst neighbourhood imaginable.

When I arrived to be processed at the SHU, even the guards couldn't resist commenting on how ridiculous I looked. The all-orange outfit was one thing, but the healthy Texas tan – which I had picked up over the long months I was living in Houston, fighting the case – meant that I looked like the man from the Tango adverts.

'You've obviously been living too well,' one guard growled ominously. 'That tan'll soon disappear.'

Next it was time for my tests. First up was a quick interview with one of the doctors, who asked a series of questions about my health, state of mind and sexual habits. The idea was to work out whether I posed a risk to myself or any of the other inmates, which, apparently, I didn't. Clearly, a few minutes with a sheet of predetermined questions is nowhere near enough time to put together a whole psychological profile, but it was more than good enough for my hosts, the US Bureau of Prisons, to give me a thumbs-up and a rubber stamp saying I was fine.

After that I was checked for TB (also fine), and then I was handed a stack of supplies to last for my first few days in the SHU: a roll of toilet paper, twelve sheets of A4, a couple of pencils, a few random paperbacks and a towel. All in all, not an easy stash to carry when your hands are chained together, but I managed to shuffle my way awkwardly into my new home without dropping anything. It was around three in the afternoon when the heavy door swung shut on my poky cell, and then I was finally alone: more alone than I had ever been at any point in my life.

The cell where I spent my first few nights could not have been further from the luxury I'd been used to in my investment banking days. It was barely fifteen feet by six, with a bunk bed pushed against one wall and nothing but a thin, blue mattress to lie on. I sat on the feeble mattress and my heart sank when I felt the cold, hard slats of the bed poking through. The only other furnishings were a stainless-steel toilet with a sink attached and a desk with an accompanying stool, all of which were bolted to the floor.

There was one small window, barred and frosted, of course, so I couldn't even distract myself by looking outside. The cumulative effect of this awful place was a combination of boredom and disorientation – something made worse by the fact that with no watch, no television and no radio, there was no way I could possibly tell the time. All I knew was whether it was night or day.

The cell may not have been much to write home about, but even so I forced myself to sit at the cold steel desk and begin a letter to the wonderful family I had left behind. During my time in prison, I would go on to write many letters to my loved ones back in England – trying to maintain a relatively upbeat tone as I filled them in on my new life.

International telephone calls were prohibitively expensive at a dollar per minute, so these letters quickly became my main connection to the world outside the prison – the real world, as I saw it. A dollar per minute may not sound like much, but inmates had a monthly spending limit for the commissary, the prison shop, which included phone time. My family regularly paid dollars into my prison account, but once I had spent enough to supplement my diet and ensure that I would stay healthy, there was not much left over for phone calls. Plus, it was hard not to get choked up when I heard everyone's voices, so I tended to stick to the letters. Writing them was a welcome distraction, and from my first moment in the SHU, I was desperate for any way to pass the time.

It didn't take long for me to grind both the stubby pencils provided down to a nub. With no chance of getting my hands on a sharpener – blades of any kind were not exactly welcomed in Allenwood – I had to use my teeth and fingernails to scrape away enough wood to continue writing, a process as slow as it was painful. By the time I gave up for the afternoon, my fingers were bleeding and the only thing I could taste was pencil lead. All that was left for me to do was to alternate between reading and napping for what felt like hours.

Eventually, the flap in my cell door opened and a tray of food appeared. I managed to make this first meal behind bars – a bowl of unidentified broth with bread and potatoes – last for all of twenty minutes, and then it was back to boredom. I have always been a very energetic and active person, so being locked up like this was a special form of torture for me. It was only day one of my thirty-seven-month sentence, and it had already become clear that I would have to adjust quickly if I was going to stand a chance of making it through the ordeal in front of me.

Gary had once said to me: 'We've got to come out of this with our health and sanity, Giles. If we do, we can come back. If we don't, we can't.' I was determined to walk out of prison with both.

One thing I did have ample time to do in that sad little cell was think. The Americans take a very punitive view of justice, and I suppose part of their idea of punishment is leaving you alone with your thoughts, without any distractions, to ponder your wrongdoing for days and months on end.

Except I wasn't really sure I *had* done anything wrong, and so instead I felt myself being consumed by a burning sense of injustice.

That first night was also filled with thoughts of the people and places I had left behind. There was my family back in Wiltshire, the local bars and pubs I enjoyed so much, Melksham rugby club, and all my friends both at home in England and in Texas. What were they getting up to whilst I was locked up in Allenwood? Were my daughters coping? Was my mum worrying about me?

All these questions and a million more nagged away, and I felt a huge twinge of guilt and sadness at the thought of everyone getting on with their lives on the outside. I wanted everyone I loved to be happy and to carry on, of course, but it hurt more than I can ever explain that I wasn't there with them. This was one of my first prison lessons: the more you have on the outside, the worse it is to be inside. If you have nothing to live for outside prison, then being inside may be easier. But if you have a full and happy life, it becomes almost impossible to bear being locked away.

Worst of all was the knowledge that my daughters were growing up quickly and I wasn't with them. As I will go on to describe, all of our lives had changed forever in mid-2002, when Gary, David and I were indicted by the Enron Task Force. We were extradited to the US in July 2006 and it was now May 2008. We had been living with the nightmare for six years already, six years out of my daughters' young lives and perhaps another two still to go. Every day that passed was another day without their Dad, one more day since I had been able to hug and kiss them and tell them that I'd always love them, and that I'd be home before they knew it. In that way, being in prison was a kind of living death, in the sense that everyone else's lives – family and friends – carried on, while mine was suspended by a depressing pause button.

In the cell that night, my loneliness and homesickness were the culmination of a truly agonising time. For the previous two years, because we weren't US citizens we had been considered a flight risk, so the terms of our bond (known in the UK as bail) had meant that we couldn't even go near an airport, let alone go home. Instead, we'd had to rely on our friends and families making the long and expensive flight out to our temporary base in Houston, Texas, to snatch a few days or weeks together. Then they would go back to their lives in England and we'd be stuck in America fighting a case that we should never have had to contest in the first place.

I tried to spare myself the self-pity, although I was convinced that we had been stitched up. We had been well and truly hung out to dry by federal officials (the Feds), the US Department of Justice (DOJ), the so-called Enron Task Force, the British government, the US justice system, by NatWest and the Royal Bank of Scotland (RBS). Other than one meeting in Houston, all of the alleged activity related to the fraud we had been accused of perpetrating took place in the UK, so we should never have faced a legal case in the States. We had even written three times to RBS – the supposedly defrauded party – inviting them to prosecute us in the UK if they thought they had been defrauded. They declined each time.

But moping about it wouldn't do me any good now. I owed it to everyone I had left behind in England to put my head down, do my time and get back to them as soon as possible, in the best mental and physical shape I could possibly be.

Lying on that cold, hard bed with its paper-thin excuse for a mattress, I also found myself replaying the previous twenty-four hours – a whirlwind of time that included a last night of freedom with Matt, my ever-present attorney. I had tried to make the best of it, but it's hard to enjoy yourself when you know you'll be in prison the next day – a prospect that loomed over me like the world's worst hangover. The judge had ordered Matt to accompany me to Allenwood, so we had flown to New York and stayed at a swanky hotel in Manhattan the night before. There we had knocked back a few final drinks, and I'd tried to focus on the positives.

My sentence could have been a lot worse, for one thing. If we had taken our case all the way to trial and lost – not that we could have afforded to do that – the federal prosecutors would have pushed for us to spend the maximum time behind bars. In our case, that was thirty-five years. At least with my plea deal, I'd be out soon and able to reclaim the rest of my life. Crucially, our deal also included the promise that the Americans would expedite our transfer back to the UK to serve our sentences.

In good old Blighty, in general, prisoners serve only half of their time before they are paroled, so moving to a prison in the UK would effectively halve my remaining time. The judge was aware of this when we were sentenced, which is why he went for the headline thirty-seven months, knowing we'd probably serve less than half of that. In America, the illusion of justice being done is all that matters: the land of the free, indeed.

But by now you're probably wondering how a high-flying British banker ended up facing the possibility of a thirty-five-year prison sentence in America. Well, to understand what happened to me, you need to understand what happened at Enron. Read on, and I will do my best to shed some light on the murky sequence of events which brought us here.

CHAPTER 1

THE SMARTEST GUYS IN THE ROOM

Enron was a giant American energy company that was the darling of the entire business and financial world in the late 1990s. *Fortune* magazine named it America's most innovative company for six years running and, at the height of its success in 2000, Enron claimed to be raking in over $100 billion in annual revenue. Headquartered in Houston, Texas, Enron was the pride of the state – as big as the Dallas Cowboys and considerably more lucrative.

For years, Enron's skyrocketing share price and charismatic young executives were so magnetic, nobody seemed to notice that some of these very executives were cheating: they were using a whole host of fraudulent accounting tricks to inflate artificially the value of the business, and to hide its mounting debts where nobody could see them. Meanwhile, thousands of investors were getting rich off the back of Enron's successes, having hitched their fortunes to the stratospheric share price. It all seemed too good to be true and, eventually, it became clear that it was.

The bigger Enron became, the more questions started to be asked. In 2001 it finally emerged that Enron was a house of cards – a flimsy tower without any real foundations. The truth, behind all the gloss and the glamour, was that the business was almost completely worthless and that some of its top executives had been fraudulently enriching themselves for years at the company's expense. Most of the employees and the people who dealt with Enron had no idea. Only a select few were on the take, but that was all it took. The entire business folded almost overnight, dragging thousands of jobs into the dirt with it, and, at the same time, the collapse wiped out every single retirement plan that had relied on Enron stock holding its value. Literally millions of Americans lost out in what quickly became known as the Enron Scandal.

Enron filed for bankruptcy in December 2001 and President George W. Bush vowed, even before the dust had settled, that people would go to jail as a consequence. I remember sitting at home watching him say so on television, and thinking that this was good politics. He, too, was from Texas and Enron had been one of his biggest donors in the recent presidential campaign, so he needed to be seen to be tough on the failed company and its bosses.

At the same time, the whole of Wall Street was furious: a handful of executives at one of the biggest firms in the world had been lying and cheating their way to vast personal fortunes, all the while screwing over the little guy. No one who had invested their hard-earned money in Enron would be receiving a cent of it back. Pensions, funds and share prices collapsed – and it was ordinary, hard-working Americans who suffered the most.

It was a classic tale of corporate greed and financial-sector largesse, which was too good for politicians and public prosecutors to resist. Pretty much the entire American media demanded blood: they wanted the so-called 'Smartest Guys in the Room', the crooks behind the Enron scandal, to be punished. The DOJ's Enron Task Force used highly controversial tactics to send more than thirty people to prison for their involvement with the doomed company. When I heard Bush say that people would go to prison, little did I know that I would be one of them.

David Bermingham, Gary Mulgrew and I were sucked into the ensuing witch hunt: never mind that we had absolutely nothing to do with Enron's collapse. The three of us were senior investment bankers; we ran the Structured Finance Group at GNW and Enron was one of our most important clients. They were extremely active in the financing markets and paid out tens of millions in fees every year to banks like ours. The companies and financiers we had dealt with in Russia were certainly not straightforward. I had turned down numerous bribes and proposals, and we were always cautious in our dealings with them, but by contrast Enron appeared to be the client of our dreams. At least we certainly thought so, until the company went bust and our association turned into a nightmare, as it did for very many people.

Throughout the late nineties, the three of us had worked with the company and their financiers on many legitimate deals but, in the end, we were tarred and feathered by association. You could also say that we were guilty of being successful bankers at a time when the press and the public were starting to realise how much they hated them.

As head of the global energy business at GNW – the investment banking and trading division of NatWest – my team and I arranged and financed deals for major players in the energy market. At that time, Enron was one of the most aggressive energy companies in the world, and their finance team was a delight to work with, because everything they touched seemed to turn to gold. We worked with them in both London and Houston and our group at GNW successfully completed numerous deals with them. We all worked hard and played hard. Looking back, we had some great times and I don't regret any of them.

At that level, deal-making is as much about who you know as what you know. It was part of my job to know as many people at the company as possible, and to make sure that when they were contemplating their next deal, we were always in the frame. There were dinners, social events and regular hospitality trips: we attended the Monaco Grand Prix, spent nights in Las Vegas and Miami and went skiing in the Alps. Because of these trips, Gary and I became good friends with some of Enron's top executives, including the Chief Financial Officer, Andy Fastow, and his right-hand man, Michael Kopper.

I also played golf regularly with various Enron people. On one memorable occasion, we were closing out our latest deal but couldn't agree on a fee. I wanted $250,000 but the Enron financier wouldn't go above $200,000. At the start of the round, we agreed that whoever won the game would prevail. The bank won – and we then used the increased fee to entertain a group of GNW and Enron executives at the exclusive Skibo Castle in Scotland so that we would be in the frame for the next deal. That was the way it was with those guys, and I loved being a part of it, though like everyone else in the financial world at the time, I had absolutely no idea that certain Enron executives were defrauding the business.

Much of Enron's apparent success came from the practice of shifting corporate debt off the balance sheet, so that it looked as if the company was healthier than it really was. For example, Enron would finance an asset like a power station, and then put it into an offshore (and off-balance sheet) company created specifically for that purpose. The industry term for these companies is a Special Purpose Vehicle (SPV). Enron had more SPVs than you could count, with the exact number and dollar amounts kept as one of the company's most closely guarded secrets.

Alongside the asset, the SPV would also house the debt from financing the asset, which would then be ring-fenced and offered to lenders, who could buy the debt and then sell it on. All this meant that Enron could make money – through cash flow from the asset itself and from deals with lenders – without any of the debt from the asset appearing on Enron's books. The debt was almost always tied to the SPV, and not to Enron itself. Only the Enron financiers knew the amounts involved.

As a market-leading financing business with some very smart bankers, we supported Enron and helped them to create many of these complicated vehicles. We were in the business to make money and Enron always paid up. We avoided becoming too exposed to Enron's debt by underwriting and syndicating their loans – selling on their debt in the financial markets – which meant that we could keep on making more deals for them. Enron, and Andy Fastow in particular, loved us because of it. The big problem for us and the financial markets, completely unbeknownst at the time, was that Enron was accumulating so many SPVs that it would become impossible to keep track of all their investments – and, more importantly, all the debt packaged in with them.

Among my closest colleagues during this period were Gary and David – the two men who would later become my co-defendants. Gary Mulgrew and I met in the mid-1980s, when we were junior bankers at NatWest. He is a smart, intelligent and very charismatic individual, who is extremely proud of his Glaswegian roots. We were great friends and we made an excellent team, rising through the ranks together. He was dynamic, visionary and the ideas guy, but he paid little attention to detail. He was also good fun and told a great story, although he was inclined to stretch the truth on occasion – something that caused problems for me after we were indicted. I was the more grounded one, who would take Gary's ideas and find practical ways to implement them.

David Bermingham and I met in the early 1990s, when we were both working in tax structuring for clients. He was quite brilliant, a real intellectual and extremely likeable. I enjoyed working with him very much. David would come up with great structuring ideas and I was the sales guy who tried to keep things simple for our clients. However, you could also say that he lacked a certain common sense, and that was something else that would land us in a whole heap of trouble further down the line.

The three of us would later come to be known as the NatWest Three, but at the time we were simply an ambitious trio of bankers doing what bankers do best: cutting deals and making money. In our most lucrative deals, we worked closely with Fastow and his team. We never suspected that he would turn out to be one of the most notorious white-collar criminals in history and the man who, along with Michael Kopper, would cause the three of us to end up in prison, our lives and careers shattered. But more of that later.

Despite the successes of our financing business, NatWest as a whole was struggling and Royal Bank of Scotland (RBS) was in the process of taking over the business. A takeover would mean a restructure, and there was a good chance that GNW would be cannibalised once the deal was done. Having been part of the dynamic, flexible and entrepreneurial set-up at GNW, David, Gary and I had no intention of sticking around to see whether we would still have jobs under the restrictive management of a large bank such as RBS, so we sounded out new opportunities. Gary quickly received a great offer to set up a new financing business at a Canadian bank and was keen for David and me to join him.

If we were going to change banks and continue making lucrative deals, we needed to know that we would still be able to work with all our existing clients, and especially Enron. Gary arranged a meeting with Andy Fastow in Houston to tell him we were thinking of moving, and to ask whether we could keep working together if we did. It was all the same to Fastow, and he told us that nothing would change on the Enron side of things. He later went on to tell Gary that since we were about to leave GNW, he had a separate opportunity that might interest us.

In the past Fastow had occasionally discussed with Gary the possibility of working together at some point and he had recently experienced great success with a private equity vehicle known as LJM, in which GNW had been partially involved. Gary (and I) took it for granted that the mentioned 'opportunity' was to do with LJM, since Fastow was setting up another vehicle, LJM2, and – we assumed – a European offshoot. Naturally, we were keen to work as closely as possible with a wizard like Fastow, and so Gary indicated that yes, such a proposal would be interesting. He then asked David to meet Kopper in New York to look at the options.

It turned out that the deal had nothing to do with LJM. Instead, Fastow invited us to invest $250,000 of our own money to buy in to a new SPV. Evidently, he needed our money because the SPV would then qualify as an outside investment, for Fastow's and Enron's purposes. He knew we would be able to provide the funds, because he was aware that we were leaving GNW.

Gary and I speculated that the money would be used to buy an asset from a telecoms start-up that Fastow wanted to sell from Enron into this new vehicle. Fastow was obviously in it to make money for himself, but we didn't know how. All we knew was that if anyone could provide us with a return, it would be him. He was *Fortune* magazine's CFO of the Year – why wouldn't we trust him?

Naïve? Perhaps. Illegal? Not as far as we knew.

By now it was early 2000, and the looming takeover (due to be finalised on 1 April) was fuelling a frantic atmosphere at GNW. The business had been offered a special one-off bonus at the end of the quarter as an incentive for staff to stay on until the takeover was complete, and as a reward for all the money we had made GNW over the previous few years. With RBS about to seize control, we were all told that we would get a pay-out proportionate to the amount of money we could make before the end of the quarter, provided that we stuck around that long. As a result we were under instruction to shift every single asset the group owned, and to cash in on as much of it as possible before time was up. One of the assets we could sell was our share in Swap Sub – a complicated package of volatile financial assets tied to Enron and partly owned by NatWest.

I asked the analysts at NatWest to evaluate how much the company's stake in Swap Sub was worth, as the value of the asset changed greatly on a daily basis. At that date, the value was minimal. Fastow had offered $1 million to buy it and our analysts agreed that this was a good price for us. I ran the deal past one of the senior executives, Neil Coulbeck, who verbally gave the deal the okay and agreed that we should take the money. Swap Sub was only one of several big-ticket sales we presided over in that final quarter, and we put it to the back of our minds as soon as the deal was done. Our business did so well for GNW in that short, frantic period that my own bonus was £350,000.

Simultaneously, David had been making progress with the Fastow opportunity, which was being handled by his sidekick, Kopper. It turned out that the company in which we had been invited to invest was intended to buy the very same Swap Sub asset GNW was now selling. We knew GNW was getting a fair price – as confirmed by our analysts – but also realised that we couldn't invest with Fastow while we were still employed by GNW.

In his excellent book, *A Price to Pay*, David describes in detail how he agreed an 'option' with Kopper to enable us to make the investment if we left GNW or, if we decided to stay (I had been offered a position by RBS at this point), to let the option to exercise the option lapse and not proceed. David explained to Gary and me that the option was not something we had to disclose to our employers, since it would only be executed if we left GNW and therefore not disclosable at that point since we would no longer be employees. Much to my subsequent regret, I accepted David's advice, safe (or so I thought) in the knowledge that GNW would be getting a more than fair price for the sale of its share of Swap Sub.

I was also labouring under the misapprehension that Gary had informed his own boss, the CEO of GNW, Chip Kruger, that we were doing a private deal with Fastow. When Gary had initially mentioned Fastow's opportunity to me, I had said that I was fine with being involved so long as Kruger was also okay with it. Gary said that he had mentioned something to Kruger, but as stated in David Bermingham's book, it was 'pretty non-specific', because at the time we didn't know what form the opportunity might take. Again, and much to my subsequent regret, when we were made aware of the detail, none of the three of us informed Chip about it.

Indeed, a few years later, after we had been indicted and arrested at Bow Street Police station, we were given the affidavits of both Neil Coulbeck and Chip Kruger. Neil stated that he had 'no recollection' of any meeting with any of us about the sale of the asset. Chip stated that neither Gary, David or myself ever disclosed to him that we were considering investing in the asset ourselves, and that such an investment represented a conflict of interest with our employers. He also stated that if he had known anything about the transaction, he would have terminated our employment immediately. That was hard to argue with, since if we had thought that we were doing anything wrong, or we had suspected Fastow was acting illegally, we would never have made the investment in the first place.

Meanwhile, we were also negotiating to join the Canadian bank, and contracts were being finalised. My own guaranteed quarterly earnings were roughly in line with the bonus I had recently been paid. I was making so much money legitimately that I had absolutely no incentive at all to do anything illegal. That was a point I made many times to my attorneys when we were fighting the case, although it was an argument that probably didn't – and still doesn't – endear me to many of our banker-bashing critics.

I chose to take the job at the Canadian bank and made preparations to leave GNW, after which there would be a three-month period before taking up the new position with the Canadians. The three of us exercised the option and agreed with Fastow to cash out of the deal in which we had invested.

At the time, we still didn't know what he had done to make so much money, but we were understandably delighted when he paid us our share of the profits: $7.3 million between the three of us, working out at around $2.4 million (£1.5 million) each. As far as we were concerned, it was a fabulous deal. We each declared the returns to the tax man and in due course paid the full tax: that's how sure we were that our deal with Fastow had been above board. We had no inkling at all that we had participated in a gigantic fraud.

Eighteen months passed before Enron collapsed in late 2001, and we learned for the first time that anything was amiss. As GNW employees, we had sold our share of Swap Sub for what we thought it was worth, but NatWest was not the only bank that held part of Swap Sub: Credit Suisse First Boston (CSFB) had also owned an equal share. Post indictment, we found out that when he was buying all the shares in Swap Sub, Fastow had paid CSFB $10 million for their portion of it – even though our analysts had valued it at a fraction of that price. This made it appear as if we had defrauded NatWest by deliberately selling our stake at an undervalue, when a rival bank had made ten times as much on exactly the same deal. This, plus the fact that we reinvested back into the asset post the sale, made taking the profit for ourselves the basis of the indictment against us.

Those two sales – from CSFB and NatWest – meant Fastow's SPV became the owner of Swap Sub. Having paid a total of $11 million for it, he collapsed it for a $30 million payment from Enron. What was so wrong is that he was in charge of the SPV while also working as CFO at Enron. It was a monumental conflict of interest and it should never have been allowed to happen.

Between acquiring Swap Sub and collapsing it, Fastow had marked the price up by $19 million – all of it profit. He gave $7.3 million of that to be shared among the three of us, and kept the rest for himself and some of his favoured Enron execs, including Kopper. It is a prime case study in how Enron's top financiers were cashing in at the expense of the company. We were used purely as cover to conceal one of the numerous crimes that were committed.

We still don't know to this day why Fastow paid so much for CSFB's share, when it had been objectively proven to be worth far less. When in 2007 we eventually agreed to a plea bargain with the DOJ, all sides had to agree to a Statement of Facts setting out the events relating to the case. In section 29 of the statement, the DOJ acknowledged that we were completely unaware that Fastow had agreed with Enron they would pay him $30 million to collapse the assets in Swap Sub, which had been the whole basis for our indictment and extradition.

So that is how we became embroiled in the Enron scandal and came to be accused of defrauding NatWest. Years later, we agreed to plead out to one count of wire fraud and, as stated, the prosecution accepted in the Statement of Facts that we had had no idea of what Fastow had done. However, for our part, we accepted in our plea bargain that we had made a terrible error of judgement and breached our contract of employment by taking from our then employer (GNW) the opportunity to invest in Fastow's deal for ourselves. That constituted one count of wire fraud for which we accepted a punishment of thirty-seven months in prison.

When Enron collapsed, it emerged that Fastow and others had taken part in numerous other fraudulent transactions – he was indicted on seventy-eight counts – and he ended up being sentenced to six years in prison for his crimes. It was originally ten years, but subsequently reduced due to his cooperation with the DOJ against other Enron executives. Eventually, more than thirty people were imprisoned because of their criminal activities, including the CEO, Jeff Skilling, plus Kopper and numerous other Enron staffers. What made our case unique was that we were extradited and tried in America even though we were British, like our alleged victim, NatWest, and lived and worked in the UK.

The argument the Americans used to get us to the States was that one meeting with Fastow had taken place on US soil and numerous emails had used US internet infrastructure, so they demanded we face justice in America. When Prime Minister Tony Blair acquiesced to the Bush government's demands (not for the first time), our case was elevated to the front pages of the British newspapers and became the subject of debate in the House of Commons.

The way a lot of people saw it, we had been sold out by our own government to appease the Americans' need for justice at any cost. Commentators suggested we were only indicted in the first place because the Feds wanted us to act as witnesses against Fastow and his sidekicks, who of course were far bigger scalps than we ever were.

In the early days of the scandal, in 2002, we were offered a chance to cooperate with the prosecutors against Fastow and the others, but being (a) convinced of our innocence and (b) utterly naïve in the ways of the US justice system, we spurned that opportunity and made the mistake of fighting the case at every turn. It ended up being drawn out for so long that Fastow pleaded guilty and was in prison before we were again offered a chance to cut a deal with the DOJ. After that, it felt as if the Feds were prosecuting the three of us for no better reason than to get numbers into jail.

Now you know how I ended up in a cell in the SHU at Allenwood prison. There was only one consolation to this whole dreadful saga: the promise from the DOJ that as part of our plea deal, we would be repatriated back to the UK as quickly as the internal administration of the US Bureau of Prisons (BOP) would allow, thereby immediately cutting our remaining sentences in half. I had tried to focus on this scant positive ever since the deal was agreed.

Realistically, I wouldn't know how badly I'd been treated until I was back in the UK and out of prison. Back then, I believed that it would be a good result if I could be home and free within eighteen months. Only time would tell whether that hope was misplaced.

CHAPTER 2

WELCOME TO THE SPECIAL HOUSING UNIT

The drive from New York to Allenwood took only a few hours. It was an easy enough journey, but the mood in the car was miserable. I could tell Matt felt bad for me, and as the Pennsylvania countryside shot past the window, we talked briefly about the case. Matt and I both wanted answers to the same questions. Was there any way we could have won if the case had gone to trial? Did things really have to end like this? Could we have struck a better deal? They were all good questions, but there was no point in torturing ourselves with what-ifs. As far as I was concerned, the deal was done, and we couldn't change it: as for whether it was a good one or not, the only way to find that out would be to wait and see whether the Americans stuck to their side of the plea bargain.

We arrived in Allenwood early in the morning, leaving a bit of time to kill before I had to report to the prison. What I really fancied was one final pint, but no such luck. Nowhere was serving booze at that hour, so I would have to spend the day the same way I was to spend the next year and a half: teetotal.

The first thing I noticed as we approached the compound was the sheer scale of the place. It was enormous, with three full-size prisons arranged over some four thousand acres of grounds. There was a separate prison for each level of security – high, medium and low – and I felt like a schoolboy on a field trip as I peered through the car window, trying to work out my eventual destination.

As part of our plea deal, the Department of Justice had decided that all three of us should be placed in low-security prisons, which are typically home to long-serving or mostly rehabilitated offenders. If we had been American citizens, we might have been allowed to serve our time in an open prison, known as a camp; but we were foreigners, the risk of us fleeing the country was deemed to be too great, and so we were stuck behind bars.

As I approached my new home, my initial assessment was an optimistic one though – or as optimistic as it could be, given the circumstances. One of the first things I saw through the mesh of security towers, barbed wire and chain-link fences was a full-sized football pitch, along with a series of basketball courts and a baseball cage. Hundreds of inmates were running around in the fresh air and a group of men were actually playing football. It helped that it was a hot, sunny day, but Allenwood didn't seem as daunting as I had imagined it would be.

I was still terrified, of course, but I stayed composed as Matt passed me the scissors to cut the electronic tag from my ankle. With a snap, the familiar band split in two, and my leg was free. That tag had been my constant companion for the past twenty-two months and I had been forced to pay some $6,000 for the privilege, since the US government insisted on levying a daily charge. It was one hell of an expensive bracelet, but at least I wouldn't be needing it where I was going next.

I don't think I slept at all that first night in prison. It was no real surprise, given the combination of the paper-thin mattress and the tremendous noise from the corridor. I had done a lot of research before coming to Allenwood, and I had come across countless stories about inmates who involuntarily whimper in their sleep, effectively broadcasting a message to every thug in earshot that they're a soft touch. This was a surefire way to mark yourself out as a victim, ripe for extortion – or worse. I knew that my first night would set the tone for how the rest of my sentence would progress, so when morning finally came, I was pleased to have got through it without drawing attention to myself.

I didn't hear any whimpering from elsewhere in solitary that night, but I did hear an awful lot of shouting. Inexplicably, there was also one inmate nearby who kept flushing his toilet over and over, all through the night.

The SHU was arranged with ten cells on either side of a walkway, so there were twenty cells in total. Many of the prisoners spent the whole night yelling to people in other cells, and their shouts took on an eerie quality as they echoed through the total darkness. That first night, one man spent a solid twenty minutes shouting in Spanish. At first, the sound was intimidating, but the monologue quickly became mind-numbing, particularly since I couldn't understand a word of it. As I listened to the shouts and endless toilet flushes, I wondered what kind of nightmare world I now found myself in.

I discovered a couple of days later that many of the inmates have their own personal radios. It was only then that I learned what the man had been shouting about: he'd heard the weather forecast for the next day, and he was relaying it to his mates on the wing. It goes to show how prison can get in your head, making you assume the worst of people who are not necessarily as crazy or dangerous as they may seem.

It was still dark when breakfast was pushed through the flap in my cell door. I was expecting gruel, so I was pleasantly surprised to see a syrup-covered waffle and an apple. It wasn't exactly a five-star meal, but it could have been a lot worse. After I had finished eating, a guard appeared on the walkway beside my door.

'Hey, Darby,' he called. 'You going out?' This was the first thing anyone had said to me since I had been left alone the previous day.

'Out where?' I asked. I knew I wouldn't be getting out of here for a long time, and it occurred to me that the guard might be winding me up. But then again, by this point I was just grateful for the interaction with another human being.

'Outside,' he said, as if it was the most obvious thing in the world. 'Exercise.'

I literally jumped at the chance to get out of my tiny cell, even if it meant that the cuffs had to go back on. With my hands clasped in front of me I was led to the yard, where inmates were milling around in a series of large cages. I ended up in a cage with an American-Chinese guy whom I later learned was called Bo, but before I had a chance to introduce myself, I was distracted by a chorus of shouts from the other inmates.

'She got tits, she got tits!' one inmate yelled.

'Get your tits out!' called another.

'Yeah, show us your tits!'

The shouts kept coming, from all directions and seemingly aimed towards our cage. The inmates had all worked themselves up into such an excited frenzy that the atmosphere was a bit like being at a particularly rowdy football match, only the spectators were all wearing orange and standing around in giant cages. I started to wonder if they were shouting at me, but then I turned round and saw what all the fuss was about.

There was a third inmate entering our cage – an attractive Mexican girl with long, dark hair and a huge chest. It was the first time I'd seen a woman on the inside and, judging by the reception she was getting, I assumed the same went for many of the other inmates. She stood in the far corner of the cage, ignoring the shouts of the men all around her. Some of the inmates in neighbouring cages were pressed against the slats by now, still hooting and yelling with delight as they implored the Mexican girl to take off her orange, prison-issue top.

I thought it was odd that Bo ignored her, turning away in what seemed to be disgust. We had to raise our voices over the shouts of the other inmates, but Bo and I managed to have a quick conversation. He was the first prisoner at Allenwood with whom I'd had a chance to speak, and I was eager to make a good impression. He told me that he had been in solitary for four months, as a punishment for running an illegal gambling syndicate over in the main prison. I said that it was my first day and he asked how I was settling in. All in all, he didn't seem like the kind of hardened criminal I had been worried about. We had been chatting for a few minutes when he looked over at the Mexican girl and pulled a face.

I looked back at the girl and wondered what Bo's problem was. A few more minutes passed, and I started to feel sorry for her. She was still getting a lot of abuse, and Bo was making a point of standing as far away from her as possible. She was being treated like a leper, and I couldn't understand why. I made my way over to her side of the cage. I asked her what her name was and she replied that it was Alexandra.

It seemed impossible that a woman would be among the male inmates at a place like Allenwood. I assumed that a processing cock-up must have sent her here and that the guards must be wondering what to do with her. After all, I knew first-hand that the US justice system was nowhere near as foolproof and efficient as the Americans like to make out. I asked her what she was doing here, and she told me she had spent the last ten months in solitary.

'They've transferred me here hoping that I'll eventually be able to go in with the general population,' she continued.

I looked at her, amazed. 'Why would they do that?'

She shrugged. 'Well, I'm a guy.'

I was stunned. After that I shut my mouth and joined Bo on the other side of the cage. All of the inmates in the yard had been watching my encounter, and I didn't want to give the wrong impression. 'Fucking faggot,' growled Bo. (Subsequently, Alexandra did get placed into the general population and made a small fortune selling her wares most days in the unit shower block.)

To pass the rest of the time outdoors, I struck up a conversation with one of the guards. He told me that I would get an hour in the yard, and then it would be time to go back to my cell until the same time tomorrow. Unsurprisingly, he picked up on my accent and asked where I was from. In my experience, most Americans don't have a great grasp of UK geography, so I replied 'England' – there was no point in being more specific.

'Why are you here?'

'Because your government thinks I'm a bad guy.'

It was the truth, of course, but it made the guard laugh. I assumed everyone else in the entire prison system reckoned they were innocent, too, and he'd probably heard it plenty of times before. 'Okay, Tony Blair,' he said. 'Why are you really here?'

Before I could answer, another guard chipped in and asked if I liked soccer. He had been listening to our conversation, and seemed eager to chat to a real Englishman.

'You ever heard of the Manchester Blues?' the guard went on. I could only assume my new friend was talking about Manchester City.

'Yeah, of course I've heard of them.'

'Well, they suck, man.' By now, a few guards had gathered around my cage and this comment set them all off laughing. I didn't care – I was glad to have broken the ice. I offered a similarly lame put-down of the New York Yankees in return, and by then it was time to go back inside.

The rest of the day passed in slow motion. In fact, time was moving so slowly for me that it was almost going backwards, and I had exhausted all the avenues of entertainment before even the morning had finished. I had been reading and writing to keep myself busy, but it didn't take long before I'd had enough of both.

With nothing to do, and twelve agonising hours before it was time to sleep, I honestly thought I was going to go mad in that cell. I wasn't particularly frightened or worried – I was just bored. The inane, unending monotony reached the point where I started saving a few meagre mouthfuls of food at mealtimes so I could eat them later and have something to look forward to. Every now and then a guard would appear and crack a joke, or ask how I was, but otherwise it was pure, unadulterated tedium. I was so desperately bored that I ended up working myself into a panic and soon afterwards I developed a thumping stress headache. The SHU experience was turning out to be the cruellest form of torture.

The worst thing was that I had served barely twenty-four hours of my thirty-seven-month sentence. I could visualise that time stretching far, far in front of me – a vast expanse of pure nothingness that terrified me in a way that I had never expected. With nothing better to do, I curled up on my miserable excuse for a bed and waited all night for my headache to subside. Even the pain was boring.

Eventually, I was able to make out some light through the murky glass of my cell window. Another day at last. A guard told me that it was a Friday (somehow, I had already lost track of the days), and today I would get a shower. As good as a thorough wash sounded, I was more pleased that I would finally have something else to do. If I could kill thirty minutes in the shower, that meant thirty minutes I wouldn't have to spend in my cell. The thought of an entire weekend in the SHU was horrendous.

After the shower, I was taken outside for my daily hour of exercise. But as soon as I stepped outdoors, I realised that I needn't have bothered with the shower. It was lashing down with rain, and I was drenched and freezing cold after only a few minutes in the unsheltered cage. Once again, I wasn't alone. This time, my companion was a huge, muscular Latino guy, who introduced himself as Cobra. I didn't dare ask why people called him that, instead I just told him my name and made some lame joke about the weather being even worse here than it was back in England.

Cobra laughed, and then he reached down to his trouser leg, pulling it up so he could reach into his sock. At that moment, my heart stopped. I had heard all the stories about people making their own shanks – improvised knives – in prison and smuggling them in their socks. All I had done was say hello to this giant of a man, and now he was reaching for something tucked away inside his sock. The nearest guard was only a few paces away, but I was trapped in the cage. If the Cobra struck, there was no way the guards would be able to get me out in time. He could kill me on the spot.

Without being aware of it, I had backed up right against the wall of the cage by the time Cobra had finished rummaging. But then he held out his hand, slick with rainwater, and I was hugely relieved to see that there was no knife: all he had in his palm was a pair of small white mints. If he noticed the look of relief on my face, he didn't comment on it. Not for the first time since I had arrived in Allenwood, assumptions had got the better of me.

I was so pleased that Cobra wasn't going to stab me that I took the mint and popped it straight into my mouth. 'Thanks,' I said. 'Um, where did you get that?'

'Don't ask.'

I nodded. I was trying to slow my heart-rate and think about anything other than the journey that the smuggled mint might have been on before it found its way into my mouth. I asked Cobra how long he had been inside.

'In the SHU?' He counted briefly on his fingers. 'About six months.'

'Oh, wow.' I may have been the newest inmate at Allenwood, but I already knew that that was a long time to spend in solitary. 'Why's that?' I asked.

Cobra smiled, and a look of pride flashed briefly across his face. 'Me and my boys beat the shit out of some dude. He kept making trouble in the unit, so we took it into our own hands to shut him up. I'm being investigated for it now, though – looks like I'll be going back up to a medium.'

By this Cobra meant a medium security prison. In the US system, violent inmates can earn their way into lower-security prisons – generally safer and more comfortable – by serving their time peacefully. The closer you are to being released, the more likely it is that you'll be moved down into a more relaxed facility. Cobra had clearly spent most of his time at the tougher end of the prison spectrum, and it seemed like he almost relished the challenge of moving back up a step.

It was still raining, and I was shivering and soaked through by the time one of the guards came to take us back to our cells. I nodded my thanks to Cobra for the mint and wondered how much longer he had left before he was released. Some people end up spending so long in the prison system that they become institutionalised, and don't ever want to leave. It occurred to me that Cobra might be one of those people, and that he might have attacked that guy so he could get more time added to his tariff. My thinking was interrupted by one of the guards, who was about to deliver the best news I'd heard since arriving at Allenwood.

'Hey, Darby, get your stuff,' he said. 'You're going out this afternoon.'

'Out where?'

'To the unit – the general population.'

'Seriously?'

I was being moved out of solitary! My mood rocketed at the prospect of an end to the mind-numbing boredom and loneliness that had threatened to consume the entire weekend. After lunch, I was taken to the SHU reception area and then shown the door. The compound was vast, and the guard pointed to a building in the distance, perhaps half a mile away. Then he removed my cuffs and chains and instructed me to report to the laundry there to pick up my uniform.

It was still pelting down with rain as I made my way across the compound, but I didn't care. After a truly awful forty-eight hours in solitary, I felt like Nelson Mandela walking to freedom. But of course there were new challenges – and new dangers – waiting for me among the general population.

CHAPTER 3

A CELL OF ONE'S OWN

As if on cue, the rain seemed to come down thicker and faster with every step I took. I found myself practically wading through the compound, hoisting up my baggy jumpsuit to stop the trouser legs trailing in the puddles. Fortunately, the first stop for prisoners leaving the SHU was the laundry, so it didn't matter that I was soaked through by the time I arrived. As I entered the dimly-lit laundry building, my orange jumpsuit was so wet that it had turned a dark shade of red, and it felt as heavy as the shackles I had worn when I was first detained in Texas. As for my deck shoes, dribbles of water leaked out from the thin canvas with every step I took.

At a long table on one side of the room, a group of mostly black inmates were folding clothes and talking quietly amongst themselves. One was grappling with a shirt so big it looked more like a tent, while the others were half-heartedly folding T-shirts and jumpsuits and dumping them in a pile. As I walked in, they all stopped what they were doing, making no attempt to hide their interest in the new guy.

Behind the folding table was a doorway that led into a room filled with washing machines, where large, blue-sided trolleys were stacked high with standard-issue prison laundry. Towers of boxers and khakis and bedsheets threatened to spill over the top. Directly in front of me was a reception desk with a sour-looking old woman sitting behind it, squinting through her glasses at an ancient computer monitor. She had a face like she'd been chewing wasps, and somehow she managed to look even less pleased when I squelched into the room, dripping as if I'd just come out of the shower.

I made my way to the counter and waited for the woman to say something. A few seconds of awkward silence were broken only by the sound of falling water droplets slapping against the lino floor. I looked around self-consciously, and it was only then that I noticed the trail I had left behind me, muddy rainwater streaked all the way back to the door. No wonder the woman looked so annoyed. Finally she spoke, opening her eyes wide and leaning forward as she asked me what I was doing there.

'I've just come from the SHU,' I answered, looking down at my orange, solitary-confinement jumpsuit. Upon hearing my accent, the inmates at the laundry table started whispering amongst themselves, until the old woman shot them a stern look. At this, they fell silent and returned to their folding, but they were doing it so slowly, and paying it such little attention, that it was patently only for show. Their eyes were still firmly fixed on me.

'I can see that,' the woman said, after a long pause to consider my statement. 'I assume you're after a uniform?'

'Yes, please,' I said.

She sighed an exaggerated, comically loud sigh, as if I was the source of an extreme personal inconvenience: never mind that this was her job. Then she made a wafting hand gesture towards the group of inmates and one – a young black guy with a mischievous smirk on his face – disappeared into the room at the back. I waited for a few seconds, the dripping finally slowing, until he reappeared with a bundle of laundry in his arms.

'Here you go, England,' he said, handing over the tangle of bedsheets and clothes. The other inmates all snickered.

I quickly looked over my provisions. There was a set of bedding, a pair of khaki trousers, a white T-shirt, two pairs of socks, two pairs of boxers, prison-issue boots and a khaki jacket. The clothes were obviously an improvement on the jumpsuit, but my heart sank when I saw the state they were in. The shirt and trousers looked like they had been worn by a hundred people before me, and the boxers as if by a thousand. They were frayed and so thin around the crotch that the fabric was practically transparent. My stomach churned when I thought about where they'd been. Still, at least they appeared clean: that was the only solace.

I thanked the elderly woman and nodded at the inmates. I didn't know it then, but the laundry room would become a significant part of prison life for me. For now, though, I was out of there. My next stop would be my cell and now I started to feel nervous all over again. I had been told that I should report to Gregg Unit, one of the four living units situated around the prison's grounds. Armed with my bundle of laundry, I set off in the direction of Gregg, my new home for ... how long? A few months? A year? Longer? It all depended on my transfer back to the UK, but I knew I'd be staying there for a while. Even a day would be longer than I would have liked.

The unit was an ugly, squat, concrete block, almost identical to all the others dotted around the grounds. I reported to the office and the cop (as the guards were known) assigned me a cell – number 59, A Wing. I knew Allenwood was a big place, but the true scale of it only started to dawn on me as a guard led me down the corridors of Gregg Unit towards A Wing. Allenwood Low alone housed some 1,400 men between its four units. My wing consisted of sixty cells, most of which contained three inmates each. A few cells had space for only two, but these were considered far too luxurious for someone like me: they were reserved for the longest-serving prisoners, the ones who were the most respected among the population. That meant I would be stuck with two other people, doubling the chance that I'd end up with at least one terrible cellmate. I had heard all the horror stories, and all I wanted was to be housed with people who were passably normal, reasonably hygienic and not violent – the ultimate virtues in a cellmate (or cellie, as they are known in the States).

I've been calling them cells but, in the low-security part of Allenwood at least, that's not really what they were. For one thing, the 'cells' didn't have doors, so they couldn't be locked. Instead, they were more like cubicles, with white-painted, breeze-block walls around seven feet high and an opening around four feet wide. This gave Gregg Unit the feel of an enormous warehouse, with sixty of these breeze-block cubicles arranged along its corridors on either side of each wing.

With nothing to trap the sound coming from each cell, the wing was incredibly loud. As I walked along through a gauntlet of shouting and whooping prisoners, I began working myself up about my cellmates. By the time I finally arrived at cell number 59, my palms were slick. I braced myself as I entered the cubicle, not knowing who would be staring back at me, and was surprised to see nobody there. There was an empty bunk bed with an equally empty camp bed opposite. Three small wardrobes were pushed against one wall and a metal desk was fastened to the other. This was my new home.

The cell was clearly lived in. Clothes were strewn on the camp bed and the bottom bunk, and shoes were huddled beneath both. Then I realised that my cellmates must be working. Almost all prisoners had jobs – making food in the cafeteria, folding clothes in the laundry, cleaning the grounds, or labouring in the federal furniture factory attached to the compound – so that explained their absence. It was early afternoon now, though, so I knew they would be back before long.

With this thought at the forefront of my mind, I changed into my new clothes and dumped the rest of my bundle on the top bunk. There were no sheets on the thin mattress, so I climbed the flimsy ladder and fitted the bedding I had been given. With nothing else to distract me from my anxiety, I settled myself on top of the bed, waiting for someone to walk through the gap in the bricks and introduce themselves.

It wasn't until about half-an-hour later that anyone did walk in. First to appear was a chubby, balding, middle-aged white guy. As soon as he rounded the cubicle entrance and saw me perched on the top bunk, above his own bed, his eyes lit up and he came bounding over to bump my fist. I was expecting a handshake at first, so this caught me by surprise, and I had to adjust awkwardly at the last second.

I'd always thought that fist-bumping was more of a young person's street greeting. But, as I quickly learned, in prison you don't shake anyone's hand. With hundreds of guys living in the same confined space, hygiene was a huge issue, even among guys who made every effort to be clean. Since you never knew where any hand had been, fist-bumping was widely favoured over handshaking – another morsel of knowledge, amongst the many I would pick up during my frantic first few weeks behind bars.

'Ross,' my new acquaintance introduced himself, smiling broadly as I knocked my fist against his. 'How's it going?'

'Darby,' I replied, immediately feeling better about my situation. There was something about Ross's smile and wide eyes that told me he was one of those people who was eager to please. 'Good to meet you, mate.'

'Ah,' he said, taking in my accent. 'You're English, right?'

It was already plain that my accent was marking me out from the other prisoners. I stood out as it was, by virtue of being older and whiter than the average inmate – most of whom were young, Latino or black – but now I knew that the added novelty of being a foreigner would earn me even more attention. I told Ross that he was right, and asked if he'd ever been to England.

'Once or twice,' he said, and then launched into an extensive monologue about life in Allenwood. I got the impression that he didn't have many friends inside, judging by how keen he was to talk to me at such length despite having only just met me. As part of his introductory lecture, he warned that the guards were spectacularly strict, adding that many of them had a deep, sadistic streak. He explained that there was a communal television room around the corner from the cell, and pointed out the way to the toilets, showers and microwave room.

Then, noticing my newly issued (but far from new) outfit, he recommended that I should buy myself some fresh clothes at the commissary, the prison shop, which our unit was allowed to visit once a week. He explained the protocol for meal times – the units were called one after the other to eat in the canteen across the grounds – and offered to lend me some of his supplies, such as coffee, chocolate, or a pair of shorts, until I could visit the commissary and pay him back. By the time he finished talking, he was almost out of breath and red in the face, but he was still smiling.

I was slightly overwhelmed by all the information but, more importantly, I was pleased to know that at least one of my cellies seemed like a decent bloke. However, I was eager to learn about our cell's third inhabitant. I asked Ross who occupied the camp bed. Immediately, his countenance changed, his smile flickering and then fading away.

'Oh,' he said, breaking off eye contact with me to look over at the bed in the corner. 'That's El's bunk.'

'What's he like?' I asked.

Ross shrugged. 'Between you and me, he's not the best person to be sharing with – put it that way.'

My heart sank. 'How come?'

'Well, his friends are always coming around to see him and they can be really hostile. They're kind of loud and obnoxious. He's been inside for a long time, you see. Fifteen years or something. You should watch out around him.'

'Shit,' I said. 'Thanks for the advice, man.'

At that, Ross started fussing around with the clothes that were scattered over his bunk. He didn't say much else as he went about folding his shirts and putting them away. He pointed out which wardrobe I should use and told me to keep my possessions locked away whenever I left the cell. Other than that, though, he was now strangely quiet. His mood had nosedived after my questions about the mysterious third cellie.

I didn't have to wait long to meet El. He came into the cubicle half-an-hour or so after Ross and did a double-take as he saw me on the top bunk. He was also middle-aged, but he was a thick-set, muscular black dude – the polar opposite of paunchy, pale Ross.

El swore under his breath. I nodded at him and he nodded back, before coming over to offer a half-hearted fist.

'Darby,' I said.

'El.' Then he shook his head and crashed down on his camp bed. He didn't say anything to Ross. He didn't even look at him: it was as if the man wasn't even there.

Ross left the cell a little while later, where to I didn't know, but it was common for inmates to drift around the premises – watching television, cooking food, going for a walk, or merely finding someone to chat to, all good ways to pass the time. As soon as Ross had gone, El, whom I had assumed to be sleeping, sat up and looked at me, completely alert.

'Hey. You been talking to that piece of shit before I came in?'

I was taken aback by the hostility in his voice. 'Who, Ross? Yeah, just a little. He told me where everything is and stuff, but that was about it.'

El nodded. 'Did he say anything about me?'

'No, not really.'

'Good.' El paused for a moment, thinking, scowling. I could tell he was trying to get the measure of me. 'This your first time?'

I sat up properly on my bunk. 'My first time in prison? Yeah. I came from the SHU today.'

'How long you in?'

'Thirty-seven months. Fraud.' Briefly I had managed to forget about the length of my sentence, but saying it out loud brought the reality crashing home.

El started to smile, and then he actually laughed out loud, taking me by surprise. He looked like a different person all of a sudden – younger, kinder, less dangerous. 'Thirty-seven months? You serious?'

I swung my legs over the side of the bunk and turned to face him so we could talk properly. 'Yeah, I'm serious,' I said. 'What's so funny about that?'

El made a show of rolling his eyes, but kept up the smile. 'Fuck, man. You said Darby, right? Thirty-seven months? That's chump change, man.'

'What do you mean?' I asked. El was shaking his head in amazement.

'I mean, thirty-seven months is fucking nothing. It'll be over before you even know it. Chump change, like I said.'

'It was a plea bargain,' I said. 'I had a good lawyer.'

'Really now?' El's smile evaporated as quickly as it had appeared. I got the impression I had said the wrong thing. 'Was yours a multiple-defendant case?'

'Yeah,' I said. 'How did you know that?'

'A lucky guess,' he said, fixing me with an intense stare. Once again, he didn't seem so friendly. 'What do you mean, fraud?'

I knew this was an important moment, and that if I tried to explain the intricacies of my case, I would lose him. It was easier to stick to the basics. Right now, I needed to be credible.

'Well, it's complicated,' I said. 'But basically, I was accused of robbing a bank. I'm supposed to have stolen a few million dollars – well, along with a couple of colleagues, that is. It wasn't just me.'

He whistled. 'Millions? How many millions?'

'Seven million dollars in total.'

'Well, that's some serious shit, Darby. Now are you going to tell me how come your sentence is so fucking short if you stole seven million dollars? You a rat or something? You sell out the others?'

In multiple-defendant cases in the US, each defendant must have separate legal representation. It's normal – and a widespread practice – to strike a favourable plea bargain by testifying against your co-accused. This may ensure leniency from a judge but it will do you no favours if you end up inside. In the world of prison, rats are the lowest of the low – right down at the bottom of the pecking order, with the sex offenders and paedophiles.

Based on what little he knew about my case, El was making a reasonable, if incorrect, assumption about me. In the American federal justice system, around ninety-five per cent of defendants cut some kind of deal – 'pleading out' as it's known. Under a system where deals are everything, ratting out co-defendants can be an attractive option. I was given the chance to do so back when we were fighting the case, but I turned the prosecutors down. I knew that I wouldn't be able to live with myself if I sold out the other two.

'No,' I said firmly, hoping El would pick up on my indignation. 'I'm not a rat. My co-d's and I struck a deal together. We each got thirty-seven months. We were going to go all the way, fight it at trial, and we knew we stood a good chance of winning. The prosecutors knew it as well, so they offered us all the joint deal.'

El thought this over for a second and then nodded. 'All right. Well, I'm pleased to hear that, Darby. I don't suppose you have your papers yet?'

'I've only just got here,' I said. 'I don't have anything yet, but I'll show you as soon as I can.'

El was talking about my case file – the document that all prisoners are issued with, showing the full details of their conviction and sentence. Since mine contained the written promise to get me back home as soon as possible, I needed that case file to start the expedited transfer process within the prison. But the files also serve another purpose among the prison community: they are used by inmates to prove that they really are who they say they are. Checking a new inmate's file was a good way to weed out rats and other undesirables, such as the despised paedophiles and sex offenders.

'All right,' El said. 'You're okay for now.' The smile returned to his face. He whistled softly and shook his head again. 'Thirty-seven months, man. I can't believe that. For seven million? You sure did good.'

'It doesn't seem like such a short sentence to me,' I replied.

'Trust me, man, it is. Look at me, right. I've already done fifteen years. Got seven more to go.'

Twenty-two years! I couldn't even begin to imagine how anyone would keep sane with a sentence that long. I didn't have the courage to ask what El had done to get such a sentence, but I presumed he must have killed someone. I didn't know it at the time, but it was a good job I didn't ask. I would quickly find out that it is taboo to ask anyone directly what they're in for: instead, the done thing is to ask how long they are serving. Then, if they want to tell you why, they can do so voluntarily – unless, that is, you suspect someone of being a rat or a sex offender, in which case senior inmates like El wouldn't hesitate to interrogate a new arrival like me.

Ordinarily, all the undesirables are kept in a separate wing, but life is so miserable there, and they are so hated by the other prisoners, that some prefer to take their chances within the general population. They use fabricated back-stories, hence the need to be able to prove your crime and establish credibility. Some get away with it, but most don't, since the normal prisoners detest the undesirables with a passion.

El smiled wistfully. 'Now you see what I mean about chump change, right?'

'Yeah,' I said. 'Jesus, El, that's a long time.'

'Sure is. I did three years in the pen at the start. That's real time, man. Not like this holiday camp bullshit they got going on here.'

Allenwood wasn't a holiday camp at all, but I could certainly believe it was far better than a penitentiary. At those places, you stay locked up in your room for twenty-three hours a day, like I had been in the SHU. I was there for only two days and I struggled, so it was impossible to fathom how slowly three years would drag in a dreadful place like that. The pens (as they are known) are bad for other reasons as well. I knew they were extremely dangerous, controlled by violent gangs, and it wasn't uncommon for inmates to be found dead after a feud. Thinking about the things El had seen – and probably done – made me shiver.

'So,' I continued, deciding it was time to change the subject, 'what's the deal with Ross?'

'Fuck that guy. Look, Darby, I don't know you yet, but you seem okay. Listen to me closely. Don't look at that guy. Don't talk to that guy. And if he tries to give you anything, you tell him to go fuck himself, okay? I bet he's already tried that one, right?'

I thought back to Ross's kind offer to tide me over until I could visit the shop. 'Yeah, he has,' I replied, more than a little confused. 'I haven't taken anything yet, though.'

'Okay, good.' El made a disgusted face. 'Those people are all the same man. Fucking manipulator, that's what he is.'

I didn't exactly know what El meant by 'those people', and I wasn't sure I wanted to ask, so I nodded along. After his little tirade, El stood up from his bunk and stretched. Then he made his way over to one of the wardrobes and pulled out a pair of trousers and some trainers. He tossed them in my direction.

'These will keep you going until you get yourself properly kitted out,' he said.

If only my friends and family could picture me now, I thought. I had only just arrived and here I was already in some kind of alliance with a serious, hardened criminal, fifteen years into his twenty-two-year sentence. I might have found it funny, if only I hadn't been so overwhelmed. I thanked El and he told me it was no problem. Then he headed out through the cell opening, doubling back when he saw I wasn't following.

'Hey, Darby,' he said, poking his head around the gap. 'Come on, man, time to go.'

'Go where?' I asked, hurriedly pulling on my new trainers, which were infinitely more comfortable than the shoes I had been issued with originally.

'Chow, man,' El said. I wasn't sure quite what he meant, but I followed him anyway, tucking the laces into the shoes to save time.

Chow, as it turned out, was what the inmates called food. A huge hall, governed by its own rigid code of etiquette, the canteen at Allenwood was unlike any dining experience I'd ever had. For one thing, all the food was prepared and served by inmates. This meant that it was beneficial to get yourself a friend in the kitchen, since it was down to the prisoners working there to dish out the portions. I saw on that first day that portion sizes could vary wildly from one inmate to the next – with workers giving their friends heaps of food, while unpopular characters and strangers were left with scraps.

To get to the chow hall from our unit, we had to cross the compound. Most of the block was on its way to dinner, so I was able to get a good look at the population of Gregg Unit. About forty per cent were black, with roughly the same proportion of Hispanic guys. White guys like me were the minority. El seemed to know absolutely everyone, and we could barely walk a few steps without someone calling out to him or stopping for a fist bump. In the end, I gave up trying to have a conversation with him, because I was being interrupted every few seconds.

When we finally made it to the chow hall, there were more calls to him from around the room, and then we lined up together, waiting to reach the servery. I already had the sense that El was a pretty useful guy to know.

'You're a popular man, El,' I remarked, looking around the hall, which must have had some five hundred people in it. 'You seem to know everyone here.'

'Well, Darby, like I was saying earlier, fifteen years is a fucking long time.'

When we finally reached the counter, we were each given a hot dog and some salad on a battered metal tray. Naturally, El knew the guy who served us, so he ended up with an extra sausage. Then El introduced me to the server, a tall black guy, and said I was his new cellie. Before I knew it, the server told me to give my tray back. When he returned it, there was an extra sausage nestled among the salad leaves.

'Cheers, man,' I thanked him, and followed El to a long table.

I was immediately reminded of those canteens you see in American high-school movies. I sensed that you couldn't simply rock up and sit at a table of your choice – instead it was your position within the hierarchy that determined where you sat. Being a new, middle-aged white guy with a relatively short sentence, I would have found myself pretty close to the bottom of the pecking order, only a few pegs above the rats and paedos; but since I was with El, it was a different ball-game. My cellie was clearly respected and senior within the hierarchy, which meant that we could sit wherever we wanted, and, since I was with him, nobody was going to give me any trouble.

As we ate, we were joined by some of El's friends, but he focused most of his attention on me. He wanted to give me a crash course in prison etiquette, something that stood me in good stead throughout my entire stay. He explained, as I had guessed, that your rank determined where you sat in the chow hall, and the same rules applied to the TV room. He told me to keep my head down and mind my own business, and warned me against taking favours from anyone. It was El who also cautioned me not to ask anyone why they were there.

'Oh, yeah,' he said, stuffing the last of his hot dog into his mouth. 'And the best advice I can give you is this: do your own time, Darby. Don't get involved in anyone else's.' I wasn't too sure what this meant, but I thanked him anyway.

One of El's friends nudged him to get his attention. 'Hey, man,' he said, pointing across the chow hall. 'Look who's just turned up.'

I turned in my seat to follow the direction of the finger. I saw Ross ambling in to join the back of the queue.

'Fucking lollipop,' El said. 'You know, I fucking hate that guy.'

We watched as Ross slowly inched forward in the line. He was on his own, and he looked around nervously, working out where he would sit. Before anyone could say any more, someone cut in to ask something about the baseball season. I half-listened to the conversation, but I didn't know anything about baseball – American football was my sport of choice in the States. Besides, I was interested to see where Ross would sit.

I turned around as discreetly as I could when he was getting served – no doubt with only a single sausage. He then carried his tray to the far side of the hall and sat at a table in the corner, alongside a group of white men of a similar age. I turned back to El's conversation. I was beginning to develop a theory about his and Ross's mutual animosity.

El continued his induction over the next few days: teaching me the rules, showing me where everything was, and introducing me to various people – the right people, as he called them. Being seen with El sent a message that I was accepted by one of the main guys, so nobody gave me any trouble during those early days. In fact, I soon learned that he was an even bigger deal in Allenwood than I had realised. Owing to his long sentence, and his spell in a high-security facility, he was one of the most respected inmates in the unit. He clearly had a reputation, and people were always keen to make sure they stayed on his good side.

To me, though, El was nothing but kind, and we got on well. It helped that we were around the same age, and I began to think that in another life he would have been precisely the kind of guy I might have chosen as a drinking buddy. He was big into his sports, and talked with excitement about the coming NBA and NFL seasons. Gradually, I also shared more details with him about my own case and, in return, he opened up about his conviction enough for me to learn that it was heavily drug-related but he hadn't killed anyone, as I had first feared.

He also warned me about the guards, explaining how Allenwood was more harshly ruled than any other low-security prison he had ever encountered. The slightest infraction could earn an inmate a ticket to the SHU, and you could guarantee that you would be spending most of your sentence in there if you marked yourself out as a repeat offender. Fighting? Straight to the SHU. Refuse to cooperate with a guard or an investigation? Straight to the SHU. Try to steal any BOP property? Straight to the SHU. Do not pass Go: do not collect $200. The cops' philosophy was that they would put you in solitary first and ask questions later.

As a result of this strict regime, the BOP deemed Allenwood to be one of the few prisons where it was safe for sex offenders and rats to be mixed in with the general population. In most facilities, these undesirables would be kept away from the other prisoners, who would be likely to view them as easy targets to brutalise. But at Allenwood, the undesirables felt able to mix in, protected as they were from the worst excesses of their fellow inmates by the iron fists of the guards.

At least, that was the perception. In reality, rats and paedophiles were still ripe for extortion, and many took severe beatings at Allenwood. As such, they weren't really safe among the general population in any meaningful sense – they were only a bit safer at Allenwood than they would have been at most other prisons.

I knew from my own experience that the SHU was a miserable place to be. But El explained that spending time in solitary – whether voluntarily (for your own safety) or as a punishment – had more disadvantages than just the crippling boredom and loneliness. Whenever a prisoner was sent there, other inmates would break into his locker and steal whatever possessions he might have accumulated during his time inside. The guards knew this went on, but they didn't care. In fact, it helped them maintain discipline, since everyone knew that getting yourself in trouble meant you would never see your 'stuff' again.

The result was that Allenwood wasn't as violent and dangerous as I had initially feared. In general, El reassured me, other than the suspected rats, paedos and sex offenders, people respected each other. However, I was still warned to be vigilant at all times – and with good reason.

Many times I saw first-hand that, despite the guards' efforts to maintain peace, violence was never more than one disrespectful move away. One evening, El and I were eating in the chow hall, having a normal-enough conversation, when suddenly I heard an almighty clattering, the sound of metal hitting the floor. I spun round and saw two guys squaring up to each other at a nearby table. One of them had knocked the other's tray to the ground, whether deliberately or by accident I didn't know. Within seconds, a punch was swung and the recipient was bleeding heavily from the mouth. Before another blow could even be aimed, let alone landed, the guards were on the scene, twisting the two inmates' arms behind their backs with such force that I thought they would be pulled from their sockets.

In an instant, both men had been frogmarched out of the chow hall on their way to the SHU, where they would stay until the guards were satisfied that lessons had been learned. Almost certainly, both men would emerge from solitary to find that they had no possessions left, forcing them to waste what little money they had on new supplies from the commissary.

That was how justice at Allenwood worked.

CHAPTER 4

ORIENTATION WEEK

With each day that passed, it became clearer that Ross was a near-total pariah. He had so few friends that they could be counted on the fingers of one hand and all of them came from the group of older white guys that I had seen him with on my first night in the chow hall. While I spent hours every day writing letters – and then, when I started getting post, reading the letters I'd been sent in response – Ross had no contact with the outside world. From what I gathered, he had no wife, and if he had children, they had nothing to do with him. He never had visits and, as far as I could tell, he never used the prison phones. He lived a life of almost complete isolation.

Knowing what I did about life in prison, I was aware that there must be a reason why almost all the other inmates shunned him. It was possible, of course, that he was a rat. But since he seemed to have no family or friends on the outside at all, and since he had volunteered nothing about his sentence, it was more likely that he was a sex offender. I reached this conclusion after a few days in the cell, and the more I thought about it, the more certain I grew. It made me feel sick to be sharing a cell with him, and soon I joined El in shunning him completely.

It wasn't long before I learned that I was right. Ross was known around the wing to be a 'lollipop' – a sex offender of some kind. Nobody asked him directly, and nobody really talked about it – it was simply one of those things that became clear over time. After all, the biggest warning signs – no friends, no family, no post, no visits – were all there. I felt even more repulsed when I thought back to how eager he had been to befriend me when I first arrived. He probably thought I was like him.

El explained that this was a reasonable thing to assume. In fact, it was also El's initial fear about me when we met for the first time. As it happened, I fitted the age and racial profile of an undesirable; a large number of middle-aged white guys in the US prison system are sex criminals of some kind. But El said that he could discount that possibility in my case, as soon as he learned how short my sentence was. That was why he thawed so quickly when he learned that I was doing only 'chump change'.

The only other thing for El to be wary about was that I might be a rat, but once I explained my case to him, he could tell that I wasn't. I was also able to show him my papers a few days later to confirm this, though the fact that I was willing to show them to him in the first place proved I had nothing to hide, so he was totally cool with me.

He warned me, however, that most inmates would take one look at me and assume I was a sex offender, exactly as he had. It was important never to associate knowingly with the 'lollipops', as he called them, in case my name was tarnished by association. People would realise eventually that I wasn't one of them, he said, and he would put the word out that I was a good guy. But he warned me to expect a hostile reception from most people until they knew for sure that I was just a regular criminal.

I thanked him for this advice, which turned out to be bang-on accurate. I would definitely have had an easier time making acquaintances at first if I had been younger, or black or Hispanic. But I remain deeply thankful to my great friend El for taking me under his wing and making those early days at Allenwood bearable.

The first few weeks passed in something of a blur. I spent most of the time adjusting to my new environment – exploring the facilities and starting to settle into a daily routine. I spent long hours walking around the recreation yard and I was pleasantly surprised at the facilities on offer to the BOP's 'guests'. I joked in letters home that it was like staying in a Hilton – a massive exaggeration, of course, but it was necessary to keep my girls in good spirits.

There was a well-equipped gym and weights area, where many of the black inmates spent their time, as well as courts for handball, volleyball and basketball, and pitches for soccer and American football. There was also a relatively large library, where I could find recent newspapers and magazines as well as a good selection of books.

Some people, particularly Americans, might baulk at the expense of fitting prisons out with these amenities. Prison is meant to be a punishment, as many Republican types will tell you, but the thing about day-to-day prison life is that, more than anything else, it is fundamentally boring. Unless you've experienced it, it's hard to understand how excruciating it is. Each and every second drags, and every inmate feels the strain. Some tedium is inevitable – it's part of the package. But when there aren't any facilities to help with the boredom, that's when things get dangerous.

Chronically bored inmates start looking for things to do. Often, they turn to violence to keep themselves occupied, to get the heart beating and the blood rushing. That's how the BOP justifies its spending on facilities: really, they're a safety feature. The more time inmates spend occupied with exercise, reading or games, the less time they're going to spend sharpening toothbrushes into shanks and sticking each other. Take it from me, I was really glad that there were plenty of things to do.

In addition to the regular library, there was a separate legal library. This was a place where inmates acting either as their own lawyers, or as lawyers for others, could read up on the ins and outs of case law and make sure that they were as well-equipped for their next hearing as they could be. I was fortunate enough to have Matt Hennessy fighting to get me repatriated even while I was in prison, so this library wasn't much use to me. But I saw how some inmates – no money, abandoned by their families, and no friends on the outside – were forced to fight their own cases, since nobody else would.

This hammered home a sad truth, of which I would become increasingly aware as time went on: many of the men I was living with had absolutely nothing. I don't mean that as a figure of speech – I mean they literally had nothing and nobody that cared. For many, the meagre income from their prison job was the only money they had. Expensive lawyers like mine were completely out of the question. It really made me appreciate what I had, because no matter how dire my own situation felt, I could find countless guys who had it far, far worse.

One thing I couldn't appreciate, however, was the food. That was one aspect of prison life that certainly didn't measure up to a Hilton. The breakfast was usually fine – cereal, milk and a piece of fruit – but the other meals were consistently awful. Lunch was always served from 11 a.m. to 12 noon, with food varying from fajitas to hamburgers and, on Wednesdays, French fries. There was always rice and beans and brown bread (sometimes we even got butter) to supplement the meals and a good job, too, because many of the dishes were truly inedible. Every few days we would be served a slab of baked fish – sewer trout, the inmates called it – which was so tough, we joked that you could use it to replace the soles of your shoes.

Dinner was served from 5 p.m. in the chow hall, with the four units called one by one to get their food. The first unit there was always the one that had done best during last month's inspection, so it was an incentive for inmates to keep their spaces clean and free of contraband. Being called first was a real bonus: it meant you got the choicest lumps of meat and, often, enjoyed larger portions. The unit called last would frequently find only scraps waiting for them: the scrawniest chicken pieces, or the thinnest ladle of chilli.

The chow hall was an important part of the prison economy. Coming from a finance background, I was intrigued to learn about the complex and surprisingly sophisticated market that operated beneath the noses of the guards. Even though officers were always stationed at the entrance, all kinds of food somehow found a way out into the units. Smugglers could make good income by secreting popular items like milk cartons, chicken legs or cold burgers and then selling them on to hungry inmates in the units. If you knew who to speak to, it was possible to acquire enough food for a banquet.

Although I knew many people who did, I never took a chance with any of this smuggled food. You've only got to ask yourself how it was concealed from the guards to lose your appetite entirely. Instead, I relied on the prison shop for my extras. Each inmate was allowed to spend a sum of $70 per week on supplies from the commissary. Most inmates had nowhere near that much cash and it was only thanks to transfers from my family and friends that I could get close to the spending limit. The commissary was a lifeline for me, though, and I have no idea what I'd have done without it.

In general, the commissary was used to supplement the poor clothing issue and the hit-and-miss food supply. It sold an array of T-shirts, trainers, underwear and other clothes (my favourite item being a pair of shiny silver shorts that were more comfortable than they were fashionable) and a selection of food, including basics such as noodles, soup, refried beans, cookies, crisps and fajita kits, which inmates could make themselves using any of the four microwaves on the unit. You could also buy toiletries, soft drinks and other small comforts there.

For me, the real lifesavers were the teabags, coffee sachets and powdered milk, which made me feel as if I was back home, for a few minutes at least, enjoying a warm cuppa while I read the papers. My mother had arranged a subscription of regular papers from the UK for me, so I really could recreate those comforting moments.

Lastly, and most importantly, the commissary was also where inmates went to buy phone credits and stamps. The latter functioned as a sort of currency in the units, with many deals, bets or transactions using stamps as the form of payment. Nobody had any cold, hard cash in prison, of course, so stamps were the closest thing to a real currency, owing to their fixed value and their usefulness in the real world as well as inside. But there was another currency also being used at Allenwood: packets of dried fish.

It sounds crazy, and at first I thought it was, but in my early days I saw many inmates exchanging packets of dried tuna, salmon and mackerel as if they were money. El explained to me that most people used fish packets – particularly the dried mackerel – as an alternative currency. Everyone was doing it. Want someone to cut your hair? Pay them in fish. Betting on the NBA? Use fish. Getting someone to rustle something up for you in the microwave room? Tip them with fish. It was an incredibly creative bartering system.

Eventually, I learned why fish was considered to be so valuable. It wasn't solely an Allenwood thing – it was a convention that was established throughout the US prison system. Cigarettes always used to be the go-to currency in prisons, but they were banned in American correctional institutions in 2004. When the supply of fags dried up, inmates started looking elsewhere for a replacement currency, and many of them settled on dried mackerel. 'Mack' sold for $1 per pack at the commissary, and it was deemed to be the best choice because of its round, stable value, and also because nobody actually wanted to eat it. Supply was also limited, so it was guaranteed to hold its value.

Of course, things only have value because other people believe them to have value, and that was the case with the fish. The packs were long-lasting, the supply was limited, and they had a practical function as well – so in many ways they were the perfect currency. Over time, fish packets became recognised bartering tools throughout US prisons, and by the time I arrived at Allenwood, 'mack' was well established as a replacement for cigarettes. It was an interesting lesson in prison economics, that much was certain.

Whether funded by stamps or mackerel, the black market was thriving. I didn't even need El to show me the ropes with this one – it was so obvious. Everywhere you looked, people were cutting deals and selling smuggled supplies. T-shirts and shorts found their way out of the laundry, hustlers slipped food out of the canteen and trades were taking place all over the unit. Betting was widespread, too. That was right in front of me, impossible to miss. It turned out that one of the reasons El was so popular was that he was also the prison bookie.

At first, I was amazed at how little the guards seemed to care about the whole bootleg culture. After all, they must have known what was going on. That it was so widespread relates to my earlier point about so many of the inmates having absolutely nothing. If nobody is paying money into your prison account, and your paltry wages from whatever job you're doing aren't enough to feed you properly, then of course you're going to resort to theft and smuggling to make your life easier. For some people, hustling was the only way to improve their lot, and I didn't blame them for doing it.

The hustlers tended to target the prison facilities more than individual inmates. For example, while people wouldn't think twice about stealing from the chow hall, they would be more likely to hesitate before nicking something from someone's locker. Even so, we kept all our possessions safeguarded by combination locks, and relied on our cellies to make sure nothing vanished from our cubicle if we were absent. The only exception was whenever someone was sent to the SHU, as I mentioned earlier – in which case their belongings were viewed to be fair game.

When I wasn't marvelling at the machinations of Allenwood's black market, I spent much of my first days and weeks getting to know people. I met more colourful characters in that one place than I had in my entire life up to that point. Unfortunately, many of these people, most of whom seemed to be regular guys, had seriously upsetting stories. Almost everyone was serving a long sentence – five years or more – with fifteen, twenty, even thirty-year sentences fairly typical. In the first week or so, I probably met around fifty guys and only one was serving a shorter sentence than me. Few had any support from the outside, which made me intensely thankful for all the people who were looking out for me. I had always realised that I had a big support network, but compared to these guys, it was truly enormous. After a few sad conversations with lonely, long-term inmates, I always made sure to write letters thanking every single person who was helping me. I had family and friends behind me, and I was still struggling to adjust to prison life.

During this orientation period, as El jokingly dubbed it, I also learned some important lessons about the TV room. Even more than in the chow hall, this was one place where prison politics reigned supreme. Each unit had three TV rooms, with eight sets in a main room and then two in smaller side rooms. To listen, you needed a radio and some headphones, available from the commissary for $60 or on the black market for a few stamps and a handful of dried mackerel. You then tuned the radio into the channel to which you wanted to listen. That way, inmates could choose from eight different screens without having to fight over the audio.

El explained that there were distinct tribes of people who used each TV room. The side rooms usually played CNN or the History, Geography or Discovery channels, and this was where the serious newshounds would congregate. The rowdy main room was where the fun was, although many of the more timid inmates refused to go in there. Two televisions were always set aside for Spanish language shows, but all the rest were reserved for sport, and sport only: ESPN played all day, every day, while you could also choose from Fox Soccer, NFL TV, and any other sport channel you can imagine.

Every evening, this room would be packed with fanatics screaming and howling at the televisions, with mackerel packets changing hands as people bet on the results. It was all a way to let off steam and pass the time, and I was grateful for it. During that first week or so, the NBA basketball play-offs were on, and many of the black inmates were glued to the screens. I had a surprisingly good time in there with El, although it didn't come without its harsh lessons in the ways of the prison.

The TV room, like everywhere else in Allenwood, was governed by a rigid social hierarchy. The longest-serving inmates were guaranteed seats, with the best spots going to prisoners like El who had already done over a decade behind bars. The rest of us, meanwhile, were forced to stand around the edges of the room or, if we were lucky, nab a seat right at the back when nobody else was using it. Throughout the day, however, the TV room was quiet enough and there were rarely any issues. I spent one of my first days watching the final games of the Premiership season. I walked in as the second half of a Chelsea game was kicking off and settled myself in a spare, front-row seat for the rest of the game.

I watched the entire half without a problem, and then the footage switched over to Manchester United being officially crowned champions. Just as the ceremony was starting, a Mexican guy sauntered over and switched the channel.

'Hey, man,' I protested. 'I was watching that.'

'No, you're not. It's finished. And this TV is for Spanish.'

I was eager to show that I wasn't someone who could be pushed around. It was the end-of-season ceremony, I said firmly, and I would be watching it.

He shook his head, like a teacher dealing with a troublesome pupil. 'Didn't you hear me? I said this TV is for Spanish.'

'No, I don't think you heard *me*,' I shot back, louder than I intended. 'I said I was watching it.'

Then a Spanish-accented voice cut into the conversation from behind me. 'If you want to watch English sport, you watch that TV.'

I turned round to see an enormous Mexican guy pointing to another screen, and then I did a double-take: I hadn't realised it, but around ten prisoners had sat down in the row behind me, all of them Hispanic, and all of them were staring at me. I knew when to back off, so I apologised and left them to it. I later learned that the group had done me a favour by waiting for the Chelsea match to finish before changing the channel – another lesson for me about the perils of engaging mouth before brain.

When there wasn't anything to watch, I spent my time writing letters. I relayed my anecdote about the Mexicans in the TV room, explained what the facilities were like, and generally tried to make it sound like I was doing okay. One line in a letter to my wife and daughters read: 'When you think of me in prison just imagine the following: a beautiful sunny day, set in a beautiful valley with picturesque scenery all around, out walking the running track and listening to the radio.'

It was true that the scenery (apart from the barbed wire) and the early summer weather was stunning, and there was plenty for me to do. But in truth I was feeling nowhere near as chipper as I made out. I was finding it really hard to be away from everyone I loved, and I was struggling to keep myself positive and motivated. With my entire sentence stretching out before me, I knew it would require serious effort to keep myself sane and healthy.

I learned very quickly that one of the hardest things was the lack of communication with the outside world. Prisoners didn't have any internet access. Emails were off-limits, so letters and phone calls were the only way to keep in touch with life on the outside. But I found the phone calls so difficult, knowing that the small, worried voice on the other end of the line was thousands of miles away. I would frequently tear up within seconds of hearing one of my daughters say hello, and it was a real struggle to hold myself together long enough for a decent conversation.

I was in Allenwood on the day my middle daughter turned eighteen, but by the time she got to the phone for me to wish her happy birthday, I was too emotional even to talk to her. She was saying, 'Hello? Dad? Dad, are you there? Are you okay?' and I couldn't bring myself to answer. I knew that if I heard any more of her voice, I would have collapsed in tears in the phone area, in view of half the unit. I called her back the next day and managed to hold it together, but even then, it was so difficult. Each phone call served as a stark reminder of everything I was missing. Over time, I cut back on these very difficult calls and relied on letters to keep up with my family instead. In the meantime, I had no choice but to forge new connections with the people around me. I wouldn't have coped if I had shut myself off completely, so I turned to El for companionship and occasional reassurance.

In El's company, I was introduced to more of my fellow prisoners every day. I quickly found out that almost everyone had a riveting story to tell, and I was relieved to learn that the majority of the inmates were friendly and surprisingly articulate. On one of these early days, I was sitting by the softball court, watching a game, next to a guy known as JD. He was in his early thirties, and perfectly respectable. After I told him the basics of my case, he said he was at the start of his sentence, too – only his would last for eighteen years. I was surprised to hear him talk so casually about such a long stretch of time.

'I was convicted of supplying crystal meth,' he said, by way of explanation.

'Wow,' I said. 'Eighteen years. I assume you went to trial to get that kind of sentence?'

'Nope. I pleaded out.'

I was stunned. I couldn't believe that a drug charge had landed him eighteen years *with* a deal. 'What?' I asked, unable to hide my shock.

JD looked at me and grimaced. 'Yup,' he said. I could see the sadness in his eyes. 'You see, my dealer got caught with a big package, and then to save his own neck, he ratted out everyone he was supplying to. He made out that I was the key guy. It was bullshit, of course. I mean, I'll freely admit that I was a user. But a supplier? No fucking way.'

He paused to let the nature of his stitch-up sink in. 'You know, I've got an eight-year-old son and a two-year-old daughter. When I get out, they'll be adults. Man, if I'd have lost at trial, I'd be looking at thirty years.'

And I thought *I* had been hard done by. I didn't know how someone like JD could bear facing all that time. But the remarkable thing was that he did: and there are tens of thousands of other men with stories like his who keep on existing. JD got up every day, went to his job, hung out at the rec and carried on, one day at a time. No matter how much he must have resented his situation, he always showed respect to his fellow inmates. In its own, unusual way, I found JD's perseverance and stoicism uplifting.

Others, too, inspired me in those early days. I got to talking with quite a few guys on the wing, and before long I had a small group with whom I enjoyed spending time. In prison, you hear so many incredible stories that you become immune to being surprised by most of them, but some people did still amaze me with their tales. Take Mel, a guy you'd walk past in the street without so much as a second glance. I guessed he was in for drug offences, like so many people, until he told me, with a totally straight and expressionless face, that he was serving twelve years for arranging the contract murder of his own wife – for $50,000. The sting was that the guy he had hired to commit the murder was an undercover federal agent!

Then there was Cliff, another man around my age, who wouldn't have looked out of place at my local rugby club. He was three years into a ten-year sentence for supply and possession of a gun, as well as using a gun in furtherance of a crime. Based on that information, he may not sound like a man who deserves sympathy, but his case was not as cut and dried as you might imagine. It all started when a trusted friend roped him in on a drug deal, promising him $5,000 if he helped to look after a consignment. Cliff had a family and was short of cash, and he thought the money would go a long way to making his wife's and two children's lives more comfortable. The friend gave him a gun and told him to sit in a hotel room and keep watch. Two people were supposed to come and check on the goods and then they would leave. After a while, the pair duly arrived and poked around the hotel room. They asked Cliff if he had a gun on him: he said he had, and showed it to them. Then they left. Cliff collected his pay-off and forgot about the whole thing.

Months later, he was arrested. The entire operation had been a set-up, and the two men were working for the Feds. Until then, Cliff had never committed a crime in his life, but suddenly he was staring at a life-ruining sentence. In the end, he pleaded out to thirteen years and at his sentencing he presented the judge with letters from his friends and family saying that he was a fundamentally good person, and begging for leniency. The judge agreed that Cliff didn't deserve thirteen years, so bumped his sentence down ... to ten years.

Cliff clearly wasn't innocent, but I was certain that he didn't deserve to lose a decade of his life because of this one mistake. Having related the whole story to me, then he came to the worst bit: 'I was taken into custody after the sentencing and my wife came to visit. I thought she was going to comfort me, but she announced that she was divorcing me, right then and there in the courtroom. That was three years ago.'

I was shaking my head, trying to imagine his anguish. 'What about your children?' I asked.

'Well,' he said, 'that was three years ago and I haven't seen my wife or kids since. She's now met a new guy and he's moved into my house, with my kids. All for a lousy five grand.' I didn't know what on earth to say to Cliff – but I did know that my own life would be unbearable if I couldn't see my daughters, or even be in touch with them.

Cliff continued: 'The thing is, I know what I did was wrong. But I'm not a bad man, Darby, really I'm not. I know I fucked up, but I don't know what I ever did to deserve all that.'

What do you say to that? What can you say?

At the same time as making these tentative new friends (I tried not to get too attached to anyone until I knew what they were in for), I tried to maintain a sense of anonymity. I understood that prison was the kind of place where gliding under the radar was a good thing, and I didn't want to draw more attention to myself than necessary. Unfortunately, my case had been quite big news in America as well as back in the UK, so some of the newshounds knew who I was.

A guy by the name of Walter was in Allenwood for securities fraud and, being a finance guy, he recognised me straight away. He told a couple of people who I was and then they told their mates and before I knew it, I seemed to be a person of note. This made me nervous, since so many Americans had lost money investing in Enron. As I said earlier, it wasn't only big-time hedge funds that were hurt by the firm's bankruptcy – lots of ordinary, working-class people had pumped their pension funds into it, and John Doe wasn't amused. I didn't know if any of the people around me had lost out personally through the crash, and I certainly didn't want to find out.

I was in the library, still finding my way around the prison, when an inmate I'd never seen before came up to me. 'Hey,' he said, 'are you that Enron guy?'

I winced. 'Well ... yeah.'

'Congratulations!' he exclaimed, breaking into a broad smile.

'On what?'

'Well, I read that book, *Conspiracy of Fools* – about the Enron collapse. It was really good!'

He was referring to a doorstop of a book that detailed the entire Enron story. It isn't one of my favourite reads – it has nothing to do with me and, where I am mentioned, I'm not painted in the most flattering light. But I didn't tell him this. I thanked him and moved on.

Something similar happened a couple of days later when I met Mike, an American businessman. He was in for ten years for tax evasion, and after being indicted, he had fled to Spain and lived there, travelling around Europe on a false passport for more than two years, before he was finally picked up at Luton airport. He then spent time in Wandsworth Prison before being sent back to the US.

During our fight against extradition, I had been offered false passports and a place to live in Northern Cyprus, as there is no extradition treaty there, but decided it was preferable to face the music rather than spend my life on the run. Mike told me that every single moment of every day, wherever he went and whatever he was doing, he was looking over his shoulder, anxious about being caught; when he was eventually arrested, it was an enormous relief. His story was fascinating, but he seemed more eager to hear about mine.

'You're that banker guy,' he said. 'Right?'

I reluctantly admitted that I was.

He slapped me on the back. 'I followed your case when I was in Wandsworth, man. You guys got the shaft.' I wasn't about to disagree with him.

The whole time I was trying to avoid being outed as 'the Enron guy', I also had to worry about avoiding the lollipops. It was far too early for me to have the measure of everyone on the wing, so I had to be careful about the inmates with whom I associated. There were some tough lessons in the beginning, and I was wary of El's warnings that my age and skin colour fitted the profile of a typical sex offender.

One warm evening, I was walking around the track with Paul, a guy who said he was serving forty-eight months for running an illegal online gambling site. We were a few minutes into our stroll, keeping half an eye on the basketball game taking place in a nearby court, when we started gaining on an elderly white guy who was ambling along in front of us with a small group. Paul leaned closer to me and lowered his voice.

'He's English, I think.' He studied the back of the man's head. 'Yeah, I've heard him speak before. He's definitely from your side of the pond.'

I went over to the elderly guy and introduced myself. 'Hey,' I said. 'I'm Darby. I hear you're English? Nice to meet a fellow countryman.'

He replied in a thick, West Country accent and, for a moment, as I listened to him rolling his 'r's, I forgot I had ever left the south-west. The man told me that he was indeed English, and introduced his two friends – both white Americans, both in their sixties. Paul joined the group and we all had a pleasant enough conversation. We covered all the usual subjects – American politics, the legal system, work, our various dealings with the Department of Justice.

We had been walking along for around twenty minutes when Jimmy, a fun guy I had got to know fairly well, walked past. He looked at us and appraised the group. His eyes then came back to me and he scowled, meeting my gaze for a moment before turning away in what appeared to be disgust. I realised then that I hadn't asked any of the new group how long they were in for, so that's what I did next.

'Eight years.'

'Six years.'

'Eight years.'

None of them offered any more information about why they were in; they answered curtly and quickly and tried to steer the conversation back to more comfortable subjects. That was when it dawned on me that they were probably not the kind of people with whom I should be mixing. I understood straight away why Jimmy had given me such a strange look, and I thought about the optics of our little group. By being seen with them, I was giving these probable sex offenders legitimacy they didn't deserve. And, worse, I was sending a message to the rest of the unit that I was one of them. This realisation hit me like a sledgehammer, and I quickly made my excuses and steered Paul away from the others. Evidently, I still had much to learn.

The funny thing was that even after a couple of weeks at Allenwood, I still wasn't sure what El was in for. I understood it was something to do with drugs, but I didn't know all the details. What he did tell me was that he was only twenty-six when his sentence was handed down. When I met him, he was forty-one. He was another of the many casualties in the Americans' draconian war on drugs. I also learned that he had two daughters, both of whom lived some five hundred miles away. Fortunately – and remarkably, given the circumstances – El had managed to keep in contact with his kids, and he still wrote to them regularly.

I suspected that this may be one of the reasons why he had such a good outlook on life – even though his was bleak by almost anyone's standards. He was one of those people who was always smiling and joking around, and it was clear that all the other black guys on the wing looked up to him. During the evenings, you could often hear El's roaring laugh from the other side of the unit – usually the result of some gentle teasing over a game of chess or backgammon, his favourite ways to pass the time.

El told me that Allenwood was the eighth prison he'd stayed in, and I suspected he had seen some horrific things on his journey through the justice system. For example, we were in the TV room one evening watching one of the Jason Bourne movies, when a scene came on where someone is garroted. El remarked casually, 'I've seen that happen.' The way he said this, it sounded like an everyday occurrence. I asked him where and he continued: 'Chow hall in the pen. Some guy had gotten hold of a chain. Walks right up behind this dude at dinner and just did it there and then, just like that on TV.'

'Why did he do it?'

'Fuck knows why anything happens in those places, Darby.'

But whatever happened, El remained upbeat; he kept his head down and gradually made his way through his sentence one day at a time. That was all he could do. And if he could do it, I started to believe that I could do it, too.

CHAPTER 5

A NEW CELLIE

After only a few weeks, I settled into some semblance of a daily routine. Fortunately, all my case papers came through fairly quickly, so I was able to lodge my transfer application (to be moved to a UK prison) before I could get too worked up about it. A short meeting took place with a warden to submit the paperwork, although I didn't know whether to be reassured or not when she studied my file and said she'd never before seen anything like the plea bargain promise of an expedited transfer. That meant one of two things: either the Feds were being unusually efficient and amenable, and I could genuinely expect a rapid transfer, or the promise was without foundation and utterly meaningless. Only time would tell which it was going to be.

Having arrived at Allenwood in May, I hoped to be back in Britain by October, and definitely by the end of the year. I couldn't even countenance the thought of the transfer being stalled or, even worse, rejected entirely, which would result in me spending my entire sentence in America. Still, the transfer request was out of my hands, and it was something of a relief to have submitted it. All I could do now was wait and I told myself there was no point in worrying about it until I heard back. Thus I was able to focus my energies on the challenges of day-to-day living.

As I told friends in a letter back home, prison was just like boarding school ... but one where you couldn't go out. In Gregg Unit, my fellow boarders and I tended to rise somewhere between 5.30 a.m. and 6 a.m. The daily routine then depended on your job. El worked at the on-site government furniture factory, making tables, chairs, desks and whatever else Uncle Sam needed in prisons, schools and courts. His shift started at

6.30 a.m. and went on until 2.30 p.m., so he spent most of the day out of the cell. I was impressed by how many hours of work some inmates put in. Since you could choose which jobs to apply for, I wondered why anyone would opt to work in a factory for eight hours a day but, as ever, El had an explanation. For one thing, the furniture factory offered the best-paying job in the prison. Although the wages were still somewhere below the minimum wage, they were great compared to the pennies per hour the menial prison jobs paid. Also, working long hours was widely viewed as the best way to stave off the tedium and prevent yourself from snapping completely.

Ross, meanwhile, seemed to come and go as he pleased, moping around the unit. If he had a job, his hours must have been short and irregular, because he never seemed to be working. Still, I tried my best to ignore him when he was in the cell. In fact, I think the combination of my quiet hostility and El's out-and-out hatred sent a very clear message that he wasn't welcome to spend any more time around us than required. This was great for me, since it meant I could get some quiet in the mornings while El was at work and Ross was ... well, doing whatever he was doing.

My job in those first weeks was as a litter-picker, one of the worst-paying gigs in the prison and with the shortest hours. At first, I thought this would be a good thing, but I quickly learned my lesson about the boredom. I worked for only one or two hours every evening, walking the grounds looking for rubbish to collect. It was about as dull as it sounds and did very little to eat through the hours that seemed to stretch endlessly ahead every day.

The only advantage of the job was that I could have a bit of a lie-in. I tended to wait until most people were out of the unit before I got up, so I could shower while the block was quiet. Then I would brew myself a cup of tea and watch the sport and news headlines at 7 a.m. This talk of lie-ins and morning television might make it sound as if life at Allenwood was a walk in the park, but the reality was that I was in near-constant emotional anguish. I could think of little else but my family and friends, whose lives were going on in the real world while mine was frozen in time.

Reading letters from my daughters about what they were doing at school, and whose birthday parties they had been to at the weekend, I wouldn't be aware that I was crying until tears started to fall onto the page. Even the morning ritual of tea and the news headlines made me sad: but I still did it, because I could forget where I was for a few seconds at a time and pretend it was the start of a normal business day. Then a chair would scrape in the TV room behind me, or I'd hear a profane shout from outside the unit, and I'd be jolted back to sad, lonely reality.

To make matters worse, every time I settled down in front of CNN, I would be reminded of the morning in June 2002 when I found out that criminal charges had been laid against us and this whole nightmare began. Let me tell you a bit more about that. I was staying with friends at the time and we were watching *BBC Breakfast*. Enron had collapsed in December 2001 and the DOJ's Enron Task Force had been established by George W. Bush in the following weeks. I was aware of the Task Force before that, but this was the day I really took notice of it.

It had started like a normal day. I had work on my mind – by then I had left the City and owned a small manufacturing business in the south-west of England – and the last thing I was thinking about was past dealings with Enron. There I was, watching the news, when suddenly a 'Breaking News' banner flashed across the screen: three British bankers had been indicted in the US Enron probe, the newsreader said, and they were facing thirty-five years in prison. Thirty-five years!

My initial thought, in the split-second after reading the headline, was that those poor bastards were screwed. I had seen the feeding frenzy going on with the Feds – they could smell blood and they were going to make sure that everyone who had ever touched Enron would pay the price. I listened as the names of the bankers were read out.

Gary Mulgrew. David Bermingham. Giles Darby.

I had this sudden sensation that the air around me had been completely sucked out, leaving a vacuum: I couldn't breathe and my heart started galloping. *Thirty-five years!* Did he really say that? It was lucky I was sitting down, because if I'd been standing up I might well have passed out. Strangely, my mind made the connection with my former colleagues before it sank in properly that one of the three names belonged to me. My first coherent thought was shit, I know those guys. Then a second thought came crashing into my head, eclipsing everything else: one of 'those guys' is me! My life is over. Finished.

The newsflash was my first inkling of any supposed wrongdoing on my part. I hadn't had anything to do with Fastow or Enron for months. It wasn't as if I had been lying awake at night worrying about my own peripheral involvement with the fallen company; yet now it seemed that I was looking at thirty-five years in prison. It was a shattering, sledgehammer blow.

In his book, David Bermingham goes into intricate detail about the events that led up to the charges but, to summarise, after Enron's collapse in late 2001, the company had made a filing with the authorities about numerous suspect transactions. One of these was the SPV that we had invested in. In the meantime, Fastow and several of his finance team had been fired.

When, thanks to Enron's filing, the details of our suspect transaction became known, we informed our then-employer, the Canadian bank, of our involvement. We also voluntarily disclosed our investment to the Financial Services Authority (FSA), who subsequently requested our permission to send our statement to the DOJ and we had willingly agreed. The optics of the investment were bad enough for the Canadians to ask the three of us to resign and reluctantly we did so. After leaving the bank, I had bought the small business in the West Country and life had moved on. Clearly, we had chosen to do the right thing and help the authorities nail the bad guys who had brought Enron down. We had no idea at the time that we were going to be cast as the bad guys – otherwise why on earth would we have gone straight to the authorities and told them everything we knew?

To begin with, the DOJ issued criminal charges against us rather than an indictment, but it was a signal of the intention to indict. In later years, and having been brutally exposed to the US justice system, we learned that rather than go to the FSA and offer ourselves up, what the three of us should have done immediately was: say nothing, hire experienced US attorneys, seek immunity from the Feds, and then – only then – tell them what we knew in return for a lenient deal.

That is precisely what Fastow's crooked sidekick, Michael Kopper, had done and in the process he had turned the spotlight straight on to us and our involvement. To demonstrate our complete naïvety, his attorney had even contacted our UK lawyer to ask if we were cooperating with the Feds. Our answer? Of course not – because we didn't believe we had done anything wrong! We didn't even have any US representation until we were charged in June 2002: we were utterly clueless when it came to the workings of the US justice system.

A few weeks later, Kopper pleaded out and became a witness for the prosecution, fingering us amongst others in the process, as I said. In our initial dealings with the crisis, we behaved like amateurs, having no idea of what we were up against. Being convinced that we had not committed any criminal offence was, in the context of the US justice system, the worst mindset to have. In a multi-defendant case, the people who are the real crooks are able to confess to their crimes and turn evidence to get lighter sentences – as Kopper did. People like us, without experience of the system or any understanding of how it works, are often the last ones left standing, by which time there is nothing or no one to offer up. This in turn means the relative innocents get dealt with more severely than if they had simply 'fessed up in the first place and cut their own deal. It's a brutal system.

We hadn't heard a peep from the FSA since our statement to them in November 2001; we hadn't been visited by the police or been asked to give more information. We had simply gone along to the FSA, told them everything, and then forgotten about it. But now I appeared to be a wanted criminal, facing the prospect of a long jail sentence.

I spent days in a state of shock. The first thing I did was to visit the premises of the small business I owned to try to reassure my employees that they were going to keep their jobs. But every moment of those first weeks was truly awful. At one point, I was so overcome with the trauma of it all that I couldn't physically stand up. I had to be helped out of the car and into my house – I had no energy and my limbs simply stopped working.

On another occasion, I walked into our local supermarket with one of my daughters, only to be confronted by a rack of local newspapers with my photo on the front page. The headline read: Wiltshire Banker Facing 35 Years In American Jail, with a big picture of me in the centre of the page. I turned round and walked back out into the street. It was more than I could face at the time. The magnitude of what was happening was simply incomprehensible.

I'm sure many people who read about the case thought we deserved everything we got. Maybe so. In hindsight, with plenty of time to think in Allenwood, I accept that we had made some bad and stupid decisions, but at the time I still didn't regard myself as a criminal. I thought of myself as a man who had let arrogance and hubris get in the way of his thinking, but not as a man who had knowingly done anything wrong. So many of my fellow inmates were in similar positions: such as guys caught with drugs on them when they were barely older than children, now facing sentences that seemed like a lifetime, or men who had been entrapped in sting operations by the Feds.

Dark thoughts about justice and fairness – or the lack of either – threatened to overwhelm me on a daily basis. I had to force myself to focus on the positives. Sometimes, that meant comparing my situation to those around me, an exercise that always left me feeling sad for the other guys, but grateful for my comparative good fortune. I figured out early on, as most did, that keeping busy would be the trick to making it through without losing anything of myself.

It didn't help that I faced an early psychological challenge. My forty-sixth birthday fell on a Friday in May, only a couple of weeks into my sentence, when I was at my most vulnerable. It was an unwelcome reminder that another year had passed without life returning to normal. Having been indicted in June 2002, we were extradited in July 2006 and imprisoned in 2008: six long years. So spending my birthday alone in my prison cell was hugely emotional, however comforting it was to receive a good number of cards and letters in the post and to know that people back home were thinking of me. To add insult to injury, my football team, Bristol City, had made it to the play-offs at Wembley on the following day. It was the first time for some thirty years that they had made it anywhere near the Premiership and there I was, stuck behind bars and unable even to follow the action. I made a phone call after the game, only to hear that they had lost, which just compounded my sense of frustration and disappointment. It was a bloody tough couple of days.

In general, I tried to focus on the few positives and the small mercies. One of these was the weather. It was gorgeous in Pennsylvania at that time of year, so I spent as much time as possible outside. I would go on long walks round the rec in the afternoons, and then join in with the games of football that took place in the evenings. Sometimes I would bring a book and read in the sun, or sit at one of the picnic-style benches dotted around the grounds and listen to the radio.

I also enjoyed watching other games between inmates – basketball and American football were particularly popular among the prisoners, and they could get very heated. As a result, these were the games that tended to attract the biggest crowds.

In those early summer days, the inmates jokingly referred to the rec as 'the beach'. There wasn't a real beach, of course, but it was so sunny in the valley that the prison campus nestled in, that the heat evoked memories of trips to the coast and foreign holidays. For me, the most powerful memory was of a business trip to Miami laid on by Fastow and his team, which had taken place only weeks before my life came crashing down.

This was shortly after Fastow had approached Gary with his unspecified 'investment opportunity' – the dodgy deal that would land us all in prison years later. Fastow and I were sitting by a pool, drinking and chatting, and eventually the conversation turned to our deal. I was in awe of his financial wizardry, and I thought he was doing us a favour by investing the money on our behalf. Of course, I had no idea he had suckered us into criminality, and I was so naïve that I remember thanking him for involving us.

Whenever my fellow inmates and I were hanging out at 'the beach' at Allenwood, I always thought back to that encounter with Fastow. I couldn't get the image out of my head of me sitting by the pool with him; raising a glass to him and thinking he was a great guy for including me in one of his deals. It took the shine off those sunny days I spent with El and the gang, watching basketball games or listening to music.

Talk about sunny days at 'the beach' probably came as quite a surprise to my family when they read my letters home. The thing is, people think that prisons are going to be dangerous, violent hell-holes all the time, and of course they can be, but most of the time they aren't. They are deeply sad places. They can be nasty and difficult environments but the Hollywood depiction of relentless gang warfare and constant lockdown is not really accurate, at least not in my experience. That is not to pretend that I enjoyed my time at Allenwood at all: I was thoroughly miserable, but there were times when the humanity of my fellow inmates made me forget where I was for a while.

I always needed to be alert, of course, but I rarely felt as if I was in real danger, in those early weeks at least. It doesn't mean that unpleasant things were not happening around me – they were, and beatings were a regular occurrence. However, prison life was such a shock to my system that it took me a while before I could even think about anyone but myself. That was the case until El pulled me over for a chat in my third or fourth week. He had decided he'd had enough of Ross, and he wanted me to help 'do something about him'.

'What do you mean?' I asked. 'You don't want to "do something" as in ...' I trailed off.

El laughed and playfully punched my shoulder. 'Fuck off, Darby. You've seen *Shawshank* too many times. I mean we need to get him moved to another cell. He's lazy, dirty – just an all-round piece of shit and I don't want to associate with him. It's bad for my reputation. I need him gone, okay?'

As I said, El was viewed as one of the 'senior' guys on the wing; certainly among the black inmates, he was one of Gregg Unit's head honchos. So as he saw it, the guards had disrespected him by placing a suspected sex offender in the same cell as him. If he didn't do something about it, El was worried that his credibility on the wing would take a hit. That's how prison worked – credibility was a very fragile thing, and one minor infraction could seriously undermine anyone's reputation.

I reassured El that I would do whatever was needed. I felt it would be a way to repay his kindness and, knowing what I knew, I hated sharing a cell with Ross anyway. It sounded like a win for both of us if we could get rid of him – the only question was how.

'Well,' El explained, 'any inmate can ask to move cells if they feel like they aren't safe. There are obviously a lot of things I could do to let him know he's not, but I don't want to get myself sent to the SHU. So the best thing for us, and for him, is if we make it very clear that he'll be best off moving. I'll have a few words with him, maybe try and fuck with him a bit, and you should keep on ignoring him – and definitely don't step in if you see me messing with him. If he says anything about me, just tell him to fuck off, okay?'

'It sounds like you've done this before,' I said.

He grimaced. 'I've had to live with some creatures far worse than that piece of shit, Darby. But now I'm finally at a low security I don't want to be sleeping in the same cell as some lollipop. I mean, his kind shouldn't even be mixed with the population anyway. You know, at any other prison, he'd have been beaten half to death by now.'

That very day, El put his plan into action. Of course I knew that Ross was almost certainly a lowlife, but he was still a human being and I found it hard to look him in the eye and mistreat him. Instead, I engineered moments when I could leave El alone in the cell with him. I didn't know what El had been saying or doing to Ross when I wasn't around – I presumed it wasn't anything nice – but I did hear him threatening our cellie once or twice whilst I was there. It wasn't anything too bad by prison standards but still El made it clear that Ross would get what was coming to him if he didn't move. The reaction was immediate. Ross had been a skittish and nervous character anyway, but now he seemed even more on edge, flinching whenever El came anywhere near him.

Thanks largely to El, although I admit my hostility played a part in it, the atmosphere in the cell became distinctly and instantly unpleasant. If Ross walked in while El and I were there, the mood would suddenly switch, and our friendly chatter would cut off. This very quickly reached the point where Ross's presence invoked the kind of on-edge feeling you get at particularly rowdy football matches. El's eyes would snap onto Ross's, and follow him around the room, all the while cracking his knuckles and oozing hostility. Although I knew El wasn't going to do anything, it felt as if violence was only one wrong move away. I never said anything – I merely let the routine continue, hoping for all our sakes that our cellie would give in and ask to be moved.

Eventually Ross could bear no more; before we knew it, he was gone. We woke up that morning with him in our cell, then went about our daily business, and returned in the evening to find that all his stuff had vanished. El was thrilled and he beamed at me. 'Thank fuck for that!' he grinned, standing against Ross's empty bunk, the one below mine. 'He made me feel so sick that I was starting to think I might have to beat him up anyway.'

El's delight became even more pronounced when he found out who would be replacing Ross – one of El's friends, a slender black guy about the same age as us, known only as 'T'. He moved in that evening, throwing his bedding on Ross's old bunk and shoving his bundle of clothes into Ross's old wardrobe. The new man greeted me with a standard fist bump, and then turned to El and whooped with pleasure. The pair bumped fists and T slapped him on the back.

'Great to be here, man.' T beamed at El. 'Hey, what did you do to the lollipop who was in here? I'm not going to find him under here, am I?' He bent down and made a show of inspecting under his bunk, and then burst into rasping laughter.

I had seen T around, but we had never spoken before. I was pleased to discover that he was chatty and friendly right from the off, telling me about his work in the furniture factory, the same place as El.

'You lucked out here, Darby,' he said. 'Practically going to be living on your own while El and I are putting in the hard hours.'

He asked me where I worked, and I told him I did the evening shifts picking up rubbish around the grounds. He tutted and shook his head.

'That's some shit, man,' he said. 'You need to get yourself something that will keep you busy. Trust me, man, I've been here long enough to know that. Hell, so has he.' He looked over at El.

'For real,' El agreed.

'Hey,' T said, still looking at El, 'you know I'm easy about who I share with, right, so long as they're clean. Is Darby clean?'

I was standing right there, but obviously that didn't matter to T. El laughed and nodded. 'Sure is, T. It was only the one white guy that I had a problem with.'

T guffawed, and that set El off laughing too. They were like a couple of mischievous schoolchildren, but I didn't mind. In fact, their energy and enthusiasm were contagious.

'Well then, Darby,' T said, turning back to me. 'I think we're going to get on just fine.'

'I hope so, T,' I said. In truth, I was merely relieved that Ross had gone.

'You know, I wasn't kidding about the job though, man. You're going to go mad if you don't get something better. You should try the laundry, I hear they're a man down at the moment, and we know some people who work there, don't we?' He nudged El, who picked up the conversation.

'Yeah, we do. Good guys they are, too. I reckon we can get you in, Darby, if you're up for it?'

I was, and I thanked them both for their help. A job in the prison laundry? I was going up in the world.

With the sullen sex offender gone, the mood in our cell improved overnight. T, as it turned out, was almost as funny and personable as El, and I enjoyed chatting to him and learning about his life. He was already eighteen years into his sentence, for some combination of drug offences, he said. When I told him how long I had to serve, he made exactly the same comment as El: 'Chump change.'

While this made me feel marginally better about my own situation, I couldn't help feeling bad for the other two. They were some of the most mild-mannered and, in the circumstances, fun guys I'd ever met – inside prison or in the outside world – and now their lives were being wasted behind bars. I knew about the war on drugs before I came to Allenwood, but it was only after coming face-to-face with the casualties that I understood how tough it truly was.

Like El, T had spent time in the pen. They both joked about the things they saw there, and they clearly enjoyed regaling me with their stories, but I got the impression that deep down they were scarred by it. Both were relatively senior on the wing, so they had to give the impression that they were unflappable and in control all the time. It was only in the cell, and then in occasional, unguarded moments, that I saw how being locked up for such a long time was taking a real toll on them, despite their attempts to pretend otherwise.

Allenwood was safer than most of the prisons El and T had stayed in. But there were still moments when the proverbial hit the fan, and I would be jolted out of the false sense of security into which I had lured myself. One such moment came during the first weekend after we got rid of Ross, still only weeks into my sentence.

Everything kicked off at the end of an hourly 'move'. Free movement was not allowed at Allenwood – prisoners could only move around the compound during ten-minute windows every hour on the half-hour. The prison was divided into sections, for example the units, the chow hall, the commissary, the rec, the laundry, and so on, and you could move between sections during the allowed time. But after that ten-minute window, you had to stay wherever you were until the next hour's 'move'. So say there was a televised football game at 4 p.m., you couldn't simply rock up to catch the kick-off at 4 p.m. Instead, you had to make your way to the TV room during the ten-minute window at 3.30 p.m., or else you would have to miss the first half-hour and move during the 4.30 p.m. window. If you miss the move, you're stuck until the next one.

This was all so the guards could keep tabs on where everyone was, and it made it easier for them to police activities in the unit. I also think it was intended to remind the inmates who was in control. It was another way to rob us of our agency and make us feel like cattle, rather than human beings. It worked. Personally it reminded me of being back at school, waiting for the teacher's permission to leave the classroom.

One day, after one of these moves, a known sex-offender came back from the rec to find a black guy in his cell, trying to break into his locker. The thief had probably targeted him intentionally, knowing that he had no allies apart from the other undesirables. As anticipated, the lollipop didn't fight back, but he did make a monumental fuss, shouting at the thief, slinging abuse at everyone nearby and generally causing a scene.

We heard the commotion from our cell on the other side of the block, and within moments, half of Gregg Unit was crowded round the cell where the fracas was taking place. Nobody cared that an undesirable was being targeted, but a group of Colombians took a special interest in the commotion. It turned out that a few of them had been robbed recently as well, and they were eager to find out who was the neighbourhood thief.

The sad truth was that nobody's locker contained that much – and certainly nothing of any real material value. The average inmate would keep a stash of food supplies, some packets of fish, spare clothes, a radio, toiletries and other basics. There was never anything worth stealing. But robberies were still taken very seriously, because most inmates had next to nothing and if they got robbed, they would lose everything – all their worldly possessions, meagre as they were. So you can imagine that the Colombians were very eager to see justice done for whatever they had lost.

Between them, they grabbed the thief, a black youth, and took him to the chief black guy on the unit. Although Allenwood wasn't dominated by racial tensions in the same way as some American prisons, there was still a distinct hierarchy for the biggest ethnic groups: blacks, Americans, Hispanics, Colombians, Mexicans, Cubans, et cetera. Having a head honcho to whom they could report any issues kept things broadly civil, and stopped minor disputes from sparking an all-out war between the different factions. In fact, the cops actively encouraged the hierarchies.

In this instance, the Colombians told the black 'shot caller' that either he could teach the thief a lesson, or they would. The thief was advised to check himself into protective custody – that is, take himself to the SHU for his own safety – but he refused. Clearly, he thought it was a matter of pride to endure whatever was coming to him. El told me what was going on, and also warned me to keep my head down that evening.

Sure enough, the Colombians took their revenge. I was in the TV room watching ESPN and, I noticed, so was the thief. It had been a perfectly normal evening, with the usual banter and the frenzy of betting stamps and fish packets on the games. In fact, it seemed to me that the earlier commotion had been forgotten and the thief had been allowed to carry on normally without so much as a peep from anyone.

But then, at around 10 p.m., the mood changed abruptly. People stopped shouting at the screens, and I became aware of a hush washing over the room. I looked around and saw the entire perimeter was lined with a small army of Colombians, all staring at the back of the thief's head. Sensing the sudden change in atmosphere, the thief also looked round and all hell broke loose. He leapt to his feet, sending his chair flying in the process, and there was a mad scramble as he tried to weave through the crowd towards the doors – but the Colombians had already anticipated this and blocked him off. There was a cacophony of scraping as everyone jumped up from their chairs and tried to get out of the way as quickly as possible, myself included. I made it to the edge of the room just as four pairs of hands seized the thief.

A second later, he was curled up on the floor, as the Colombians rained a hail of punches and kicks down on him. They beat him relentlessly for what felt like a long time – and must have felt even longer to him. Meanwhile, the guards had heard the commotion and were trying to get into the TV room. But the Colombians had planned for this, too, and some of the larger men used their bodies to block the doors. With the guards unable to get in, the Colombians dispensed their justice, prison-style, as we bystanders looked on.

Nobody was going to risk getting involved, and with the Colombians on the warpath that was a wise move. Instead, we all watched, in silence, as blood streamed from the thief's face and pooled on the floor. I was worried that they were going to kill him, but I knew there was no intervening. By the time the gang decided enough was enough, their victim was barely moving. A feeble moan came from him, reassuring me that he had been left alive, even if only barely. The attackers, meanwhile, had blood all over their shoes and fists, and I noted that some had a glint in their eyes that suggested they would have happily beat him some more. Now that they had their revenge, the men blocking the doors stepped aside and guards streamed into the room. Two of them went straight to the prone form of the thief, while another declared it was a lockdown, and ordered everyone to return to their cells.

It was my first lockdown, so I didn't know quite what to expect. I anticipated there would be something a bit glamorous about it, and I would finally feel as if I was in one of those prison movies. But in reality it was mind-numbingly boring. In hindsight, I don't know why I was surprised – after all, a lockdown meant everyone had to stay in their cells for an unspecified amount of time. In this case, nobody was allowed to leave until the beating in the TV room had been investigated.

On lockdown, you can't watch television, you can't go to the microwaves, and you can't shower. El and T had horror stories of lockdowns in the penitentiary that lasted for days on end, so that by the time normality was restored, everyone was stinking, starving and desperate for something to do.

We had been in our cells for only a few minutes when a squad of guards invaded the wing. They wanted to check us all for cuts, bruises, bloodstains or any sign that we had been involved in the beating. After the three of us had been checked, the guards left us alone and went to work checking the rest of the inmates. In the end, the lockdown lasted all night. It was excruciating to be trapped in our cubicle, but at least the lockdown had the desired effect of calming everyone down.

In the first few hours after the beating, there was a frenzied, febrile tension in the unit. Although I had only El and T to talk to, I could sense it in the air. Even those two seemed more on edge and alert than usual, and they were veterans of the prison system. It was as if the unit was full of sharks, and one sniff of blood had brought out everyone's inner craving for violence. But after a few hours in lockdown, the tension seemed to melt away. El and T eventually went to sleep, and I dozed off myself shortly afterwards.

I had been asleep for only a few hours when I was woken by a commotion. I couldn't see what was happening, but I could hear a scuffle down the hallway, and a lot of shouting. I looked at my watch and saw it was shortly after 4 a.m. I learned later that day that the disturbance had been caused by the return of the guards. They had swooped in while everyone was asleep and dragged six inmates off to the SHU, all of whom were Colombians, and all had been involved in the beating.

The penalty for fighting was that you were moved to a medium-security prison, so several of these men could expect their time behind bars to get a lot harder. The ironic thing was that the next day, with the Colombians in the SHU, all their lockers were busted open. They had almost beaten a man to death for stealing their things and now they were being robbed again – only this time nobody did anything about it.

I had been there only a few weeks, yet I was already learning that Allenwood could be a strange, cruel and dangerous place.

CHAPTER 6

THE LAUNDRY NAZI

True to their word, El and T used their connections to land me a job in the prison laundry. It definitely beat the short hours and almost non-existent pay of my old job picking up litter, a task so mundane that it was somehow more boring than sitting in my cell and staring at the wall. I was glad to be moving up in the world.

Before reporting for my first shift, I had only been to the laundry on a handful of occasions – none of them particularly pleasant. When inmates first arrived at Allenwood, the laundry was where they went to get their hygiene packages (toothpaste, toothbrush, four razors and a bar of soap) as well as their clothing issue.

After I was kitted out for the first time, I was told that I could come back once a year to exchange my clothes for new ones. I hoped beyond hope that I wouldn't be in America for long enough to get a crisp new T-shirt, what with the wheels of bureaucracy turning on my transfer request. But I still had to go back every two weeks to collect a fresh hygiene pack, and whenever I went, there always seemed to be some sort of problem.

I didn't mind waiting in line for ages while the workers messed about – after all, I was in prison, a place where standing around is a core part of the experience. Instead, what always irked me was the attitude of the sour old woman who ran the laundry, a real battleaxe called Miss Anderson. Nothing was ever easy with her, and she always made out that the inmates were an enormous personal inconvenience. It made me wonder why she had ever decided that a prison would be a good place for her to spend her days, if she hated dealing with inmates so much.

As a result of her totally obstinate manner and unwavering rudeness,

Miss Anderson developed something of a legendary reputation among the population. She was a bit of a comedy figure, but at the same time she was known as a woman who delighted in making other people's lives difficult. The tiny shred of power she held as the boss of the laundry room had gone to her head, and she ruled her patch with an iron fist. She was known to most as the Laundry Nazi – a fitting nickname for an ageing authoritarian and a stickler for even the most arcane of rules.

I had hoped that Miss Anderson would be different to work for, but she held her employees in much the same contempt as she held all the other inmates. Over time, once I proved myself to her, her attitude towards me gradually thawed. But it was a slow process, and for most of my time at Allenwood I had to put up with her relentless complaining and constant pettiness. I had worked with my share of grade-A assholes in my time, which helped to put Miss Anderson into perspective.

The main problem with her was that she was inherently distrustful of us all. There was a real aura of misanthropy about her – she thought that we inmates were all scum who deserved everything we got. I didn't bother to explain the intricacies of my case to her when I saw that she was the same with everyone: she was one of those people who believed in tough justice, to the extent that the justice part ceased to matter.

Over time, I did come to know her as a complex woman whose heart wasn't as bad as I had thought. But at first, I could easily picture her as the kind of person who would be in favour of bringing back hanging – a blind believer in American justice and the first person to throw a rotten tomato at whoever was unlucky enough to find themselves in the stocks. She was a real 'electrocute first, ask questions later' kind of woman. You get the point, I'm sure. Not an ideal boss.

It didn't take long for me to learn the ropes. I was never particularly gifted when it came to domestic chores, but I was competent enough to work a washing machine. A lot of my job consisted of funnelling clothes into washers, then drying and folding them in large batches. The folding all took place on a long table towards the front of the laundry area, not far from Miss Anderson's desk. She wanted us to do the folding there for a reason – so she could watch us.

A part of me completely understood her suspicion. Clothes did have a habit of 'walking' from the laundry room and ending up on the lucrative black market, so she wisely kept a beady eye on everything her employees did. When new batches of clothes arrived from outside the prison, she was extra-vigilant, such as one day when two hundred brand-new, white T-shirts were delivered, all of them rejects that the Bureau of Prisons had bought at discount prices from mainstream US retailers. To the man on the street, a poorly-stitched, plain T-shirt may not be worth the risk of time in solitary confinement. But in Allenwood, where most of the clothing issue had been worn by large numbers of different inmates before you, the chance to get your hands on a brand-new shirt that nobody else in the world had sweated in could drive you to take extreme risks.

When these sparkly new shirts arrived, Miss Anderson made sure to stop what she was doing and oversee our folding operation. She was so paranoid that she insisted on watching us until every single shirt had been folded and literally locked away in one of her cupboards. We could feel her eyes boring into us as we worked, so we all made sure to go as slowly as physically possible – in fact, we spent almost an entire shift folding those shirts. Anderson must have known that we were messing with her, but she was so concerned about her haul that she didn't take her eyes off us for one second. As soon as the shirts had been safely stowed, we had a good laugh at her expense. It amused us that she was so concerned – truly a case of small things and small minds.

There was usually another CO (Correctional Officer) stationed nearby, keeping an eye on us laundry workers and making sure little old Miss Anderson could handle herself. She was tougher than the fish they served in the canteen, though, so I don't think anyone needed to worry about her. Unfortunately, the other COs were as unpleasant as she was and many of them had a habit of overreacting to even the slightest infraction.

One day an elderly black guy hobbled in to collect his hygiene package. There was something very depressing about seeing really old people in prison – there weren't many of them, but the ones who were there always made me feel a twinge of sadness on their behalf. This old timer had comically thick glasses on, and he was clearly a bit on the frail side. A CO had left his cup of coffee on the counter next to the hygiene packs, and the old inmate reached for the white cup instead of the bar of soap.

'Hey!' the CO shouted from across the room. He bounded over. 'Don't touch my coffee!'

The old guy groped along the counter, squinting through his glasses. 'Sorry, sir, I thought it was the soap. I can't see very well.'

I couldn't bear to watch any more, so I reached over and picked up the soap for the old guy. I passed it to him and he nodded his thanks, the CO hovering behind us.

'Lucky you didn't touch my coffee, or I'd have put you on a shot!' the CO barked. A 'shot' was a written warning for bad behaviour, which could result in a loss of privileges and even a trip to the SHU. The old guy didn't say anything after that; he shuffled out, shaking his head to himself. It was an encounter that typified the uncompromising attitude shared by the majority of the guards.

Working in the laundry bore little comparison with my old job as an investment banker, especially financially. Naturally, I wasn't expecting to be rolling in it, but I was still stunned when I received my first paycheck. It was for $13.10, which worked out then at around £6.50 – for the whole month. In an entire month, I had earned the equivalent of one hour's work at the minimum wage. I could only laugh when I worked out that this amounted to a daily rate of 20p, literally pennies per hour.

The real cherry on top was that $4 of this monthly salary was given to me as a bonus! My report card said that I had 'done a good job folding'. If this wasn't so comical, I would probably have been insulted. Even in Allenwood, I was topping up my salary with bonuses: once a banker, always a banker, I guess.

Of course, I was in a position to see the funny side in all this, but then I was lucky. I was one of the fortunate few with money on the outside, and with friends and family members willing to make deposits into my prison account. For the guys with nothing, their measly monthly salary was all they had, representing the difference between living a life totally devoid of pleasures and obtaining the small comforts that are essential to keeping any inmate sane. That is another reason why so many prisoners opted to work in the on-site factory, where pay was higher and the hours were longer. For them, surviving on my laundry salary would have been next to impossible. It also explained why so many guys in the prison turned to theft. It's so easy to judge – as I'm sure Miss Anderson did, plenty of times – but if you've never been in that kind of situation, then you have no idea what depths you would sink to if it meant your life would become a little less painful.

As it happened, there was a committed smuggler within our group of guys working in the laundry, a bloke called Shane. He ran a nifty little scam, using the carts that we wheeled around the prison to collect and deliver bedding, clothes or whatever else needed washing. Shane was concealing odd items of clothing – a few socks here, some shorts there – amongst the mounds of bedding and then carting them out of the laundry. As soon as he thought he wasn't being watched, he would pull the smuggled goods out and stash them somewhere on the unit to collect and sell later.

Shane had probably been at this for months, if not years. The funny thing was that before he was found out, he was Miss Anderson's laundry clerk – the most senior position an inmate could hold within the laundry, with the most responsibilities attached. When Miss Anderson caught him with an illicit pair of pants one day, she was doubly furious. Not only had she been ripped off by one of the prisoners, but now she had to find a new clerk: this must have confirmed her suspicions about us all being good-for-nothing lowlifes.

I hadn't been working in the laundry for very long, but it seemed I was the surprise candidate to be Shane's replacement. Miss Anderson beckoned me over.

'I know about you, Darby,' she declared, as if she had made a major discovery. 'I've investigated your crime and decided that you're responsible enough to be my clerk.'

The job involved overseeing all the laundry and clothing supplies for the entire prison. What a career opportunity! From a high-flying, globe-trotting, fast-living banker to the custodian of all the Y-fronts in Allenwood – even I could see something deliciously ironic in that. All I can say is, I must have done a hell of a job folding ... and as I wrote about this bizarre job opportunity in my next letter home, I was chuckling to myself. My sense of humour appeared to have survived so far and I knew I had to preserve it if I was going to make it out of prison in one piece.

It might be hard to believe, but I ended up turning down the promotion. The trouble with being the clerk is that you have to get up earlier – at around 5.30 a.m. – to report to work at 6 a.m. Then, once you're in at the crack of dawn, the job consists largely of handing out toiletries, exchanging clothes and collecting all the day's dirty laundry in good time for it to be washed. I had already spent years of my life getting up early to commute to work, and I didn't fancy doing that in prison as well. Also, I wasn't expecting to be in America for that long and there was another inmate in our laundry group who would benefit far more from the pay rise. Bob, a Vietnam veteran and an all-round nice guy, had been under the weather recently, so he struck me as a better candidate. I got straight back to Miss Anderson with him in mind. 'Thank you, ma'am,' I said humbly, addressing her with the respect her title, Correctional Officer, demanded. 'It's a lovely offer, but I'm hoping to be transferred back to the UK in a few months. I'm worried it won't be worth the effort of training me up if I'm only going to leave again.'

'Oh,' she said curtly. Clearly, she had thought I would jump at the chance. Her face displayed the usual miserable expression – tight lips, sucked in cheeks.

'I'm happy to fill in and help you out, though,' I continued, in the same deferential tone. 'And I know a guy who'd be perfect for the job. Bob is your man, I'd say.'

'When are you leaving?' she asked.

'How long is a piece of string?' I shrugged.

'What?' She had never heard that expression before, so I tried to explain what it meant. She scowled at me from behind her boxy computer monitor. 'Well, Darby, you tell me. How long *is* a piece of string?'

'If you're the US government,' I replied, 'then I expect it's however long you want it to be.'

The best thing about working in the laundry was the time I spent with my colourful co-workers. Quite a few of the guys were close with El and T, and when I told them who I was, they immediately treated me like one of their own. One of my favourite people there was called Russ. He was a charismatic Italian-American, in his early fifties and full of life, and one of those people who saw the funny side to everything.

It was Russ who warned me from the off about Miss Anderson's foul attitude.

'That woman has perfected the art of rudeness,' he said, looking over from the folding table. Miss Anderson was behind her desk, arguing with an inmate, an obese black guy whom I had never seen before. We watched as the inmate complained that his clothing issue, which he'd only had for a month, was ruined. His trousers had been too tight, and now they had split right down the backside, requiring a belt to hold them up.

'Well, why did you take the clothes in the first place if they weren't the right size?' Miss Anderson was in full computer-says-no mode.

The inmate floundered. 'I thought I'd be out of here before now, but I've got a visitor coming to see me next week and I really want to look smart.'

Miss Anderson appraised him. 'You don't look very smart right now.'

'I know, ma'am, that's why I came here. My other clothes don't fit me and these ones are split.'

Miss Anderson argued back for a few more minutes and then, once the inmate had been well and truly humiliated, she relented. She sent Russ off to find the poor guy some bigger clothes, and then made him put them on and tuck the shirt in to prove everything would fit. Only then did she let him go. It's not as if the woman was openly abusive, but she was the perfect living embodiment of the unhelpful prison system, devoid of compassion and stripped of all humanity.

At any given time, there were usually at least eight of us working in the laundry. Four inmates were stationed at the enormous folding table, while a couple of others sat at sewing machines in the back, working on repairs to particularly distressed articles of clothing. Everyone else was tasked with keeping the storeroom in good order, putting away the clothes we had folded and retrieving things from the back whenever they were needed. It was all very well-organised.

We had to report for our shift at 7.30 a.m. and we were usually finished with most of the folding from the washing machines by around 8.30 a.m. That left us with a lot of time to sit around and chat, often with a cup of tea in hand. You can take the man out of England …

Normally the rest of the morning's work was done by 10.30 a.m., by which time lunch wasn't far off. Working in the laundry took a significant chunk out of my days, and I was grateful for it. An added perk of the job was that the laundry had its own toilet, which meant that we could all enjoy some peace and quiet and didn't have to rush. This was in stark contrast to the toilet situation on the unit, where there was only one for every twenty-five of us and a constant queue.

I spent many of my working days chatting to Russ, and gradually he shared his story. He was in for ten months for mortgage fraud – not a long sentence, even compared to my own – but being sent to prison had ruined his life regardless. His wife, whom he had been with for fourteen years, had recently sent him a 'Dear John' letter saying she had met someone else and wanted a divorce. After that, he didn't hear from her and she never accepted his calls. The next thing he knew, the divorce papers arrived in the post, complete apart from his signature.

I had often wondered how Russ always seemed so upbeat and soon I had an answer. He had only three weeks left to serve before his release, so he was very much on the home stretch. Knowing that he would be going soon, I started to make more of an effort to get to know the others, and quickly gravitated towards a very well-read and articulate white guy called Brian. He was an erudite character, who always kept abreast of the news, and as such we found we had lots to talk about.

As Russ's release date crept closer, Brian, myself and the rest of our laundry gang shared in his excitement. Some people would get funny when it was time for their friends to leave, but there was no jealousy in our group. We were all truly happy for our mate, and wished him well. Unfortunately, the same couldn't be said for one of Russ's cellies, who had stopped talking to him as soon as he found out he would be leaving.

He was also having trouble with a couple of his fellow Italian-Americans in the unit, who seemed to be dripping with resentment that one of their number was nearly out.

I was stunned at the spitefulness. Russ told me that one of them had even tried to stitch him up so he would have to spend more time inside. This man had stolen a rolling pin from the kitchen and then planted it in Russ's locker, hoping the guards would find it during an inspection, classify it as a potential weapon and write him up for it, which could easily have resulted in an extension to his time. Meanwhile, someone else had started stealing his clothes from his cubicle while he was at work, viewing the things as fair game because Russ was on his way out. In fact the situation became so bad that he reluctantly told the head honcho of the Italian-Americans about it, who instructed the others to lay off.

'Russ, why are they doing all this stuff?' I asked, bewildered.

'It's not personal,' he said. 'It's just that some of these guys, they have years and years left. When somebody close to them leaves, they start to see it stretching out in front of them and it all becomes too much. There's no one else to take out their frustrations on, so they go after the guy who's leaving.'

We were all hovering around the laundry room, making ourselves look busy, and Brian was listening in to our conversation. Now he piped up.

'Darby,' he said. 'I've seen groups of guys actually beat up the guy who was leaving, because he was going around shooting his mouth off and being too happy. Seriously.'

'Yeah,' Russ said, with a wry laugh. 'And then they all end up in the SHU.'

'Well,' Brian went on, 'I've seen guys check themselves into the SHU just before getting out precisely to avoid that kind of thing. Otherwise you can say goodbye to your good time and have a few more years added on to your sentence.'

'Good time' is the way inmates are rewarded for behaving, since prisoners are not generally paroled in the US. If you don't cause any trouble and don't get any major black marks on your file, you are eligible for a small sentence reduction, known as good time, which works out at fifty-four days for every year you've served. Russ wouldn't have been eligible for release without his good time factored in, so the campaign to get him in trouble could have had serious consequences.

I could only shake my head in disbelief. It bothered me to think that Russ might have ended up serving more time because his supposed friends were jealous about him leaving. Human behaviour doesn't get much lower than that.

Russ also had something else to worry about. In addition to his federal charge, for which he was serving his time in Allenwood, he had a state charge – I didn't know what for, exactly – hanging over him. The state system deals with state crimes, while the federal system handles intra-state crimes. He had hoped, and assumed, that the state would dismiss its charge, given his federal jail time, but he hadn't heard anything either way. The prison authorities hadn't heard from the state attorney's office either. Unless a message reached Allenwood quickly, Russ would be released straight into state custody, earning him a ticket to a county jail.

After a long time banged up in Allenwood, the misery of a county jail was hardly the triumphant release Russ was hoping for. As the date loomed, he grew ever more anxious. He confided that he was taking medication for this, which was a bit of a surprise given how chirpy he always seemed. Understandably for a place like Allenwood, Russ wasn't the only inmate who required medication to keep his emotions under control. Many of the prisoners took anti-depressants and other drugs, collecting them at the 'pill line' three times a day. I joked in one of my letters home that my own day-to-day concerns could have been taken care of by a few pints, but obviously there was no chance of that.

Brian and I tried to console our friend as best we could, but it was hard to know what to say. Our little group had grown quite close over the previous weeks, and I was finding Brian to be excellent company. He was in his mid-forties, and I thought he had a great attitude. He wasn't one for moping; he just wanted to get his sentence done and get back out into the real world. He had two sons on the outside and, by the sound of it, had had a very interesting life before he was locked up. He had served in the military for more than twenty years, was a senior officer, and had completed tours of duty all over the world.

Perhaps the most remarkable thing about him, however, was how tolerant and sympathetic he was. Comforting, even. You don't meet many tolerant people in prison, but Brian seemed to be one of them. If someone in the laundry was having a tough day, he would always be the first to stop what he was doing and listen to their concerns. He didn't care what they had done or whether he knew them, he saw a human being in distress and wanted to help. I thought he was a sound guy. The only thing that disturbed me about him was that his tolerance extended to literally everyone in the prison, including the undesirables. I had even seen him associating with known and obvious sex offenders before – something I would never knowingly do. I made a point of bringing this up once, saying that he was kind even to allow those people the time of day. He shrugged and said, 'You shouldn't judge anyone, Darby, and definitely don't believe all that you hear.'

During our breaks, those of us who worked in the laundry would routinely make a cup of tea and then gather round whoever had brought a newspaper with them. We liked to sift through the news together, discussing the state of things and generally putting the world to rights. Russ, myself and Brian were usually there, as well as a couple of other guys. One morning, I came across an article about a Supreme Court ruling that said the death penalty could not be used for child rapists. Instead, the maximum sentence for child rapists would be life imprisonment – a fate that I think is as bad as being executed, if not worse.

Our group launched into a debate about the ruling, with many of us disagreeing with the court's decision that child rapists should have their lives spared. The prevailing view was that anyone who could do such an evil thing couldn't possibly be human, so their life should be forfeit. Brian was unusually quiet throughout our discussion, particularly for someone who normally had an opinion about anything and everything, but I didn't think too much of it.

We were on our way to chow, later that same morning, when Russ pulled me over to one side. 'You know why Brian's here, right?' he asked.

'I don't know,' I said, 'but I assumed it was drugs.'

'No. Did you notice he didn't say anything in our conversation?'

My heart sank. 'Yeah, I noticed.'

'Right. Well, my cellie knows Brian – they're both from Boston – and a little while ago he had his wife check him out. She found some cuttings about him. He was arrested in a sting operation trying to arrange a meeting with a young boy.'

Russ and I were standing to one side as the rest of our unit poured into the chow hall. I didn't want to believe what he was telling me. 'Are you sure?' I asked. 'Please tell me you're joking.'

'I wish I was. I was knocked sideways too when I found out.'

I was speechless. We walked to the back of the chow queue in silence. I felt so disappointed that I was almost in tears by the time I reached the counter. I had trusted this man and enjoyed his company. But now?

This revelation didn't just make me mad about Brian: it made me hate the whole system and the people who had put me in this place. I was surrounded by animals, and required to make judgements about people I barely knew based on the word of other inmates. I felt that it was a disgrace that we were all mixed in together like that.

When Russ and I left the chow hall, I was feeling as low as I had at any point since arriving at Allenwood and he knew exactly how I felt. He gestured towards a man eating his lunch. 'See that guy? He walked in on his best friend having sex with his wife. He killed him and got thirty years. That guy there?' Russ pointed. 'Contract killer. Thirty-five years. That one? Drug deal went bad and he killed a guy. Thirty years again. I'd still rather be locked up with any of them than I would a fucking paedophile.'

We headed back to our cells. I was off to the rec that afternoon and I said I'd maybe see him there, but I needed to get my stuff first. I found El and T in our cell, taking a long lunch break from the factory. I told them what I had learned about Brian, but neither of them was surprised.

'Darby, it happens all the time,' T said. 'Don't beat yourself up, man – how were you supposed to know?' He then proceeded to tell a story about a guy he had known who was in for four years for some minor crimes. When he was released, the guy was swabbed for DNA, and the DNA linked him to the rape and murder of a child in California, earning him a place on Death Row. T had no idea that his supposed friend was capable of something like that. 'I liked the guy,' he said. 'But I had no idea what he was or what he had done. How could I?'

The Brian situation ate away at me for the rest of the day. I had thought I was a better judge of character than that, but it seemed I had allowed him to slip completely under my radar. The thought of anyone doing harm to my daughters made me seethe with rage, and I directed all that hatred towards Brian. I felt as if he had deceived me, which only made me angrier.

I told Paul – the illegal gambler – about it that afternoon while we were out on the rec watching a softball game. He was sympathetic, but his response was measured.

'Darby, you've got to remember that it's an illness. Yeah, it's the sickest one imaginable, but it's still an illness.'

I wasn't in the mood for nuance. 'For fuck's sake, Paul,' I said. 'That doesn't make it any better though, or any more acceptable. I don't care if he's ill.'

'Okay, sure. But where do the paedophiles rank in here? How do you compare their crimes to drug peddlers, smugglers, robbers, murderers, gangbangers or any of the other criminals we exist with – and get on with – day by day?'

I sighed. 'There are plenty of bad people in here, no doubt about it. They've done bad things and I don't condone any of them. But the sex offenders disgust me on a whole different level. They're different. They prey on the weak and defenceless, and even in the rankings of seriously bad people, I'd say they're the absolute lowest.'

Paul knew Brian fairly well, and the conversation soon steered back to his specific case. 'I almost feel bad talking about him behind his back like this,' I said. 'If he knew that we knew, he would be horrified. He must have that fear weighing down on him every day. Imagine the stress, constantly worrying that you're going to be caught out. It serves him right.'

Paul nodded. 'He must be worried about his safety, too.'

'Yeah. And I can't imagine how it must feel to tell people you're in here for drugs when you know it's a lie and you can't ever tell the truth for fear of how people will react.'

Paul didn't say anything. It seemed as if there was nothing more to say.

I had such mixed feelings about Brian; he had been a good person to talk to and I had genuinely grown to like him, but now I knew the truth I couldn't bring myself to associate with him any more. The whole situation seemed to be the perfect example of the cruelty and senselessness of my new life in prison. The Feds had taken away my freedom and now, by placing me with so many sex offenders, they had taken away my dignity. I felt betrayed, hurt, angry and confused, all at the same time.

Russ could see I was struggling. He found me walking around the track one evening and came over to chat. There was another man with him, whom he introduced as Scotty, his cellie. Scotty was also Italian-American, and although he was probably in his mid-fifties, he still appeared to be pretty street-smart.

'Hey, man,' he said. 'Russ told you about Brian, right? I know him as well.'

'Hey, Scotty,' I said. I bumped his fist. 'Yeah, he did. I wish it wasn't true.'

'Me too, man. He's such a likeable guy that it genuinely shocks you when you find out about what he did. I was the same.' There was a pause. 'Look, anyway, I know you're upset about it, so I thought I should tell you. I was the guy who got the newspaper cuttings. I talked to Brian about it, and he denied it at first. But then I showed him the cuttings and he had to admit to it. It's all true, man, I'm sorry to tell you. He lost everything when he was found out. He also asked me if he should check into the SHU. I told him that wouldn't be necessary, because I didn't want to tell too many people. But Russ says you deserve to know.'

'Thanks, Scotty. I appreciate that.' I turned to Russ. 'You too, mate.'

'It's fine. It just goes to show, I guess. You never really know someone until you do.'

I saw Brian at the laundry the following morning. He smiled and said hello as soon as he saw me, and I found myself torn over how to respond. Ultimately, I couldn't bring myself to be rude to him, so I said good morning back, in a tone that was more polite than friendly. He would be so upset when he found out that I knew, but I didn't want to have that conversation with him right then. I decided to wait until Russ left before I did so, as I didn't want to put Russ in the middle of it and make things awkward for him.

When the day eventually did come for Russ to say his goodbyes, I couldn't help feeling emotional. Thanks to his unresolved state charge, the poor guy didn't know what his fate would be when he left Allenwood, but he was certainly glad to be on his way back to the real world. He was always so full of energy and such a joker, and he made me laugh so many times. He did a lot to alleviate the daily grind in the laundry, and I was very grateful to have known him, although it hadn't been long at all. We hugged on his final morning before being shipped out.

'Have a good life, mate,' I said.

'You too, Darby, you too.'

I was left to reflect on the transient nature of relationships, and the way people come and go from one's life. Russ was like a shooting star, I thought. He had suddenly appeared, brightened my life briefly and then vanished. It was a pleasure to have met him, and I was sad knowing that I would almost certainly never see him again.

CHAPTER 7

UP IN FLAMES

My moods became more volatile after Russ left. I certainly found the laundry a less enjoyable place to be without his cheery smile and his constant stream of jokes. At the same time, I was yet to hear anything about my transfer, and I was starting to worry that I might have to spend my entire sentence here in Allenwood. Also, I still hadn't resolved the Brian issue.

He must have noticed that I was being off with him. Despite my best efforts to act as if everything was fine, I hated being around him and I think that showed. One Friday morning, with the boredom of the weekend looming, I arrived in the laundry in a foul mood.

'You're about to take someone's head off, aren't you?' he asked.

I tried to blame my stony face on my frustration with the transfer process, but I knew Brian and I needed to have a serious conversation. I decided to confront him after lunch, when the laundry would be almost empty and we could have some privacy. That afternoon, I was able to catch him alone. We had just finished the day's work and were having a quick coffee before the next move was announced. I had fifteen minutes.

'Brian,' I began, 'I know you aren't really here for drugs.' He looked up from his mug with expectant eyes. 'I'm sorry to do this – I *hate* that I have to do this – but you know that I have five lovely daughters and that makes me feel how I do about the whole ... paedophile issue.'

He set his mug down, a resigned look on his face. 'Oh,' he said dully.

'Brian, when I found out I refused to believe it. I was so upset to learn that about you. I mean, I just couldn't believe that you could be involved in stuff like that.'

He waited for me to finish and then sighed deeply. 'Darby, look. The guy you've met in here is the real me. I'm not the person some people would have you believe.'

This attempt to defend himself renewed my sense of betrayal. 'Brian, I liked you. I respected you. You've been kind to me, but I'm sorry, I can't – don't want – to spend time with you. I thought I owed it to you to tell you this face-to-face, so you heard it from me. But from now on, and for my own self-respect, I don't want to be seen with you.'

These were hard words for me to say, and hard for him to hear, but I knew I had no choice for my own sake. I couldn't be seen socialising with someone like him. Now I knew the truth, I didn't want to be around him anyway: it was so disheartening, because I really liked him. Brian looked more disappointed than surprised and I suspected this wasn't the first time he'd had a conversation like this.

'Well, thank you for saying it to my face,' he said sadly. 'Not many people have had the guts to do that. Look, I can't lie, Darby. I did what I did. But every day I ask myself why. You know, I've lost just about everything. Everyone who has ever known me on the outside knows what I did. I have to deal with it every day. And I'll have to keep on dealing with it every day until I die. It's not just the shame. Every day I worry about my safety as well – and that's why I lied to you. I'm truly sorry that I wasn't honest from the start. But then you would never have spoken to me at all.'

Another heavy sigh. I could see tears pooling in his eyes.

I set my empty mug down next to Brian's. This conversation was proving even harder than I had thought it would be. 'Just so you know, I didn't tell anyone else. I heard it from Russ, but he was discreet. He didn't tell many people, and neither will I.'

'Thank you for that. If it makes you feel any better, just know that living with what I did every day means I can never forget it, and I can never forgive myself. I don't blame you for anything.' Brian had clearly condemned himself and he didn't need me to condemn him any further.

Again I said I was sorry as I stood up to leave. It was nearly time for the move, and at that point I wanted to be anywhere else but there. Brian stayed where he was while I made for the door. I had taken only a few steps when he called out to me.

'Darby,' he said. 'Really – thank you.'

I turned away and set out on the walk back to the unit. I spent the whole of the rest of the day mulling over our conversation. That evening, on the rec, I tried to enjoy the sunshine but I was still feeling miserable about the whole thing. El saw me sitting on a bench by myself and came over to join me. He knew about my issue with Brian, and he guessed correctly that was why I was moping around. He started to tell me that it wasn't my fault, any of it, when our conversation was interrupted by a loud crackling noise from the loudspeakers. After a few seconds of static, a strong, clear voice came booming out across the grounds: 'Yard recall! Yard recall! All inmates return to their units immediately. All inmates to their units!'

Everyone rose to their feet and started to make their way back inside. Even the basketball and softball games were interrupted, so that's how I knew it was something serious. I asked El what he thought it was.

He gave a shrug. 'Can't be anything good. I've seen a few yard recalls before – it means we're all going on lockdown. Almost all the yard recalls I've seen have been for fights, but I haven't heard about anything going down today.'

A few of El's friends caught up with us. They were sweating through their T-shirts, having come straight from the basketball court. El bumped their fists and asked if anyone knew what was going on. After all, gossip travelled at lightning speed in the prison yard.

'Someone just told me there's a fire at the laundry,' one man said.

'Yeah, someone told me that just now as well,' added another one of the group. 'They said they heard it from a guard.'

El laughed and turned to me. 'Sounds like you're going to get some time off work, Darby.'

We couldn't see any smoke from where we were, so I had to take their word for it. On the way back to our cell, however, two more people told us that there was a fire on the compound.

We had been confined to our cell for about an hour when there was a burst of activity on the unit. A swarm of cops appeared from nowhere, and we were ordered to stay in our cells until we had been inspected. Cell by cell, they worked their way down each wing.

'Body inspection!' an officer shouted at us. 'Everyone get your shirts off!' Our hands were checked for blood or cuts, and we were examined around the mouth, behind the ears and all over the chest and back – all the places where you might be likely to take a punch. El, T and I were given the all clear and then we waited expectantly to see who from our unit would be hauled off to the SHU. But the guards didn't drag anyone off, and left the unit as swiftly and suddenly as they had come. This was getting stranger and stranger.

Dinner earlier that day had been utterly miserable – wet beef tacos with flavourless rice. To make up for this, T sought out one of the known chefs on the unit and ordered a pizza, paying him in fish packets. Using a microwave pizza kit brought from the commissary, the chef whipped up a sausage and chicken number for T, even delivering it to the cell for him, just like a prison version of Domino's. I was grateful when T gave me a slice. You really could get anything on the Allenwood black market – if the price was right, of course. Satisfied by the late-night treat, we went to bed without finding out what the yard recall had been about.

It wasn't until the following day, a sunny Saturday, that I learned the truth. It was a scorcher of a day, and I made my way straight to the rec as soon as I got up. With no work to be done, I planned to occupy myself by relaxing in the heat. I found it far easier to stave off the boredom when I could kill time outside.

Throughout the course of the morning, a few guys I recognised came over to say hello. One of them told me that the rumours about the fire at the laundry had been true. The prison officials had been forced to call in the fire brigade, and they were worried about any of us using the distraction as an escape opportunity – hence the yard recall. I wondered whether I would have a job to go to on Monday morning. It also crossed my mind that the fire might have been a deliberate act of sabotage by one of Miss Anderson's disgruntled employees. I didn't know of any arsonists in Allenwood, but I suspected there must have been one or two among us. For the first time that day, I thought of Brian, but I immediately dismissed the possibility of him ever doing anything like that.

I spent the rest of the day milling around, killing time. The whole prison was counted at 4 p.m. every day, and then it was post time. I was always pleased to see a bundle of letters from my loved ones: they never failed to cheer me up, and reading all the latest news kept me busy for a few hours or so. I had also been set up with a subscription to a couple of British newspapers, so I was really pleased to see a back-edition of *The Daily Telegraph* too. I knew that reading it might even help me to forget where I was for a few precious hours.

I had always enjoyed reading the *Telegraph* and, in truth, I felt like I owed a lot to the people who worked there. When our case was making waves back in the UK, the paper always covered the developments fairly and accurately and even ran a campaign to try to prevent our extradition – arguing that British citizens should not be handed over to foreign powers before being tried on home soil. At one point, on the eve of our extradition, the newspaper backed a group of hundreds of businessmen who marched from the City to Parliament to protest about our treatment.

After all, the UK is one of only a handful of countries that will willingly hand over its own citizens to be tried abroad without any proven evidence. The fears shared by our supporters, many of whom had dealings with American firms, were that anyone could find themselves whisked away to the States if a deal went sour. Nobody defended our actions necessarily, but many people agreed that whether we were innocent or guilty, our fate should be determined in our home country.

A lot of civil rights organisations agreed with this stance, making the same argument that the UK's extradition arrangement with America was supremely one-sided. At the time we were preparing to be sent overseas, the US hadn't even ratified its side of the bilateral agreement. That meant while the authorities there could demand the extradition of British citizens, we could do nothing to get suspected American criminals over here.

It must have been strange for civil rights groups to find themselves on the same side as the (supposedly) greedy bankers: we weren't exactly natural bedfellows. But this alliance of views did help to raise the profile of our case, and for a while it looked as though we might even be able to win our extradition fight. We made countless appearances in the British courts as various judges debated our case – our alleged victim (NatWest) was British and we were British, so surely we should be tried in the UK? Moreover, throughout all of this, and despite our numerous direct requests to do so, NatWest itself refused to bring any charges against us. Even so, we were paraded in courtrooms and our faces splashed all over the newspapers. You didn't have to be sympathetic to our case to understand that the extradition procedure applied to us was completely wrong. The only justification produced by the US authorities, deep into their Enron bloodlust, was that we had had one meeting on US soil – with Fastow in Houston, discussing our change of employer – and that emails had been sent via US internet wires.

On the day we were initially charged, Gary was in Tokyo at the 2002 FIFA World Cup. I tracked him down to his hotel room and over the phone we exchanged our utter amazement and shock at the charges that had been levelled against us.

'Have you read the indictment, Giles?' he asked.

'Of course.'

'Mate, based on that, we did it. What on earth were we thinking?'

'Gary,' I said, 'it's a cut-and-paste of a bunch of different emails to make us look as bad as possible.'

'Well, it worked. Even I think we must be guilty.'

Getting newspapers and PR agencies on board to help us raise awareness of our plight was David's idea, heavily supported by Gary. Right from the off, I was dead against this strategy and we had some bad arguments about it between the three of us. I didn't want to kick up a fuss, because I believed it would provoke both the British and American governments, and the last thing we needed was to make the authorities want to punish us even more. Unfortunately, in my opinion, by becoming a thorn in their sides, this is exactly what happened. The Americans intensified their demands for us to be extradited, and we became such an issue for the British government that Blair and Co. were glad to see us gone.

The day before we were frogmarched onto a plane at Heathrow airport – with a BBC News helicopter circling above – we thought there might be one final hope. Nick Clegg, then a Liberal Democrat MP who would later become Deputy Prime Minister, called for an emergency debate in the House of Commons. Our fate was discussed by the unlikely cheerleaders of the Lib Dems, but the debate was really all for show. Nothing substantive came of it, and the plane took off the next morning with me, Gary and David handcuffed to US marshals on either side of us – two each.

Despite my own objections at the time, and to be fair to both David and Gary, there is no doubt that in the long run the PR campaign was absolutely vital to our cause and I was completely wrong to be so reticent about it. When we arrived in the US, we were treated far better than we would have been if nobody had known who we were. In fact, I came to suspect that someone in the British government was looking out for us and pulling strings on our behalf.

For one thing, I'm certain that without the campaign, we would never have been granted bond. Jeff Randall wrote in *The Daily Telegraph* on 5 July 2006 that 'stripped of easy access to family, friends and legal support, bankrupted by the horrendous cost of US litigation, Bermingham, Darby and Mulgrew could not possibly defend themselves properly. Banged up in Houston, they really would have a problem'.

If we hadn't been released on bond, we would never have been able to conduct a defence and introduce the necessary doubt to the prosecutors' minds. Without that, we would never have been offered a deal, and could have ended up serving something in the region of seven to ten years – maybe even longer. If you get bonded, you can defend yourself. If you don't, you can't. It really is as important as that.

Whenever I collected my out-of-date *Telegraph* from the post room, I would get a painful flashback to that whole protracted publicity campaign. A lot of good people had believed in us, and I was grateful to them. The sad thing was that, despite their best efforts, I had still ended up in prison, thousands of miles from home.

Back to my cell, as I leafed through the *Telegraph*'s business section, it occurred to me that if the laundry had burned down, I wouldn't have anything to do in the week. The weekends were hard enough to get through without the welcome routine of work, but a whole week without any distractions was tough to contemplate. All I could do was hope that things would be back to normal by the time Monday morning rolled around.

I didn't hear anything more, so after the weekend I duly reported to the laundry as usual. I quickly learned that, sure enough, there had been a fire on Friday afternoon – one of the clothes carts had mysteriously burst into flames, and the fire had spread to Miss Anderson's desk. Evidently, nobody was willing to admit to being in the laundry at the time, so the cause of the fire remained a mystery.

The sprinkler system had kicked in before the blaze got out of hand, so there wasn't too much fire damage. The smoke damage, however, was appalling. It took the whole workforce a few days to get everything scrubbed clean, so that it looked and smelt like a laundry again. The funny thing was that nobody had bothered to tell Miss Anderson about the fire, so she had spent the weekend in blissful ignorance, only to turn up on Monday morning to find her beloved laundry looking like a crime scene. If she'd known, I suspect we would have been called in over the weekend to do the cleaning work.

We spent most of the morning sharing excited speculation about what had happened. A guard had already spoken with some of the guys to find out whether anyone had a grudge or resented working in the laundry. I had visions of us all being hauled up and threatened with the SHU unless one of us confessed, but the guards were satisfied that none of us were responsible. Brian, the last of us to leave on the Friday afternoon, had been out of the laundry hours before the fire started. Only the guards would have had access at the time of the blaze, so they were content to call the incident 'spontaneous combustion' and forget about it.

As I cleaned, I got chatting to Bob – the man I had previously recommended for the post of laundry clerk. He was a good old boy from Georgia, a Vietnam war veteran and tough as nails. He told me he was only eighteen when he was put on a plane to Vietnam, having joined the army straight out of school at sixteen. He was still three years too young to be served an alcoholic drink – five, when he signed up – but Uncle Sam had no qualms about sending him to die in the jungle. It is indeed a strange country, the good old US of A!

Bob spoke candidly about his time in Vietnam. It was real *Apocalypse Now* stuff, the way he told it. 'It was hell on earth, boy,' he said, more than once. 'Hell on earth.' He spent a whole year there as a communications guy, radioing coordinates back to base so the enemy positions could be lined up for artillery strikes. That meant he spent a lot of time in advanced positions, far closer to the action than anyone would have liked.

'I'm not really sure how I'm still alive,' he said, shaking his head. 'The number of times I was under fire and I could hear the bullets whistle past me. I never knew which way to move, so I would just put my head down and pray.'

'Would you rather be here then?' I asked.

'Too right I would, boy. This place is a cakewalk in comparison – I mean, we used to go days, weeks even, without washing. We lived in fox-holes and we all used to get so bad that we could smell ourselves. I saw some awful things.' He shook his head sadly. 'Lost a lot of friends.'

Bob was in for a long stretch – ten years, again for drug offences. His son was also doing ten years of his own. The father and son had been caught in the same bust and were ratted out by the third co-defendant, a (former) family friend. Bob also had three daughters, one of whom was serving in Iraq.

'That's a lot of kids, Bob,' I said. 'Nearly as many as me.'

'You know, I saw so many terrible things in Vietnam – so much death – that when I came home, I decided I wanted to repopulate the world!' He burst into good-natured laughter.

'Any grandchildren?' I asked him.

'Seven. And I love each and every one of them dearly.'

'You know, one of the things I'm most looking forward to is having a whole bunch of grandkids one day. I know I'll love it.'

Bob smiled. 'You sure will, son.'

For a few moments then, we weren't prisoners. At least, it didn't feel like it. We were simply proud parents, a couple of doting dads who were sad to be spending time away from home, but grateful that we had a home to go back to. Bob was a fantastic man and our chat that morning put me in unusually high spirits for the rest of the day. I'd had – was having – a great life and considered myself incredibly lucky. Even at my lowest points in Allenwood, I knew I would never swap places with anyone else in the world.

By the end of the week, things were back to normal in the laundry. Miss Anderson had been even more irritable than usual, and I was looking forward to not seeing her over the weekend. On Friday morning, after a week of snapping at us and making a big deal out of every tiny mistake, she called me in to her little office. I had a worrying feeling that I was in trouble for some slight, real or imagined. Like the rest of Miss Anderson's workforce, I was guilty of smuggling clothes out of the laundry in return for packets of fish. Most of the men on my wing knew I worked there, and often sought me out in the evenings to ask if I could 'walk' an extra pair of boxers or some socks out of the laundry for them.

We had a system for nabbing articles without Miss Anderson noticing: we would grab T-shirts, boxers or socks while we were folding and stuff them into our pockets. Then, in the privacy of the laundry's toilet cubicle, we would put the extra clothes on top of what we were already wearing and go back to work as usual. It was impossible to tell if someone was wearing two pairs of boxers under their prison trousers or two socks on each foot. It was the perfect crime – or so I thought.

Miss Anderson had a computer on her desk, and she gestured for me to come over and look at the screen. I really thought I was in big trouble and braced myself to see something incriminating on her monitor.

'Look at that,' she said, jabbing a finger.

I joined her on the other side of the desk and was surprised to be staring at my own face. She was looking at pictures of me, all of them used in various news articles about my case. I was taken aback.

'Did you know you have sixty-seven Google pages?' she asked. 'Look at all these pictures of you.'

'I'm not exactly proud of it,' I mumbled. Why on earth had she been Googling me?

The old woman scrolled down the page, past endless photos of me. I recognised one of me in chains outside the courthouse in Texas. 'I've never met anybody with so many Google pages!' she exclaimed.

In an effort to divert her attention, I pointed out a photo where I was standing alongside Gary and David. 'Those were my co-defendants,' I said. I pointed at Gary. 'He's in Big Spring, Texas, and David there is in Lompoc, California.'

Miss Anderson nodded. 'I know all about you now. Five daughters, two marriages.' She tutted.

'Not at the same time,' I said. Talk about airing my dirty laundry. 'Can I go now?'

When I got back to the laundry, I caught Bob laughing.

'She does that to everyone,' he said. 'She's already checked the rest of us out.'

I thought it odd that she would be so interested, as she seemed to hold us all in such low regard that I couldn't imagine her caring about my past at all. Still, I suppose even old Miss Anderson had to pass the time somehow.

I didn't see Bob again until Monday, but this time he wasn't in his usual good mood. Bob was a born hustler – he always had something going on. One of his most profitable side-lines was a shop he ran from his locker, selling sweets, chocolate, cookies, donuts and other in-demand food items. He would load up at the commissary and then sell his produce throughout the week for stamps or fish. Because he could provide supplies around the clock, rather than at the once-a-week trip to the commissary, he was able to charge a decent mark-up on his treats.

However, over the weekend his unit had been 'shaken down'. That meant guards had been through everyone's lockers to make sure nobody was hoarding anything they shouldn't. The upshot was that most of Bob's stock was confiscated and, to make matters even worse, he had been banned from visiting the commissary for sixty days. Not ideal.

Bob was understandably hacked off about all this but, as a resourceful businessman, he had quickly developed a plan. Plenty of people around the compound owed him money, including one man – 'a fucking lollipop' – who owed him $120, an enormous debt in prison terms. The commissary had been open for his unit on the previous day and Bob had intended to drag his debtor to the shop and get him to buy everything he needed. That way, he could get around the shopping ban and still restock his locker.

'So,' Bob told me, relaying the events of the night before, 'I gave the guy my list. He had just taken some medication or some shit like that and he was complaining about not feeling well. I told him to get on with it and hauled him to the commissary, but he was walking so slow I thought we'd never get there. We were dead last in the line.'

We were folding clothes as we talked. I looked up from a shirt to give Bob a nod of encouragement. 'Right.'

'We handed in the slip and then went to chow while we waited. But guess what? After dinner, this guy tells me he doesn't have any fucking money. I was like, "You motherfucker, you ripped me off! Why the fuck didn't you tell me that before we went all the way to the fucking commissary?" He doesn't say anything. The man's a fucking freak, son, trust me. So I say, "You've got a week. Then I want all the money you owe me." Fucking piece of shit, man.'

I shook my head. 'What are you going to do if he doesn't get the money together?' I knew that the man almost certainly wouldn't.

'I don't know yet. I've got to figure that out. But that motherfucker ain't going to get away with it – I'll see to that.'

I was more than capable of guessing how that story would end. Thankfully, the following morning we were able to switch back to our usual conversation topic, our families. By then, Bob was back to normal, determined not to let the small things bother him. We were laughing and joking as we folded shirts and shorts and bedding, chatting away as if we were a couple of old mates down the pub, when I felt a presence by my shoulder.

I turned round and saw Miss Anderson staring at me, hands on hips in a pose of obstinance and defiance. I asked if everything was okay and she told me she was just supervising the folding. Bob and I shared a quick glance. She hated spending time around her employees, so we suspected that wasn't true. We folded in silence for a few minutes and then she told us that we didn't have to stop our conversation. It was awkward with her looming behind us, but Bob and I picked up roughly where we had left off, although the atmosphere at the folding table wasn't the same with the Laundry Nazi around.

What was really bizarre was that she then started to join in our chat. Maybe she was as lonely as the rest of us, I thought, listening as she talked about her own family. It turned out that she had four children, one of whom was pregnant and still living at home, not far from the due date. Hearing Miss Anderson talk about her children like that was surreal – it was hard to imagine her having any affection for another human being at all, and it was even stranger to think that she had spawned offspring of her own. It was a completely new side to her and, as strange as it was, it was nice to be finally seeing it.

Bob asked whether she was still married and she told us that no, she wasn't. It sounded like she had fallen out quite spectacularly with her ex-husband. I certainly got that impression, and I became sure of it when she told us in a very casual way that he was dead now. The rumour among the inmates was that he'd had an affair and had left her, subsequently coming to grief in a motorbike accident.

Miss Anderson didn't seem bothered by it at all. In fact, she went on to tell us that he had been cremated and now she had no idea where his ashes were. Perhaps her dead ex-husband's misdemeanours accounted for her terrible attitude towards all the men in prison – and perhaps all men in general. As suddenly as she had appeared, she drifted back to her office. Bob and I looked at each other in surprise. Of all the things I might have expected to happen that day, Miss Anderson opening up about her family life was not one of them.

For the first time, I found myself thinking that maybe there was more to her than we all assumed. Perhaps Miss Anderson, just like the rest of us, had reasons for being the way she was. Perhaps she was human after all.

CHAPTER 8

LIFE ON THE INSIDE

Back on A Wing, El and T had been preoccupied for days. They were both awaiting news on various appeals relating to their cases, and it was an anxious time for them. It didn't help that another thief had emerged on the unit. I had been led to understand that most of the inmates had a loose ethical code that forbade stealing from one other, but obviously that code was breaking down. Honour among convicts, maybe, but at Allenwood I was learning there was no honour among thieves.

It was a few weeks after the incident with the Colombians in the TV room when I heard some anxious chatter about things disappearing all over Gregg Unit. After what had happened to the last guy who was caught stealing from his fellow inmates, I couldn't believe that anyone would be stupid enough to follow in his footsteps, but I had underestimated the desperation of my neighbours. I suspected that part of the problem was the high turnover on the wing. In a typical week, four or five inmates left our wing and four or five more arrived to replace them. Perhaps some of the newer arrivals didn't know what had occurred the last time someone tried stealing from a cell.

Most of the thefts took place on commissary day – the one day of the week when we were allowed to visit the prison shop. The way the commissary worked, you filled out an order form in advance, and then handed your form in at the counter in return for a number. Behind the scenes, workers then scurried about looking for the right items to fill each order and when your number was called, you could return to the counter and collect your items. This was Allenwood's take on shopping at Argos. But with 350 inmates in each unit, the wait to be called could be exceptionally long – often in the region of a couple of hours. While you were waiting, you couldn't leave the room. You had to stand around and hope you would be next. If you weren't there when your number was called, tough luck: you had missed out and you would have to try again the next week.

Because of the long waits, it wasn't uncommon for someone to collect their purchases, dash back to the unit and throw their bag of goodies on their bed while they went to the toilet. On a few occasions, an inmate returned to find the bag had gone – nabbed by an opportunist while they were relieving themselves. El and T suspected that the thief had been noting the people who had made big purchases and then stalking them back to the block, knowing that they would probably be desperate for the loo after a two-hour wait.

A couple of weeks after the first such incident, one of the toilets on the wing overflowed. When it was unblocked, the plumber found that a commissary bag had been flushed down it – perhaps evidence that had been disposed of after a theft. This whole saga made many of the inmates a bit paranoid, so El, T and I agreed that we needed to be more vigilant. From then on, the last person to leave our cell would always check that everyone's stuff was locked away.

Other inmates were less rational, instead responding with anger and threats. A big group of black guys on the wing claimed that the thefts had been orchestrated by the Latinos, while the Latinos blamed the blacks. Never mind that people on both sides had fallen victim – the blame game was the natural response to any problem the inmates faced.

With our new agreement in place, El and T started to feel less paranoid. The atmosphere in our cell was generally very relaxed, and I couldn't help thinking that I was lucky to have both these men as cellmates. After a couple of months or so, El, who had initially been very guarded, finally told me all the details of his case. He had been a drug dealer, and had earned his twenty-two-year sentence for supplying large quantities of crack cocaine. He was fifteen years in now, and so the end was in sight: but he confided that he had recently heard some fantastic news that could get him out even sooner. Since I had arrived at Allenwood, it was all around the prison that the sentencing guidelines for crack-cocaine dealing had been downgraded. El was one of many inmates affected by this news, and he believed this could bring about a reduction to his own sentence. His attorney had submitted a motion to the courts, and was awaiting a decision from the judge. As the motion crept through the legal system, El got more and more excited about the prospect of an early release. Before long, it was all he could talk about.

I felt rather sorry for T in all this. He was serving a whopping thirty-five years and had a long way to go before he could even think about getting out. He was totally broke, and had no friends or family helping him to get through his time. Because his only income came from his prison job at the factory, he couldn't afford any decent legal representation either. I kept wondering whether there was any way I could help him, and I resolved to talk to him about it privately when I got a chance. Still, despite the bleakness of his own situation, T seemed happy for El. That's what true prison friendship was all about.

T's situation really was grim. He had recently been given a glimmer of hope regarding his case, only to learn that he really was stuck in prison for the next two decades. Of his thirty-five-year sentence, fifteen years were related to two separate charges of carrying a gun in furtherance of a criminal act, while the other twenty were for drugs. However, the law had changed so that two similar gun charges could now run concurrently rather than consecutively. T's hope was that this might knock at least five years off his sentence, and maybe as much as ten years. Before I had even arrived at Allenwood, T had filed his own motion to the courts, asking his judge to review the thirty-five-year sentence in light of the new gun laws. He was aiming for a reduction to twenty-five years – still an incredibly long time, but it would help him to reclaim an entire decade of his life.

When T told me that he had filed his own motion, he really meant it. Having no money, and therefore no attorney, he had been forced to read up on the procedure and go about the whole thing on his own. He did all the paperwork and submitted it without anyone's help, despite having no legal background. Dealing with the courts could be frustrating and arcane even with an experienced attorney by your side, so T must have known he was walking into a minefield by going it alone.

After filing his first motion, he heard nothing back. Not a peep. Then, around six months later, not long after I checked into prison, he filed another motion asking about the status of his earlier motion. On the day he heard back, El and I were in the cell talking about El's possible sentence reduction. But when T walked in, reading and re-reading a letter in disbelief, we both went silent.

The letter said that the judge had already ruled on T's motion months ago, rejecting it. Only nobody had notified T. Now, by the time he finally learned the fate of his original motion, six months after filing it, it was already too late to appeal the judge's decision. He looked sick and, having missed the narrow window for appeals, I could understand why. He had put all his hopes behind that motion, and he had learned in the cruellest way possible that they had been dashed.

It is hard to put his devastation into words – the pain, the anger, the injustice and senselessness of it all was too much for him. He collapsed onto his bunk, deflated, and didn't say anything for days. He was crushed, a broken man. I really felt for him. I didn't know the details of his case, but I knew he hadn't killed anyone. It was hard to see how he deserved to spend that much time behind bars for anything solely drug-related.

Throughout the following days, El kept working on his own legal action, but he made sure not to mention it when T was around. He kept calling his attorney to ask about the status of his appeal, but after hearing repeatedly that it was 'with the prosecution office', he got tired of waiting. He wrote his own letter, addressing it directly to the judge, and sent it off. He thought that he could knock as many as six years off his sentence, which would mean he would be eligible for release as soon as his motion was rubber-stamped.

He really believed his case was watertight, and started telling people around the prison that he was getting out. Every day he checked his post expectantly, looking for that letter from the judge, his golden ticket out of this place. For days, he was the first in the queue outside the post-room, and every time he came back to the cell empty-handed. Then, one day, he came flying into the cell. He was dancing about, shadow-boxing and jumping from foot to foot. 'This is it, Darby. It's next week. Thursday, I get news. I'm going home, man, I know I am.'

He had spoken to his attorney on the phone and then came straight to tell me. While he didn't yet know whether his motion had been successful, his attorney had talked to the prosecutor, who said they would have a response by the following Thursday. For El, it was a relief simply to hear the wheels were turning. I knew where he was coming from – I felt the same way about my transfer application, which was slowly making its own way through the many blind alleys of the American justice system.

'I'm going home, man!' El repeated. He punched at the air, a couple of quick jabs followed by a hook. 'I just know it. Fifteen years. Can you believe it?' He was beaming from ear to ear, seemingly oblivious to T's presence.

T had been sitting on his bunk, watching El's antics with a straight face. I couldn't bring myself to look at him. El was still dancing about when T stood up. 'I hope so, man,' he said, deadpan, and walked out of the cell.

I watched T go around the corner and then turned back to El. 'El, mate,' I said. 'T's still got seventeen years. That's longer than you've served already.'

El's smile faltered. 'I know, I know. I'll try to be careful with it, but I can't help myself. Fifteen years, Darby. I've been in fifteen years. I've got to go home. Shit, I *need* to go home.'

Later, once El had calmed down, we sat and talked about all the things he had missed while he was inside. He was about to be released into the twenty-first century and wanted to understand how much the world had changed since the early nineties, when he was last free. Mobile phones were completely new to him, as were text messaging and computers. He had never sent a text or email in his life.

'Shit, Darby,' he said, after I explained how texting worked. 'Can you really do all that?'

I laughed and told him that we were only getting started. We covered PCs, hardware, software, the internet, Google, iPods, iTunes, iPhones, downloading, uploading, digital cameras. All the technology that had changed our lives and which guys like El knew nothing about. He just couldn't take all of it in, so we stopped our lesson. Clearly, he would need more time to understand the magic of the modern world.

Later that day, I caught T on his own. Talk about agony and ecstasy. To T's immense credit, he was dignified and relatively serene about the whole thing, and he genuinely wished El well. 'I do hope it comes off for him,' he said. 'Trouble is, in here you keep getting kicked in the face by the system. You ain't out until you out. You get me? You gotta prepare for the worst and hope for the best, because if he don't get told he's being released next week, imagine how he's gonna feel.'

A couple of days passed, and El's enthusiasm didn't wane. It was Independence Day that week – a particularly miserable holiday for a Brit locked up in an American prison. It didn't help that public holidays on the inside were dreadful at the best of times. Not only were they a reminder of the life you were missing on the outside, but there tended to be major staff shortages throughout the holiday seasons. This meant our movements were even more restricted than usual, and we spent most of Independence Day locked up in the unit, unable to visit the rec.

It was safe to say that I didn't feel particularly independent as I listened to the shouts of stir-crazy prisoners echoing around Gregg Unit. Lunch and dinner were both predictably disgusting, and by the evening I was glad the day was nearly over. That night I was sitting with El in our cell, complaining about what a boring day it had been. It would have taken more than a miserable public holiday to dampen El's mood, though, since he was still bouncing off the walls with excitement about his imminent release – not that his motion had even been approved yet. It was still pretty much all he could talk about.

'What's the first thing you're going to do when you get out?' I asked. 'Apart from the obvious.'

He told me about his plans to see his daughters and his grandson, and how he wanted to spend a few weeks catching up with them. 'But then,' he said, 'after all that, I just want to take a road trip. I want to be alone. I'm going to get me some jazz and some blues music and drive across the country by myself.'

'Why?' I asked. 'Why not go with someone, or take your family along?'

'Because I want to be alone. Properly alone.' He laughed. 'Darby, during these last fifteen years, the closest I've come to being alone is in the damn shower. Do you have any idea how that feels? I don't want anyone bothering me or watching me. And I want to be able to do what I want, when I want. For fifteen years I've been controlled, I've been moved around by the cops, I've done whatever they asked of me. For once in my life, I want to be able to do my own damn thing. I just want to feel like a human being, rather than like a fucking farm animal being moved from one enclosure to another.'

El didn't have a wife any more, and I suspected that he would soon get lonely without someone by his side. Still, I admired his dream, and couldn't wait to get a postcard from somewhere in the middle of nowhere with his name on it.

It wasn't surprising that El's wife had left him, of course. In fact, my friend Paul told me that something like eighty per cent of all federal prisoners get divorced or separated either while they are inside or within one year of coming out.

Four in five marriages would die at the hands of the justice system. That was a shocking proportion, I thought, although at the time I didn't know that I too would eventually fall into the eighty per cent. It felt like an enormous amount of emotional pain was inflicted on people who were already being punished, and on their innocent families.

In truth, I don't think that anyone can go through an ordeal like prison and not be changed by it. That's true regardless of which side of the fence you're on. If you're the one in prison, obviously you won't emerge the same person, and if you're the one with a partner in prison, that is going to have a serious effect on you as well. It's an emotional obstacle course for all involved, from start to finish, so I suppose it's to be expected that most married couples stumble before reaching the end.

Keeping myself busy in Allenwood was the most important thing. If I could occupy my mind, then I hoped I would be able to emerge from this ordeal the same man I was at the beginning – or at least close to it. To this end, I decided to take up a hobby: playing the guitar. A smattering of music classes was included as part of the prison's educational offering and the guitar class appealed to me straight away. My second youngest daughter, then a teenager, had a flair for music, and I thought she'd be impressed to hear her dad was learning to play an instrument. The classes were more involved than I had been expecting – I had to study music theory as well as learn to play the guitar itself, and it took a while before I could even be sure I was holding it right.

The guy who taught us was Jack, a paunchy American who was a natural teacher. He was very patient with me, although after my first couple of lessons he could see that I still had a long way to go. He approached me at the end of a class, while I still had the guitar in my lap and a pick between my fingers.

'Darby, how would you feel about some one-on-one tuition?'

My fingers hurt from all the strumming, but I told him I would be eager to learn more. 'How much?' I asked.

He thought about it for a second. 'Two packs of tuna would do it.'

That was two dollars' worth of fish. At those prices, lessons were a bargain, so I told him sure. We arranged a time and agreed to meet back in the classroom later that week.

It turned out that Jack was an even better teacher one-on-one. As we worked through some chords together, he opened up a bit about himself. Like so many decent people I had met, he was in for drugs – another life ruined as part of the crusade against narcotics. He didn't say how long he was in for, but I got the impression it was going to be a few years.

I saw Jack again the following week at our guitar class, but I didn't get much of a chance to talk properly to him. After the lesson, however, I did get chatting with one of the other guys there, an enormous bloke in his fifties called Steve. He was a giant, something like six foot four and 250 pounds, not the kind of guy you would want to mess with.

Despite his brutish appearance, I knew that Steve was a very good guitarist – he had obviously played before he got sent inside – and he often lingered on his own after classes to keep on playing. Incidentally, he was also a gifted pianist, and he taught the piano lessons when he wasn't practising guitar. He was one of those people who loved music, and it seemed to me as if he could have been a professional musician in another life.

He was halfway through writing a song when I came over and introduced myself. He was scribbling lyrics on a sheet of paper and plucking experimentally at his guitar. It sounded great to me, but Steve looked somewhat frustrated with his efforts.

I sat next to him and bumped his fist. 'Darby,' I said. 'Nice to meet you.'

'You too, Darby. I've seen you around. Name's Steve.'

'That sounded really good,' I said, gesturing towards his guitar. 'Sorry to interrupt.'

'Nah, it's no trouble.' His American accent had a distinctive country twang to it. 'To be honest, I'm struggling to get the sound right. But thanks.'

'Are you writing it for anyone?'

'Always, man. It's for my girl.'

'Does she know?'

He plucked absentmindedly at a string. 'Nope. Haven't seen her or heard from her since the day we got arrested.'

'We?' I asked. 'You got arrested together?'

'Yessir. And we fought together against the cops who came to pick us up.'

'Well, how come you haven't seen her since?'

Another string twanged between his fat fingers. 'Well, she testified against me for a better sentence. She got probation, I got six years. Now I'm told she's got another guy, but when I get out, I'm going to find her and win her back.'

'Will you? Why would you want to do that?'

He sighed heavily and tapped his fingers on the wood of his guitar. 'Because I was with her for years, man, and I miss her. You know, I don't even blame her really. I just got out of three months in the hole. I can tell you, that's a lot of thinking time and I spent all that time thinking about her. That's why I'm writing for her. Perhaps one day I'll be able to play this for her, you never know.'

Steve was an intriguing guy. Something about his desperately sad story captivated me, and I wanted to know more. I asked why he had been in the hole and he explained that it was because he got into a fight over use of the piano room. Supposedly, some other guy had 'cheated' him, by claiming that he had booked the room when really Steve had. It was juvenile stuff, but in prison these tiny altercations could be magnified into major issues.

'So anyway,' Steve was saying, 'I told this guy to fuck off and he left the room. Then, five minutes later, he comes back. Only he's got a sack with him, which he had filled with rocks from the compound. He starts swinging this thing and trying to hit me. Thankfully he missed, but one of the guards saw what happened. Next thing I knew, I was in the hole. But that's not even the worst of it, right? I had to share a cell in there with some guy who claimed he was in for drugs, but the guards told me he was lying. They said that he was really an undertaker who had been arrested for interfering with the dead bodies, if you know what I mean. Imagine sharing a cell with that animal, man. It was awful. Fucking awful.'

I thought Steve's situation was absurd. He was clearly trying to improve his situation, dedicating himself to his music, and yet he had still come unstuck. It was people like him who exposed the lie behind the name 'Allenwood Federal Correctional Facility'. The reality was that there was nothing correctional about Allenwood or the US prison system at all. Sure, the BOP offered a handful of courses for inmates to do, but they made the most cursory efforts to rehabilitate people and, even then, they did it only to tick a box.

For example, I met another guy, an accountant in his former life, who wanted to put on a book-keeping course at Allenwood. The prison authorities gave him permission to run the course, but they said he would have to pay for any photocopying or resources out of his own commissary budget. That of course torpedoed the idea completely, closing off what could have been a path towards genuine rehabilitation for some prisoners.

It is no surprise that the US has the highest rates of both incarceration and reoffending in the developed world. The per capita incarceration rate is staggering: for every 100,000 people living in America, 655 are currently incarcerated. The next highest incarceration rate is Russia, with

381 prisoners per 100,000 people. The absolute numbers are equally shocking: over 2.1 million people were incarcerated in the US in 2019. China's estimated prison population, by comparison, is 1.65 million, and China's total population is roughly four times the size of America's.

The reoffending rate in the US is also shameful. A study by the Bureau of Justice Statistics found that 67 per cent of American prisoners reoffended within three years of being released. Within five years of release, the recidivism rate rises to 76 per cent. In the UK, where prison is generally more rehabilitative, the recidivism rate is estimated at around 50 per cent. There are many reasons for this, but one is that prisoners across the pond simply aren't equipped with the skills they need to live in the world outside the prison walls. Justice there is purely punitive, so education isn't taken seriously enough and, years after they have been released, convicted felons are still required to follow a restrictive set of rules as part of their 'rehabilitation'. The result of this is that it is very hard for the typical American offender to find a job and reintegrate as a productive member of society. All that is left for many of them is to revert to their old ways and continue living in the only way they know how.

Allenwood wasn't really a correctional facility, but a giant holding pen – nothing more than a warehouse. It was home to 1400 men simply because the government had nowhere better to put them. Some facilities were provided to keep us from getting too bored, but otherwise all the authorities were interested in was keeping us inside, secure and away from day-to-day society. Without any serious attempt at rehabilitation, most of my fellow prisoners stood not a chance of turning their lives around.

There was nothing I could do about this of course, so my focus had to be on my own situation. That meant getting stuck into the Allenwood way of life, adapting as quickly as possible and tackling the long days one at a time. I tried to throw myself wholeheartedly into the prison lifestyle, but there was one thing missing: family visits. I had hoped that I wouldn't be in Allenwood for more than a handful of months, so I told my family not to come and see me. Mainly I thought it would be too upsetting for them to see me there, but I also knew what a massive effort it would be for them to fly to the States, travel to Allenwood, and then submit themselves to the finickity rules and regulations for visits.

Saying goodbye on their visits whilst I had been in Texas had been hard enough, so it was impossible to imagine how difficult we would find it if they came to see me here. This was reason enough to discourage them from visiting me until I could get back to a UK prison, where we could be only a couple of hours' drive away from each other, rather than a transatlantic flight. In the UK, everything would be easier, and we would be able to establish a routine of visits. That's what I told myself, anyway.

I did still have plenty of friends in America, of course – people I had grown close to while I was out on bond. I had been in Texas for two years, awaiting trial and working the case with David, Gary and our brilliant legal teams led by Dan Cogdell and Dick De Guerin, two legal legends from Houston, as well as Reid Figel, an eminent and well-respected attorney from Washington. I had passed on the details of where I was imprisoned to a few of my friends, telling them to drop by if they ever found themselves in Pennsylvania. I didn't expect anyone to make the effort, but I explained how visits worked and made sure people had access to the relevant paperwork.

So, one sunny afternoon on the rec, you can imagine my excitement when the PA system crackled into life and my name was called. I was playing racquetball when I heard a screech of static and then: 'Inmate Darby to the rec office! Inmate Darby to the rec office! You have a visitor.'

I wasn't expecting anyone, but that didn't dampen my enthusiasm – if anything, it heightened it. I left my racquet on the ground and practically sprinted to the unit. I was so excited that I got myself a telling-off for running in the compound, another strict rule that could have landed me in serious trouble for breaking it. By now, my thoughts were racing about who the mystery visitor could be. A lawyer? A friend? I had no idea.

When meeting visitors, inmates had to wear the full prison uniform, so I was forced to change into my khakis and boots and then made my way to the visitation area. A guard noticed me and walked over.

'Darby?'

'Yes, sir. That's me.'

'Good. Someone important is here to see you.'

I handed over my ID card at reception and was led through to the visiting room, a large area that consisted of numerous small, circular coffee tables with chairs arranged around them. There was no glass screen between visitors and inmates like you get in high-security facilities, just the tables to sit at and a vending machine in case you wanted a coffee or some food. Guards lined the walls, searching if necessary and making sure nobody was smuggling anything in or out.

There was also an outdoor seating area, but that had been temporarily closed because visitors kept throwing contraband over the walls to the inmates inside. As a result, the guards were being tetchier than usual about visits, and keeping a close eye on the inmates. There were strict rules about physical contact with visitors – no touching, no hugging, no holding hands – and equally strict time-limits imposed on visiting hours.

I was pointed towards a man in a suit, sitting on his own at one of the tables. I had never seen him before in my life, and my excitement increased. He looked smart and official, and I wondered whether he was here to tell me my transfer had been approved. Perhaps he was here to take me to the airport today?

No such luck. 'Hello,' he introduced himself, in a posh British accent. 'I'm from the British consulate in New York. I'm here to check up on you and to make sure you're okay. Is there anything we can do for you?'

I was immediately deflated. 'Yeah, sure. There is something you can do for me,' I said. 'How about getting me home?'

Mr Consulate offered a sympathetic smile. 'Well, we are aware of your situation and we know about your transfer application. Unfortunately, though, we can't get involved in the process.'

My heart sank. 'Right.' I said. 'What can you do?'

'We can monitor it.'

'Fine. Monitor away.'

I would be wasting my time to moan, and I knew my visitor was only doing his job. He asked me a few questions about my health and how I was being treated, and I told him everything was fine. He took a few notes and then asked me for my home address and next of kin. The whole thing took about five minutes. After he was done with me, he had meetings with the two other British guys in the compound, including the suspected sex offender I had spoken to once briefly on the running track. I can't imagine that would have been a fun conversation.

When I left the visiting room, I had to be searched. Guards made me take off my clothes and gave me a good once over. So much for the important visitor, I was thinking. Basically, all the British government had succeeded in doing was getting me an unnecessary strip search.

CHAPTER 9

EXTRADITION

All the talk about my cellmates' cases, and the time they had left to serve, was a constant reminder of the point when things had really started to get serious for me. In the years after the initial indictment, I would wake up in the morning and, for a split-second, feel happy to be alive. Then I would remember that I could be facing thirty-five years in prison. My heart would sink and it would take all my mental strength to face the day. What would happen today? Nothing to do with the case was ever good. It seemed that we were being tossed around in a whirlpool, inexorably getting closer to the vortex.

Gary would say that whenever he heard the song 'Trouble' by Coldplay, he would think of us: 'It's a spider's web and I'm caught in the middle.' At that point it was July 2006: all the legal arguments were exhausted and we were being extradited. I was given just two weeks' notice of the extradition date in which to organise my affairs. The ordeal was real. We had reached a point of no return. This is really happening, I kept telling myself, and I have to deal with it.

Extradition Day itself was truly unforgettable. The previous evening, we had some friends over to say their goodbyes. We all knew there was a strong chance that we would get thrown straight into prison as soon as the plane touched down, so none of us – families and friends – knew when we would be able to see each other again. It was terribly emotional saying goodbye to everyone, in the almost certain knowledge that the next time we saw each other, it would be on a prison visit somewhere in Texas.

In the morning, my father-in-law drove me to Croydon police station, where we were due to report, be arrested and handed over to the Feds.

Our case was big news by this point; there had been a protest march in the City of London and the emergency debate in the House of Commons in the days beforehand. We were greeted by a throng of reporters and cameramen when we arrived, despite the fact that it was only 6 a.m. I made my way into the police station through a side door, eager to avoid the scrum of journalists.

David, meanwhile, insisted on entering through the main doors, stopping as he did so to deliver a speech about the injustice of the extradition on the front steps. The authorities were gunning for us as it was, but he couldn't resist airing his opinion in front of the flashing cameras. Once Gary had joined us, we were driven to Gatwick airport in a police van, escorted by motorbikes and trailed by television news vans. A news helicopter beat us to the airport, and was circling overhead when we arrived. I waved up at it. We were led into a room where the television in the corner was tuned in to the BBC news. Imagine my surprise when I saw a shot of myself waving up at the helicopter. Talk about a bizarre moment.

We were given a final cup of tea and some sympathetic words from the police officers escorting us before being handed over to the US marshals. There was an instant cock-up, which amused the three of us greatly: apparently a vigilante hacker had cancelled our Continental plane tickets overnight. The somewhat clueless marshals were left scratching their heads, trying to work out what they should do with us. In the end, one of them had to use his credit card to buy new tickets – economy, of course.

We were escorted to the plane, two marshals to each of us, and spent the flight with a marshal cuffed to each hand. It all felt a bit over the top for three white-collar criminals. It wasn't as if we were the types to make a break for it – we'd had four years to do that – but it was probably all for show. The rest of the plane filled up with reporters and a handful of bemused members of the public, who probably had no idea what was going on when Gary, David and I were frogmarched to our seats at the back, the marshals trying awkwardly to shepherd us along in the confined space.

The real fun started when the plane touched down in Houston, Texas, after an uneventful eight-hour flight. The pilot's voice came over the speakers: 'Ladies and gentlemen, please can you remain in your seats and allow some special guests to disembark the plane first.'

We were the special guests, of course, although I didn't feel particularly special as I was paraded down the aisle, still cuffed, as photographers tried to get more shots of us. At the gate, we were greeted by around twenty police officers waiting to escort us to the Federal Detention Centre (FDC) in downtown Houston.

David was the first onto American soil. He's not the tallest of blokes, and after he was uncuffed he was heaved up by two enormous cops – both well over six foot. The officers, with an arm each under David's armpits, started speed-walking through the terminal, carrying him between them. I will never forget the sight of David's little legs frantically working away in the air, his feet never coming close to touching the floor. It was a moment of levity in a traumatic day.

Next we were taken to immigration, in a similarly undignified manner, and strip-searched. Then we were put in wrist and ankle chains and 'processed' by the ever-efficient Feds. Although the three of us were strangely calm, that was a low moment for each of us, chained up in leg irons like terrorists and unsure of what would happen next. We assumed we would be sent straight to prison and would have to stay there for months or maybe even years, since foreign criminals in America were rarely released on bond before a trial. We had absolutely no idea how we would ever begin to mount a defence to the allegations against us from behind bars.

A group of immigration officials came over to our FBI handlers and started asking about our immigration status. They had a little bust-up right in front of us, which was quite extraordinary. Gesturing at us, one of them demanded of his FBI counterpart, 'Are you going to leave their passports with us?'

'No,' said the head marshal. 'Why would we?'

'Well, are they going to get bonded?'

'Maybe. I don't know right now.'

'Well, if they do, we're going to throw their asses right out of the country.'

'What? Why?'

'They're illegals. They'll be here illegally from the moment they're bonded.'

'No, no!' stammered the head marshal. 'You can't do that!'

'Yes, we can, they're illegals. We gotta deport them back to wherever they came from.'

'No way. That's not happening. We just spent four goddamn years getting these guys here – you can't send them back!'

'Well, I'm just telling you our position.'

The head marshal glowered at us, and then shot a look back at the clowns from immigration. 'I'll hang on to these,' he declared, brandishing our passports. 'The judge can decide what to do with them.'

My eyes met Gary's. It was impossible not to smile. The government to whom we were apparently such a challenge was so disorganised that there was a chance we would be deported as soon as the marshals released us! It was utterly farcical, but it was also rather encouraging. It made me dare to think that maybe we wouldn't be locked up after all. In due course, it was that same ineptness – or was it arrogance? – that would give us a break in the case, leading from a potentially life-ending sentence to a plea bargain and a bearable eighteen months.

Our next stop was the FDC in downtown Houston. We were taken there in a police van under blue light. Rain was lashing down, and the car behind us, carrying a complement of FBI agents, skidded out of control on the slick road and crashed into the back of our van. Cue more amusement on our part. It felt like we were being escorted by the Keystone Cops rather than the FBI.

When we arrived at the FDC, a pack of photographers and reporters was waiting there, many from English newspapers. We were hauled out of the van, still wearing shackles around our ankles and wrists, with a chain running between the two. When I stepped down onto the pavement, I had to be careful not to fall over as I certainly didn't want to take a tumble in front of the assembled media. I looked down as I walked, taking care as to where I placed my feet. As I headed up the steps of the FDC, a cameraman snapped a photograph that I believe changed everything for us: it showed the three of us on the steps of the detention centre, but the focus was on me, chained up like a Guantanamo inmate, staring down at my feet. I looked for all the world like a broken man. It was a photo that screamed injustice – these mild, middle-aged English businessmen being mistreated and degraded at the hands of the mighty American state. The photo flashed up on news coverage around the world and, the next day, it would be on the front pages of many influential newspapers, including *The Daily Telegraph,* which had been campaigning hard to prevent our extradition.

That photo seemed to show that all of our worst fears had come true, and it shamed the Blair government. The point we had been continually making – we are British, our alleged victim is British, why are we being tried in America? – would be made all over again, and with renewed vigour, thanks to that photo. I hate that my daughters had to see me like that, but the photo was about to do us a lot of good.

As that powerful image made its way back to news editors in London, the three of us were being processed all over again: we were fingerprinted, photographed and interviewed until the officers had recorded everything they needed to know about us. Then we were led into a cell and told to wait. It was a nervous time. After all the talk, all the fighting and the misplaced hope, we were finally in custody in Houston, Texas. As the reality hit us, we had no clue as to what was going to happen next. How long would we be in prison? How would we see our lawyers? When could we speak to – never mind see – our families? How the hell could we defend our case, gain evidence and access witnesses? Our situation was simply too terrible to contemplate.

We had been stewing for about an hour, perhaps more, when a distinguished-looking man wearing a suit was allowed into our cell. 'I'm from the Secretary General's office,' he said. 'Are you guys being treated well?' We replied that we were. 'We're going to get you out of here,' he went on. We looked at each other, stunned, as he left the cell and disappeared down the corridor.

A while later, one of the lead marshals – Agent Dave – came in to join us. He was the very same guy who had searched me earlier in the day and offered to stick his finger up my ass. 'You guys have friends,' he said, a weird mixture of awe and surprise on his face. The three of us shared a look, mulling over this cryptic statement. 'Come with me.'

We followed the agent out of the cell. He called a guard over and announced, loudly enough so that we could hear, 'We just had the Attorney General's office on the phone. We've got to make special arrangements for these guys.'

Moments later, the sharply-dressed man caught up with us again. We had been milling around in the corridor while Agent Dave made his special arrangements, whatever they were. The man asked us some more questions about how we were being treated and assured us that things would be okay. Then he vanished and we were led back out of the prison by the marshals and put in the back of another police van – this time, without chains – and driven to a nearby hotel. Agent Dave checked us into a connected suite and told us we'd be staying the night. Several federal officers were with him. The whole thing seemed utterly bizarre and the three of us looked at each other in total amazement. Having been in prison only moments ago, the last place we expected to spend the night was a hotel.

'Is there anything I can do for you boys?' Dave asked, in a suddenly friendly tone of voice. We were all gathered in one of the rooms. 'You hungry?'

'Sure,' I said.

'Right. I'll get some food sent up.'

'Any chance we could get a beer as well?'

He laughed. 'Don't push it now,' he said.

Not long after, plates of burgers and fries were delivered for all of us by room service. Still baffled by what was happening, we ate our food under the watchful eye of Dave and his colleagues. As we did so, we chatted about sport and our families like any group of ordinary blokes would, even though our situation was about as far from ordinary as you can get.

'You know,' Agent Dave said, between bites of his burger, 'this has never happened before. At least, if it has, I've never seen it. Who the hell are you guys?'

'They're fucking lucky,' growled one of the officers. 'That's what they are.'

After the meal, Dave got up to leave. Guards were posted outside in the hallway in case we tried to escape, he warned, but the doors to our rooms wouldn't be locked.

'You guys promise you won't disappear, right?' he said, only half-joking.

So, we weren't being released, but we weren't being held in a prison either. What did that mean? Our guess was that someone high up had seen that photo of us, and had intervened on our behalf. Obviously, the Americans would have come off worst from a PR perspective if we had been sent straight to prison. Instead, we were being given the hotel treatment, which certainly made for a better night's sleep than we would have had in the FDC, that was for sure.

The next day we were taken to court. By then, the photo of us in chains had made it into the newspapers, and the story of the NatWest Three was top of the agenda once more, with the events being covered live on Sky.

That morning was the first time any of us had met David's defence attorney, Dan Cogdell, in person. Dan was a legal wizard with a legendary reputation in Texas, so naturally we were all delighted to have him on board. He was a larger-than-life character with a wonderful Texan drawl, a great line in snazzy suits, and some brilliant one-liners. He was, and eventually remained, the only attorney to go to trial in an Enron-related case and get a not-guilty verdict for his client. Hiring him was an inspired move by David for which I for one remain eternally grateful.

After a very short meeting with Dan and the other attorneys, we made our appearance in front of the district judge and went for broke. Knowing full well that it was an extremely long shot, Dan applied for us to go back to the UK while we awaited our trial. We had been praying for this outcome, and in preparation Gary and I had managed to persuade more than fifty friends and family members to stand surety for us. Each guarantor had pledged $50,000 in bail money, amounting to a total exceeding $2.5 million, to be paid in the event that we absconded. What staggering generosity this was from our many friends and supporters in the UK.

Even with those assurances, however, the prosecution was having none of it. After all, it had been a four-year process for the Americans to get us here in the first place. Their argument was that if we went back home, it would be an even bigger headache to get us back again. The judge agreed with the prosecution and our application was thrown out.

This left us in a profoundly sticky situation. As far as I knew, there was no precedent for anyone extradited to the US being granted bond (bail). Without bond, we would be sent to prison to await trial, with no hope of preparing an adequate defence from behind bars. We wouldn't stand a chance at trial and would inevitably receive a long, punishing sentence, which didn't bear thinking about.

Of course the previous day's events had given us hope that someone high up was trying to help us. Perhaps we would be given a break today as well and get bonded out? I dared to hope so, at least. Even if the requirements turned out to be extremely restrictive, being out on bond was infinitely better than being in prison.

Our hopes proved well-placed. I could barely believe my ears as I heard the judge grant Dan's request for us to be held on bond. We were bonded for $1 million each (then just over £500,000), although I would be required to post a whopping $500,000 (£250,000) in cash up front. David was required to post the same, while Gary was asked to post $250,000 (£125,000) – a reduced sum because he had recently been divorced and forced to make a hefty pay-out to his ex-wife. Fortuitously, we had recently sold the family home and I was able to use the proceeds from the sale to cover the bond.

Our bond came with strict conditions. We would be forced to wear an electronic tag at all times, and were to be curfewed between the hours of 10 p.m. and 6 a.m. We had to report to probation weekly and our travel would be restricted to the local Harris County surrounding Houston. The judge also required us to get jobs – no mean feat, given we were foreigners with no visas or work accreditation, as well as accusations of a multi-million-dollar fraud hanging over us. When Dan pointed this out to the judge, his reaction was that there were plenty of British companies to which we could apply, and name-checked Shell and BP as examples.

The toughest of all the conditions and the sting in the tail, however, was the requirement that we had to be released into the custody of an

American citizen, who would accept total responsibility for us until we could post the required bond money. The judge must have known that this was an enormous ask – we had arrived only the day before and we didn't know anybody in Texas. We felt sure that, along with the requirement to post such a large sum of cash, this bond condition was included by the Feds in the certainty that we would not be able to meet it. That way, they could claim that we were offered bond, but weren't able to fulfil the court's demands.

As the requirement was read out, the three of us looked forlornly at each other and our hearts sank. Everything else would be just about doable – we could post the cash and even go through the motions of applying for jobs – but it was surely a stretch too far to find someone who would take us in there and then, straight from the courtroom, and make themselves liable for us. We had no chance. We knew nobody in the area and, even if we did, they would have to be mad to agree to take all three of us in until we could get the money together, something which could have taken months. We were going straight to prison, I was sure of it.

Suddenly, Dan, the attorney we had met only minutes before, stood up.

'Your Honour,' he said, 'what do you mean when you say someone has to take responsibility for these guys?'

'Mr Cogdell, was I not clear? I will release them into somebody's custody so long as they agree to take full accountability for them until they post their bond.'

Dan looked from the judge to the three of us. 'So that person would have to be responsible for them twenty-four hours a day until then?'

"Yes. Twenty-four hours a day."

'Well, Your Honour, I just met these men an hour ago, but they seem honourable to me. I've already been divorced three times. I guess a fourth won't matter.' Dan shot us a wicked glance and smiled. 'I'll take responsibility for them.'

I've never been so thankful in all my life. I couldn't believe it. We had only met the man today, and yet here he was staking his entire reputation on the three of us, not to mention putting out himself and his family massively in the process. The judge seemed as staggered as I was.

'Mr Cogdell, you understand that you will have to be responsible for these men at all times until they each post bond – and that it may take a while for them to do so?'

'Yes, Your Honour. I understand.'

From the look on his face, the judge had been knocked for six by Dan's unbelievable generosity, and by his faith in us. 'Well, Mr Cogdell, in that case they are to be released into your custody.'

Incredibly, that was how we avoided being sent straight to prison. Dan had turned out to be our guardian angel, and we all knew we would never be able to repay him. As soon as we were out of the courtroom, he took total charge. A full press pack had assembled outside, and many of the reporters were equally surprised to see us being released. Like me, they had expected us to be escorted out of the courtroom in chains. Yet here we were, walking out not exactly as free men, but a lot more free than anyone ever thought we would be.

Dan bundled us into a car with Troy, one of his associates, and we were taken to his office. After a quick debrief there, we were driven to his home. His poor wife, Robin, put on a brave face when she learned that a trio of alleged fraudsters would be staying at her house for the next few weeks, but she turned out to be a fantastic hostess. If it hadn't been for the kindness and generosity of these wonderful people, we would have been stuck in the FDC in downtown Houston for a long time, and who knows what the outcome of our case would have been then.

In the meantime, the prosecution remarkably supplied us with work permits, so we could fulfil the ludicrous bond requirement that we all get jobs. Unsurprisingly, no employer in Houston was remotely interested. We were all over the newspapers, tarred and feathered as financial criminals, and accused of helping to bring down Enron, which had been the city's shining light. It was like telling Bonnie and Clyde to get jobs as bank clerks. Thankfully, we were all able to find firms in Britain who were willing to take a chance on us and let us work remotely – in my case, my own manufacturing company.

It took three weeks before we could get the bond money together, and in the meantime, aided by Dan's wonderful assistant, Jimmy Ardoin, I found a flat in the city where I could base myself. But I was a little sad to be leaving Robin and Dan's home. We all became close friends very quickly – they were great hosts with a wonderful sense of humour – and I knew I would miss their warm hospitality. Robin and Dan, Troy and Jimmy did a fantastic job of introducing us to Houston, showing us all the wonderful places that the city had to offer and helping us to get settled.

There is no way we can ever repay the great kindness that they and many others showed us during that difficult period of our lives. There were even days when I could forget about my situation and snatch some happy moments. For a few hours at a time, I did not feel like a man whose life was falling apart.

With the up-front bond money posted, however, it was time for us to let the couple have their lives back. Besides, there was a case to fight.

The story of our extradition also contained a tragedy that was far greater than our possible prison sentences or anything else that might happen to us. This involved my former colleague Neil Coulbeck, the managing director in charge of business operations and balance sheet management at Greenwich NatWest at the time of Enron's collapse.

When we were selling the contentious Swap Sub asset at the heart of our case, I had met with Neil to seek his approval for the sale. As I explained earlier, at that point, the value of Swap Sub was minimal, so $1 million had seemed like a tremendous offer. Neil had agreed that it was a good deal for us, and he gave his verbal approval to the sale.

After Enron collapsed in 2001, the company released information about some of its potentially fraudulent transactions, one of which was Fastow's dealings surrounding Swap Sub. As soon as we learned this, David, Gary and I went voluntarily to our then employers and the Financial Services Authority (FSA) to report our involvement, as you will recall.

During their subsequent investigations, the FBI wanted to talk to anyone connected to this particular deal. We had told the FSA that Neil Coulbeck had signed off on the sale, so the authorities interviewed him to ascertain whether this was true. We knew it was, but when we eventually saw his affidavit after our arrest, we were genuinely shocked to see that he had claimed to have 'no recollection' of any meeting relating to the sale. If only he had been able to recall the meeting and told the authorities that he *had* given his approval of the sale – and explained the good economics and circumstances behind it – then in all likelihood they would have found it very difficult to charge us with knowingly committing a fraud by deliberately selling the asset at an undervalue. Ergo, the extradition may never have occurred.

However, with Neil unable to confirm the meeting where he had approved the sale, allied to our disastrous decision not to declare the option we had to make the investment, and the cut-and-pasted use of separate emails in the criminal complaint, the case against us now had traction. Our protracted fight against extradition failed, and in the summer of 2006, the media was full of stories about our imminent departure for America where we would be facing a life ending 35-year prison sentence. It was at this point – two days before we were due to be extradited – when Neil Coulbeck was found dead in a park in London. Most unfortunately, our former friend and colleague had taken his own life.

At the subsequent inquest, reported in various media, Mrs Coulbeck said that her husband feared being 'dragged into' the case against the NatWest Three. He had reportedly been nervous about his involvement, even though the FBI agents who interviewed him made it clear that he was not a suspect. Mrs Coulbeck also told the inquest that her husband's mood had changed suddenly at the beginning of July 2006, after he had read a series of newspaper reports about our case, essentially stating that we were facing the rest of our lives in a US prison. He was reportedly 'very troubled' by our fight against extradition.

At the time, she was quoted in the press as saying: 'I think ... his mother had read out something from the paper about the extradition. I'm only speculating, but I think that could have been the reason.'

It was also reported in the press that Neil had made fourteen calls to the USA on 30 June and three more calls to the head of legal services at the Royal Bank of Scotland on 4 July. Tragically, he was found dead on 11 July 2006. We were extradited to Houston two days later.

I spent a lot of time contemplating all these events whilst I was locked up in Allenwood, where the days soon took on a predictable rhythm. My daily routine – breakfast, work, lunch, rec, television – was well established in no time, and after a few weeks I felt as if I had been in the prison for my whole life. That's not a good thing, of course, but that was how it was. The days were punctuated by constant head-counts, as the BOP always wanted to make sure that we were all there and exactly where we were supposed to be.

The routine counts by the guards took place at 12 midnight, 5 a.m., 9 a.m., 1 p.m., 4 p.m. and 9 p.m. You had to be in your cell, standing by your bed, except at 9 a.m. when we were counted at work and at 1 p.m. when the count normally coincided with recreation time. This meant you had to plan your day in advance to accommodate not only the hourly moves, but also to make sure you didn't get stranded where you shouldn't be when it came to a count.

A strange thing about the routine at Allenwood was how much I dreaded weekends. On the outside, weekends were an oasis in my busy work life. They represented two glorious, back-to-back days when I wouldn't have to worry about clients or constantly check what the markets were doing. When I was still a banker, weekends were golden, pure quality time to spend with my family and my friends. But at Allenwood there was nothing good about them. Sure, I didn't have to report to the laundry or do any other work, but that was why they were so hard to endure. They dragged and felt never-ending, and I always found myself miserable on a Friday afternoon knowing that forty-eight hours of nothingness was lying between me and another week. Without work to break up the days, the boredom became all-consuming. I would become listless and agitated, desperate for something to do. If I could have worked seven days a week, then I would have. We all would have. As I've said before, work kept us sane.

The same went for public holidays, when there were fewer guards around. On these days nobody got moved out of solitary, nobody's post came through and, worst of all, we often couldn't spend time on the rec unless enough guards were there to watch over us.

On days like that, it was hard not to think of the lifers and other long-term prisoners, many of whom had been nothing but kind to me. Some of them had been wronged by the system but most of them were genuinely repentant. Some knew it was unlikely that they would ever see their families again. Every time the same national holiday came round, another metaphorical nail was hammered into their coffins: the Fourth of July, Thanksgiving, Christmas and all the rest were landmarks on the roadside of their wasted lives.

Memorial Day came relatively early in my stay. To give them credit, the prison staff did try to make the best of it, and they laid on a barbecue for us. It was a sweltering day, and this went off without a hitch – but the only trouble was that we then had to troop back inside early, to give the guards time to clean up and pack everything away.

The strain of being separated from my family was starting to weigh down heavily on me. Something about Memorial Day brought the feelings home. I suppose this was because I had celebrated the previous one while I was living in Houston on bond, working on my case. This holiday passing on the inside was something of a reminder that we had failed. Either way, I must admit that I was very grateful for the distraction of the barbecue – and the grilled burger was one of the best things I'd eaten at Allenwood.

Food in the prison was usually a lucky dip, without the luck. You could always guarantee that something of yesterday's leftovers would find its way into today's meal, which led to some unusual culinary experiments. The day after the barbecue, chopped-up bits of burger were mixed in with our mac and cheese, and the day before, a soup had been made from the reheated and watered-down remains of a beef stroganoff. The more time passed, the more repulsed I grew at the atrocious food. Weight was falling off me, and I started to become concerned about my gaunt appearance. On some nights, the food was so bad that I could barely stomach more than a few forkfuls.

By the end, I was living almost entirely off microwave noodles, which I bought from the commissary in bulk. On their own they were nothing special, but if you added in some fish and some spices – if you could find them – then they became a lot more enjoyable. I started to think of my trips to the chow hall as a social occasion above anything else, and if I could force down a few mouthfuls of food as well, then that was a bonus.

One of the guys I spent time with over dinner was a real joker known as Klepp. I had been in Allenwood for about four weeks when he approached me.

'You're Darby, right? The Enron guy?'

'Yeah.'

'Well, here's a word to the wise. People say you're a decent guy, but I'm telling you for your own benefit that you're hanging out with a few of the wrong kind.'

'Okay, thanks. But who?'

'Well, you gotta figure that out for yourself.'

After that, whenever I saw him, I always asked if I was improving my company!

He didn't give me an answer, but I knew from others that he was a money launderer for the mob, a serial criminal. When I met him, he was serving his third spell in the care of the federal government. He had already served six years at Allenwood, and was due to get out after one more. His rap sheet included running an illegal gambling ring and a smattering of other financial crimes, with the money laundering topping it all off. All in all, he and his co-defendants were indicted for 300 counts between them, with ninety or so against Klepp. He told me all this over an anaemic chicken dinner. It's fair to say I found his anecdotes far more enjoyable than the food.

'I knew I'd get a long stretch,' he was saying. 'The Feds really had the hots for me, but the trial was a long way off. I was on bond when a group of my guys went on a golfing trip to West Virginia. I went too and we had a great time. A friend of mine down there owned a strip club where we went on a few of the nights. I was looking for something to put money into and the club was so much fun that I asked the owner how much he would take for the place.

'He said $150,000. I thought, fuck it. I knew that in a year's time I'd be going away for a while, so what better place to wait for the trial than a place like this? Me and my pals all had a blast – you can imagine what it was like, Darb. I went mad. Well, you would – drink, drugs, strippers –

and the place made a lot of money, too! When I got sent down, I had to get rid of it, unfortunately. That was a shame.'

He looked wistfully out of the nearest window while the rest of us burst into laughter. 'I did try to get my girl to take over the lease and keep it, but she wasn't interested.'

'Funny that.'

Klepp was one of those guys who managed to keep positive all the time. I found his optimism contagious, and after a few minutes or so in his company, I would generally start to feel better about my own situation. He told me he had been in Allenwood in 2001, a comment that elicited a few whistles around our table. 'I watched the fall of the Twin Towers in here,' he said. 'I watched as it happened.'

His comments got me thinking: that was a long time to be in a place like this. I had been here only a few weeks and I was already going mad. It was amazing to me that anyone could survive in prison for the best part of a lifetime.

CHAPTER 10

ANGER MANAGEMENT

Allenwood was a place where you could find heartbreak anywhere you looked. Sad stories abounded, and there were many times when I felt unspeakably guilty for complaining so much about my own situation. I was being emotionally tortured, don't get me wrong, but at least I didn't have to endure the ordeal on my own.

I've already mentioned the scores of men who found themselves locked away with nobody left to support them on the outside. Wives disappeared, parents disowned them, children stopped writing. It was a shockingly common story, and it made me wonder how the US government expected these men to lead wholesome, rehabilitated lives after their release, when they had nobody to turn to and little chance of earning a decent living.

Many of these abandoned men, left to their fate by friends, family and country, still insisted on fighting their sentences. They requested appeals, they lodged complaints, they did everything they could within their limited means to get themselves back in front of a judge, hoping this time to get a break. I don't think they did it because they genuinely expected their circumstances could be changed. I think it was because they needed something to cling on to – even if it was only the slimmest sliver of hope.

Hardly any of these guys had their own lawyers, so they had no choice but to work their cases themselves. The prison's legal library was always full of desperate inmates, poring over textbooks and reading case files, searching endlessly for that one, lucky loophole that might help them. There were a few ex-lawyers amongst the prison population – all of them disbarred for some manner of misconduct or impropriety – and these jailhouse lawyers often touted their services. They charged their fellow inmates extortionate rates in black-market goods, fish or stamps in return for a few hours' work.

I found something unsavoury about this. These sharks were pitching their services to those at rock-bottom, knowing full well that nothing they did would make a difference. And that was the truth. The chance of an inmate successfully appealing his sentence was next to nil. Consider the numbers: something in the region of ninety-five per cent of prisoner petitions fail, and that's assuming that you could make a case coherent enough for a judge to hear it. I thought our own story of fighting against the juggernaut of the US justice system was a David and Goliath situation: but having met so many desperate inmates, working on their own petitions without any legal background, I realised our odds could have been substantially longer.

Of course I never said that when I was chatting to these guys. I could sense the expectation, hear the desperation in their voices as they told me about the latest courtroom chicanery they thought could bust them out of Allenwood. I smiled politely, telling them each time that it sounded like this really could be the one, the appeal that would make all the difference. Deep down, they must have known themselves that it was hopeless. But they all needed to keep trying, otherwise what did they have?

Meanwhile, I was developing anxieties of my own. Everything had gone quiet on my transfer request and it seemed to be taking weeks longer than it should to be sent round to all the right people. A part of me wondered whether I was as deluded as everyone else. I knew that the promise of an expedited transfer wasn't worth anything until I was actually back in the UK; if the transfer didn't happen, then I would have to serve my whole sentence here at Allenwood, with no chance of parole. That thought weighed heavily on me.

Thankfully, there was someone I could talk to about it. Rob, an English guy, was in for twelve years for drugs and gun possession, although like many others he was adamant that he had been set up by the Feds. He, too, was seeking a treaty transfer back to the UK, and we regularly discussed our applications. He had applied more than two years earlier, although an expedited transfer had not been part of his plea. He had heard nothing and was having a much tougher time of it than me.

In a bureaucracy as big as the BOP, the wheels are bound to turn slowly. I worried that maybe the whole process would take us years after all and after the shenanigans we had endured around the bond conditions, nothing seemed beyond the Feds.

Through casual conversation with my fellow inmates, I learned a great deal about the workings of the justice system. I was particularly impressed with Paul, the guy who was in for running an illegal gambling operation, for devising a way to get his sentence reduced. On the advice of his (clearly very good) attorney, strait-laced Paul had deliberately failed a drug test, turned up to a clinical evaluation drunk, and managed to get a psychologist to say he was substance-dependent. He wasn't, but by being classified as such he qualified for the drug rehabilitation programme, a nine-month course offered to all American inmates with substance issues. Here's the masterstroke: completing the programme would make any inmate eligible for a one-year sentence reduction. When I met Paul, he had recently finished his rehab.

A few weeks later, he had been summoned to the counsellor's office. The counsellor told him that his commitment to the programme had earned him not only the full, one-year sentence reduction, but also got him an additional six months off, with that time to be spent at a halfway house (an institution where prisoners can complete their rehabilitation with more freedoms than in a prison). Paul said he was so thrilled that he started crying on the spot. Even as he was relaying this story to me, I could see him welling up at the joy of reclaiming eighteen months of his life.

Paul's tale reminded me of my own counselling story. After Gary, David and I were bonded, we too became aware that if alleged wrongdoers had issues with substance abuse, stress or anger management, and sought help, the judge might take this into account when it came to sentencing. I had never had any issues with substances, but there were certainly anger management issues, caused by the events surrounding the indictment, extradition and bond.

Despite the terrible stress the three of us had been under during the four years between the indictment and extradition, our personal relationships held up well, even with regular disagreements regarding the management of the case. David and Gary had worked hard with a PR agency and other media to push our side of things in the UK and, despite my own reticence, they had ultimately succeeded in keeping us out of prison in the US, for which I was deeply grateful. While we were bonded in Houston we were able to work together on our defence, and we approached the task as if it was a full-time job.

We worked from 10 a.m. to 4 p.m. in Dan's downtown office almost every day of the week, ploughing through the thousands of documents with which the DOJ had presented us. David, in particular, spent night and day working the case and developing different theories and strategies about our situation. The government's claim was that we had knowingly and deliberately undersold the Swap Sub asset in order to reap a vast profit through Fastow's fraud. For our part, and as the Statement of Facts confirms, we had no knowledge of Fastow's actions. We knew that it was vital for us to find a way to demonstrate this to the prosecution, to cast doubt on their theory.

I was aware that in a couple of crucial aspects of the case, both David and Gary had not been one hundred per cent honest with me, but they were my close friends and were both good men. We had each agreed to stick together, no matter what.

In mid-2007, we were having a frank discussion over lunch when David made a particularly insulting comment to me. Tensions were already running high, and his idiotic remark pushed me over the edge. I was holding a meatball sub at the time and, in my fury, I threw it across the desk at him. David was sitting no more than three feet away from me, but somehow the sub managed to miss him. Splatters of meat sauce arced across the ceiling behind me, and the sub collided with the far wall in an explosion of sandwich filling. It was a complete mess, and red flecks of sauce ended up all over Dan's conference room, like something from a horror movie.

Later that week, I had to attend one of my regularly scheduled meetings with my probation officer. He asked me a tick-box list of questions whenever he saw me. Had I associated with felons? Had I consumed alcohol? Had I been adhering to my curfew? Finally, he asked if there were any other problems. Aware of the potential for sympathy from the court if I sought treatment for mental issues, I confirmed to him that, yes, I had anger problems and told him about the meatball incident. He suggested that I should go on an anger management course and I readily agreed.

At my first class, the facilitator asked me to say something about why I was there. I explained that I was awaiting trial for robbing a bank and his eyes lit up.

'Dude!' he exclaimed. 'No way ... I robbed a bank too!'

He then proceeded to explain how he and two friends had held up a series of local banks, but were eventually caught in the act. One of his friends had turned prosecution witness to get a lighter sentence, and he swore from that moment that he wanted the rat dead. 'I used to pray that he would be struck down,' the facilitator said. 'I hated him so much – the anger just consumed me. The motherfucker had betrayed me, and I thought he deserved to be punished for it. My mother would regularly send me newspaper cuttings in prison and, sure enough, one day she sent me one about a guy who had been killed after another man walked in on him having sex with his wife. Well, the dead guy was the same dude who ratted me out! My prayers had been answered. I praised the Lord and swore never to let my anger get the better of me again.'

This was a truly extraordinary story and the class erupted with laughter. Things got even funnier when he went around the circle and asked whether anyone had had any 'wins' that week.

'What do you mean by that?' someone asked.

'Well, a win is when you stop your anger from getting the better of you. If you can resist your urges, or stop yourself from doing something stupid, then that's a win.'

A tough-looking guy put his hand up. 'I've had a win this week,' he said.

'Oh, that's great!' the facilitator said. 'Would you like to tell us about it?'

'Sure. I was stitched up in a drug deal. I paid someone a lot of money, but he didn't show up with the goods. I wanted to kill him, but I didn't.'

'That's good,' the facilitator said. 'Can you tell me how you overcame your anger? Why didn't you act on your urges?'

'Well,' the drug dealer said, 'I haven't found him yet.'

Again, howls of laughter. If I thought my anger problems were bad, they had nothing on that guy's. I told Paul the story and he fell about laughing, too. It was so ridiculous you really couldn't have made it up.

Almost every day I spent in Allenwood, I would come across another story that made me feel fortunate by comparison. For every tale of hope, like Paul's, there was one of despair. Take the case of Frankie, a hilarious Italian-American guy who enjoyed regaling anyone that would listen with stories about his life. We got chatting one day and he asked me who my cellies were. I told him about El and T, and their extreme sentences. Frankie whistled when he heard about T's thirty-five years.

'That's a big number without a body,' he said.

'It sure is,' I said. 'How big is your number?'

'Eight.' He caught my eye. 'That's also without a body, in case you were wondering.'

Frankie told me he was in for conspiracy to murder. He was a mobster who had cooked up some crazy scheme to kill someone years before, as payback for a deal gone wrong. His best friend was in on it too and, although the pair never made the kill, when his friend was arrested, he ratted on Frankie. When Frankie heard he had been indicted, he went on the run.

He spent almost a year in a constant state of anxiety, always looking over his shoulder. It sounded like torture. The pressure was ratcheted up after a few months when he found he was on the FBI's list of the ten most wanted men in the US. After they finally caught him, he was incarcerated in the Metropolitan Detention Centre (MDC) in New York and told he was looking at twenty-five to thirty years.

The MDC sounded like a uniquely terrible place. Bizarrely for a prison, it was located on the fourth floor of a high-rise building, lending it an air of claustrophobia. The whole prison was essentially one enormous room with 120 bunks, one television, three toilets and no air-conditioning. The guys stewed all day in that same room through the cold of winter and the heat of summer, without exercise yard or fresh air, sharing their already-crowded space with an infestation of mice. Every time Frankie opened his locker, he would find fresh droppings, and clusters of mice would dart away across the floor whenever anyone approached the dingy corners where they lived.

On the outside, Frankie had worked in the bar trade, so he never slept at normal times. When he arrived at the MDC, he found it impossible to get any rest, what with all the noise from 120 guys living on top of each other. He said he didn't eat much either. When you know that you're sharing the kitchen with a family of mice, it's probably hard to work up an appetite. 'It was the worst time of my life, Darby,' he was saying, one afternoon out on the rec. 'Honestly, it was just an awful place.'

'So how long did you spend there before you pleaded out?' I asked, expecting him to give me an answer in the region of a few weeks.

'Eighteen months.'

Eighteen months? A year and a half in an overcrowded holding cell, where human rights were thrown out of the window? (Not that there *were* windows at the MDC, of course.) It sounded like something you hear about happening in Soviet Russia, not in twenty-first century America – the so-called land of the free. Whatever he had done wrong, Frankie was a human being who deserved his dignity. Throughout those eighteen months, he was still technically innocent in the eyes of the law, having never been proven guilty in court.

When Frankie said how long he had spent there, the cruelty of the MDC started to make some sense. It sounded to me as if the Feds used it as a way to extract guilty pleas. If you stuck someone in that hellhole and told them their trial was months away, and then kept postponing the trial date (as often happens), you can imagine the defendant would be ready to confess to anything if it meant being moved somewhere more habitable. Effectively, it was a state-sanctioned way to extract confessions and pleas out of men who were, until proven otherwise, presumed to be innocent.

After this miserable period in the MDC, Frankie struck a plea agreement for eight years. I admired his stoicism. By the sound of it, I wouldn't have lasted a week. However, unfortunately for me, I suspected that I would have to endure much longer than a week in the MDC's sister institution, the Metropolitan Correctional Centre (MCC). The MCC is where foreign inmates are sent once their transfers are approved, and it's where I would have to kill time while the logistics of my move home were being arranged.

I suspected that this place, another skyscraper prison with no exercise yard and no fresh air, would be the hardest obstacle between me and the UK. I had already heard terrible rumours about the MCC before Frankie described the goings-on at its sister institution.

As for Frankie, his arrest had cost him almost everything, and he didn't seem to be holding up too well. I saw him one evening at dinner, on a day when he was supposed to be getting a visit from his daughter and son-in-law. They never showed up, and Frankie was visibly upset to have been let down.

'I was looking forward to it, man.' He forked at his food, moving it around his plate without eating any of it. It reminded me of something a teenager would do. 'I was fucking looking forward to it.' He let out a heavy sigh. 'Well, I guess they'll come another time soon, right? At least they haven't forgotten me completely like all the other fucking amnesiacs from the street. I haven't had so much as a letter from most people I knew.'

'Frankie,' I said, 'people just don't write these days. You shouldn't take it personally. When you get out, they'll still be there and everyone will be pleased to see you.'

He looked at me sadly. I'd never seen him so dejected – he was usually brimming with life, but tonight he looked utterly deflated. 'Darb, it's easy for you to say. I'm doing eight years, not eight months. I've been there for so many people over the years, and now I'm the one who needs the support, there's nobody around for me.'

I felt a twinge of guilt thinking about all the letters I had been sent by my own friends and family. I looked across at the sulking mobster sitting beside me. 'Frankie, man, it is what it is. You've got to just get on with it, mate.'

It wasn't all bad news, though, and I found myself clinging to the rare moments of joy that always seemed so incongruous within our bleak setting. El's appeal was one such source of joy. After weeks of waiting, he came bounding into the cell with the news. His motion had been granted and he was finally getting out. The wheels of the BOP were turning, and all that stood between him and the rest of his life was a judge's signature.

He was obviously ecstatic, but there was something else in his expression as well: disbelief. After so many years of being downtrodden, it was a strange feeling for him to have something go right. I looked at him intently, sharing his joy, and he returned the look. We didn't need to speak. We knew how momentous this was.

El and I were so similar and yet so different at the same time. We were both outgoing, gregarious types – and risk-takers by nature. One of us was a black hustler from the streets, his father killed in a shoot-out when he was only a boy. His life story of crime and drugs had been written before he even left home. Prison time was all but inevitable. And me? A well-educated, well-raised, middle-class white guy with a successful career mapped out in front of me. Prison time? You'd never have guessed it, but there we were, thrown together by circumstance, and now good friends. I was so happy for him that I felt tears in my eyes as I digested his news. It was a truly magical moment and I was honoured to have been part of it.

All this was beyond fantastic for El, but it left T in even more of an unpleasant situation. He forced himself to put on a smile for his friend, but I could see that he was suffering inside. El's joy was salt in the wound – a reminder of what he could have won too.

It was only around this time that I learned that T had a son, a guy in his early twenties who lived in California. T hadn't seen him in over ten years, what with being on the opposite side of the country and neither of them having the money to pay the airfares. They talked on the phone, but that was it. I hadn't seen my daughters for months by this point and it was agonising. I can't imagine how he must have felt going years without seeing his son.

Later, I was able to catch El on his own. 'El, when you get out, I want you to find out where T's boy is. He won't tell me, because he doesn't want me to give him anything. But I'll give you the money if you can organise for him to get out here and see T. How does that sound?' El beamed. He would be riding the high of his imminent release for weeks to come. 'Darby, that really would be something special. Yes, sir, let's do it.'

I also wondered whether there was another way I could help T, potentially by getting him some proper legal representation. I knew that he was still waiting on news from the courts, but without anyone working his case on the outside, it was unlikely he would ever get a decent result. Thankfully, I knew several attorneys from my time on bond – and I was good friends with a couple of them.

'Hey, T,' I said one evening that week. We were hanging around in the cell, killing time. 'Did you go to trial?'

T nodded. 'Yeah. I didn't want to, but my attorney fucked up. Before the trial, at the last minute, a witness turned on me. I told my attorney I would take fifteen years, but she couldn't get the deal done. I would have been out now if she had, but instead I'm stuck here.'

'Have you heard anything more about your sentence reduction?'

'No. Still waiting for news, man. What I really need to do is get someone to go down to the courthouse and talk to the clerks.'

'You know, I have a friend in Texas who might be able to help you. He's an attorney specialising in drug cases. He's a good friend and he owes me a favour anyway, so I think he'd agree at least to take a look at your situation. If you'd like me to ask him, that is.'

T's eyes lit up. 'Really? You'd do that?'

'I can't promise it'll achieve anything, but he will be able to tell you if there's anything that can be done. If you give me your papers, I can send them off to him.'

T reached out for a fist bump. 'Darby,' he said. 'That would be really cool, man.'

Perhaps there was hope for him yet.

Throughout this period, the highlight of my day, every day, was post time (or mail time, as the Yanks called it). At 4 p.m., after the count, those of us lucky enough to have correspondence from the outside would be called to line up outside the post room to collect our letters. On a good day, I could expect one or two from family and friends, as well as an edition of *The Sunday Times* or *The Daily Telegraph*, usually a good week or so out of date.

I didn't mind that my subscriptions were so slow in getting to me – I was grateful for the reading material and, in the case of the *Telegraph*, a fiendish sudoku to keep me occupied. That's the bit you don't see in *Shawshank* – where the old man sits on his bunk messing around with a sudoku puzzle for an hour a day. Who says crime has to be glamorous?

My newspapers would end up travelling around half the unit before everyone was done with them. Before long, they became quite sought-after on the compound – lots of guys enjoyed reading them, and having one to give away helped make a few extra friends. First the paper would be parcelled out to a couple of other newshounds, including Rob, when I was finished with it: after he had read it, it would often be divided up into sections based on what people were interested in. A couple of white-collar guys would always ask to see the business news, while a Russian football nut called Oleg got the sport section. It was nice to know that I could help some of my fellow inmates relieve the boredom for a few hours at a time. If only the writers at the *Telegraph* had any idea that their work was so popular in the American penal system.

By then I had been in Allenwood for a few months – long enough to understand how things were done. I was waiting to collect the latest edition when I noticed there was a new guy lining up outside the post room with us. People came and went all the time, so it wasn't unusual to see new faces every week. But there was something about this guy that was intriguing. He was a couple of places in front of me in the queue, an Italian-American guy with a thick *Sopranos* accent.

The post queue could move very slowly, and the guards were never in any rush to sort all the letters and hand them out. Nobody had moved for a few minutes, all eyes on the dozy guard juggling envelopes and newspapers in front of us, when the new guy spoke up. He brazenly shouted at the guard that he was an idiot, using a stupid system that was making the wait much longer than it had to be. I don't think the guard had ever been spoken to like that by an inmate before, and he seemed more shocked than annoyed. Absolutely furious, he put down the mail, stepped out of the post room, shut the door behind him and locked it, and started to walk off. 'If you're gonna be like that, you can all wait for your mail!' he barked at us over his shoulder. 'I'll come back later.'

There were angry groans from among the inmates. We were desperate to receive our post, and now the cocky newcomer had earned us all a longer wait. He watched the guard disappear around a corner. 'Fucking cocksucker,' he called out, quietly enough that the guard wouldn't hear it.

Later that same day, the post room reopened for our delayed letter collection. I looked around for the troublemaker, but he was nowhere to be seen. In fact I didn't see him again until a couple of hours later, when we both happened to be heading to the chow hall at the same time.

'Hey,' I said to him, 'you know they're still doing the mail, if you want yours.'

'Thanks,' he said. I was struck by the thickness of his Italian-American accent. 'I don't know how you guys put up with the shit from the guards here. I just came down from the medium and I can tell you it's completely different there.'

'How so?'

'Well, in the medium you've got guys doing serious stretches of time, so the guards and the inmates have to get on. There's a degree of respect between the two. But here, people are just working towards getting out, so the guards don't see any point in playing nice. I mean, look at you. You don't look like a guy with long to go. How long have you got?'

'Three years.'

'There, see what I mean? You're waiting to get out, right? Well, not me. I've got thirty years and I'm not taking any shit from any of these people. What's a few days in the hole against thirty years, right?'

'Right,' I said, ruminating on his sentence. 'Thirty years, eh? That's a big number without a body.'

He laughed. 'Oh no, there's a body all right. I deserve every year of it.' A pause. 'Let's just say someone had to be put to sleep.'

'Oh.' What more could I say? It was the matter-of-factness that stunned me. He was the first person I had met who had admitted to killing anyone.

I knew there were plenty of killers in Allenwood, but when someone says it to you so casually, it takes your breath away.

A couple of days passed before I saw my new acquaintance again. It turned out that he had moved into the cell opposite mine, practically making us neighbours. He introduced himself and told me that he knew all about my case. For the sake of this book, I'll refer to him as Ralph – a name from *The Sopranos* seems fitting.

'You Enron guys,' he said. 'You practically stole all that money from behind a desk, right?'

I didn't know where he was going with this. 'Well, some people certainly did.'

He chuckled. 'Now that's much smarter than going on the street and robbing people with guns.'

I saw Ralph again that same evening. He was a few places ahead of me in the chow queue, talking to the oldest guy on the compound – a little guy in his early eighties. I had no idea what he was in for, or how long he had been in, but it was always sad to see him shuffling about the place in his khakis. Ralph spotted me and pointed me out to the old guy.

'See, there's that Enron guy,' he said. 'Millions, he stole. Millions.'

I laughed. 'Well, the Feds have it all now.'

'Yeah, yeah.' Ralph gave me a knowing wink.

'No, seriously,' I said. 'Mate, I declared every penny I made. I even paid tax on it.'

'Smart!' Ralph commented. At that, he turned back to his elderly companion and resumed his conversation. I still had no idea what he was getting at with all the Enron talk and I wasn't certain that I wanted to find out.

Things became clearer a few hours later. I was on my bunk, reading, when I heard movement outside the cell. I looked up and Ralph's head appeared in the doorway. Oh great, I thought: my mobster neighbour has turned up to borrow some sugar. El and T were in the TV room, so I was alone with him. My heart started to beat a little bit faster as I tried to guess what he could possibly want.

'All right, Ralph?' I asked him. 'Come on in.'

'Hey, Darby,' Ralph said. He perched on El's bunk. He paused for a moment, perhaps planning what he was going to say, and then launched into it. What he came out with wasn't exactly what I was expecting.

'Listen. I got a couple of kids, a boy and a girl in their teens. They talk a lot about college courses and stuff like that. If they want to get into business and corporate stuff, what kind of courses should I be pushing them towards?'

I was completely taken aback that Ralph was coming to me for career advice, but I was happy to help. Needless to say, a discussion about internships and business studies was not what I'd been expecting. I gave him some suggestions to pass on to his kids and told him how I had got into banking – working my way up from the very bottom. He listened attentively, and I could tell that he was pleased to hear what I had to say.

'Do you see the kids often?' I asked.

'Yeah,' he said. 'They come when they can, you know, but my ma has to bring them here. I saw them a couple of weeks ago actually. We sat outside – it was a really nice day – and I was able to hug them and kiss them and properly talk to them. It was our best-ever visit, I'd say.'

'That's good.' I thought carefully about what I would say next. 'You know, Ralph, I'd say you're a reasonable, sensible guy. You don't seem like the kind to kill somebody.'

'Man, I did a lot of shit. I was a bad guy, Darby. I was into all sorts.'

'Like?'

'Racketeering, extortion, armed robbery …'

'Armed robbery?' I interrupted.

'Oh yeah. Me and some guys held up an armoured van. Millions of dollars.'

'Wow,' I said. 'Was that the time you killed someone?'

'No, no.' Ralph waved his hand dismissively. 'That was different. He was in the same line of work as me. It was an occupational hazard for him, you could say.'

He saw the look on my face. 'Look, Darby, I wish I had never done it. If there was some way I could bring the guy back then I would, but I can't. So, I'm doing this time instead. I did it. I shouldn't have. I'm guilty.

I accept it and now I got to pay my dues.'

There were a few moments of silence.

'You know,' he said, 'I only pleaded out to avoid the death penalty. When I was sentenced, I didn't know if I would get a number or get life.'

'But you got thirty years? How many have you done?'

'I've done seven. With good time, I should be out after twenty-six or twenty-seven years. I'll be around sixty when I get out.'

Like so many of the people I had met, Ralph had an incredibly blasé attitude to the amount of time he was doing. It was as if it hadn't really sunk in for him – thirty years was an abstract concept, rather than a real stretch of time he would have to spend in prison.

I was trying hard to keep a neutral expression, but he must have noticed something change in my face again. 'Hey, man, it's fine. I've accepted it and I'm getting on with it. You know, the hardest part was losing my wife. That's what hurt me the most. She was with me twenty years – the only woman I've ever been with. She's got somebody else now. Divorced me. It was awful, man. I lost forty pounds because of the stress – the emotional pain of what she did was worse than my fucking sentence.'

'Ralph, it must have been hard for her too, though. To see her husband go down for thirty years. I mean, I'm guessing that must have destroyed her?'

'Look, I see what you mean, but I'm the one in here. It's me who's gotta serve the time. When I went to work, I did it for her and the family. And now she's at home with the kids, in the house I built and paid for, all the money taken care of, and she's fucking moved another guy into the house. Into my bed. I heard her new guy even wears some of my old fucking clothes! How much do you think that hurts?'

'I can't even begin to imagine.'

He sighed and forced a smile. 'My kids are what get me through it. They're on my side, you know, and they're just fantastic. That's why I'm so keen for them to get a good education. I got to keep my boy out of jail, out of the same way of life that I had. I mean, look where it got me. I couldn't bear for it to happen to him.'

I admired Ralph's desire to make a better life for his kids. I knew that him loving his children didn't make up for killing a man, but even so … I certainly felt the same way about my children. And I knew for sure they were never going to go the same way as me. I'd make sure of that.

CHAPTER 11

IT'S ALL ABOUT RESPECT

The most prominent Mafia guy in Allenwood was John Carneglia – a notorious mobster who had established a fearsome reputation as a member of the Gambino crime family and a close associate of John Gotti, the former boss of the Gambino family known as 'The Teflon Don'. Heroin distribution, loan sharking, hijacking, murders ... you name it, John Carneglia had been accused of it. Just reading his Wikipedia page is enough to give you nightmares.

I first met John in the microwave room. In the evenings there would be queues of twenty or so inmates for each of the four microwaves that served Gregg Unit, with everyone arguing about who was next in line and different groups claiming ownership of each microwave. I quickly learned to avoid the most popular times. Instead, I tended to do my microwaving in the early afternoon, usually after the 1 p.m. move, when it was quieter and there were no queues to speak of.

John was often in the room when I got there. He was something of a celebrity and he would swagger around Allenwood as if he owned the place. Whenever he appeared in the TV room, most of the inmates would leap out of their chairs to make sure he had somewhere to sit down, and he never had to queue for a microwave like I had to. I knew he was serving a mind-bendingly long sentence, which commanded respect in and of itself.

After seeing me a few times, he spoke to me. 'You're that Enron guy, right?' He had obviously asked around about me. 'You're a financial guy?'

'Yeah, that's right,' I said. 'My name's Darby.'

He held out his hand for me to shake – a rarity, given that I was used to fist bumping by now.

'John,' he said. 'Pleased to meet you. I wanted to ask you something.' My heart raced. What the hell could he want with me? 'My son wants to go into Wall Street. Where should he be applying for jobs? I was thinking about Goldman, Merrill Lynch ... the investment banks.'

'Yeah,' I said, taken aback. 'Well, that sounds very sensible. Those are the best places to make your name.'

'How did you get to where you were?'

'I started at the bottom. I joined straight out of school and made my way through the ranks.'

John nodded. 'And what about stocks? Got any tips for me to tell him about?'

I shared a few ideas and we talked some more about the world of finance. I couldn't believe that a senior mobster like John would want to spend his time talking to me about his son's career trajectory, but that's the kind of place Allenwood was. From then on, John and I always said hello whenever our paths crossed.

There was another mobster whom I met around the same time, one of John's crew, known as Bones. I saw him talking to Ralph on the running track and made my way over to say hello.

'Hey, Bones,' I said. We bumped fists. 'I'm Darby, nice to meet you.'

'You too, man,' Bones said. 'Ralph said you're cool.'

'Thanks,' I said. I couldn't help but ask. 'So, why are you called Bones?'

Bones looked at me as if I was stupid. 'Because I've put a lot of bones in the ground.' Ralph burst out laughing.

'Darby,' Ralph said, 'you don't want to ask any more questions.' We changed the subject.

One day, not long after that, again I was in the microwave room when John walked in, looking particularly chipper.

'Hey, Darby, it's been a real pleasure to meet you and I've enjoyed our conversations, but I'm leaving here tomorrow and I won't be back – so I wanna wish you the best of luck with things.'

'Thanks, John,' I said. 'Where are you going?'

'I've got a parole hearing in New York. I'm hoping to get out – probation and the cops are supporting me.'

'That's good to hear. How long is your sentence?'

'Fifty years. I've done twenty-two.'

'Well, I'm pleased for you, John,' I said. 'I wish you well.'

Three weeks later, I was once more in the microwave room when who should wander in but John.

'John?' I said, slightly surprised.

'Hey, Darby.'

'It didn't go well then?'

'No.'

'Well, what did they say?'

'Come back in ten years.'

Sure enough, John was released in 2018.

Being part of the mob, as John was, conferred some handy privileges in Allenwood. For one thing, a solid reputation would ensure that you got larger portions of food at dinner time. On multiple occasions, I watched as known Mafia guys got double helpings and the choicest bits of meat. Starving and jealous, I was often given the usual scraps and a measly helping of the day's side dish.

The Mafia guys I met were all sound, but I was always very careful around them – and with good reason. Once, a young guy in the laundry, known as Junior, almost got himself into serious trouble with one of the Mafiosi. Junior was a new arrival at Allenwood, a young American computer wizard who was serving five years for hacking and a litany of related frauds. We called him Junior, because although he was twenty-two, he looked even younger. From the moment I first met him, I wondered whether he would be cut out for prison life. There was an arrogance and naïvety about him that marked him out and, for all his intelligence, I doubted whether he had an ounce of street smarts.

He constantly recycled the same line about his crime: 'Nobody got hurt, Darby. We just fucked over the big banks … and a few credit card companies.' I was well beyond using that kind of logic on my own case, but I never said that. Junior's biggest problem, however, wasn't his lack of perspective. It was his lack of discretion. He simply could not stop gossiping about who was in for what, who had done what to whom, and who had how much time left to serve. It was relentless, tactless stuff – the kind of behaviour that wasn't welcome in a school playground, let alone a prison yard. The first rule of Allenwood was very much to mind your own business; Junior never stood a chance of sticking to that.

Despite this character flaw, he was likeable enough. He was an interesting young guy and I sensed that his time at Allenwood would be transformative for him. Either it would straighten him out and set him on the right path, or he would decide to double down and pursue a life of crime when he was out. That's assuming he made it out, of course.

Junior had almost gossiped himself into the hole within weeks of arriving. He had been spreading stories about someone who was known to be associated with the mob, telling people that this guy was behind a recent theft at the commissary. Four watches had gone missing and the prison authorities were keen to find out who took them. With a combined value of $160, it was a lucrative heist in prison terms.

Whether true or not, Junior landed himself in a lot of trouble by sharing his suspicions about the Mafioso. I don't know exactly what happened, but I do know this Mafia guy arranged a one-on-one with Junior on the rec. I can't imagine it went well, because that was the last time he ever mentioned the guy's name.

The trouble with Junior was he didn't have enough respect. It was respect that kept things ticking over at Allenwood: it was respect that kept you alive and respect that kept you out of trouble. Keeping to yourself was respectful. Doing your own time was respectful. Gossiping about people was not respectful, and if Junior didn't learn that soon, then I knew he would be in for a rough ride.

Every week I heard a new and shocking story about what happened when respect broke down. At the laundry one morning, Miss Anderson, clearly feeling a bit lonely and wanting to chat, struck up a conversation with me. She told me that there had been an incident in one of the other units the day before, involving a group of Mexicans and one black guy. The Mexicans had come at the black guy and beaten him with a piece of wood that had been removed from a desk. The wood was part of the cross support and had somehow been unscrewed, leaving a heavy metal hinge attached at one end.

The Mexicans took turns to lay into their victim with this improvised club, getting him as he was coming out of the toilet. Miss Anderson said he had been so badly beaten that he was whisked straight to the nearest hospital, while the Mexican assailants were taken to the SHU to await an investigation.

As ever, word spread on the prison grapevine and, within a couple of days, I had heard the full story. What Miss Anderson didn't tell me was that the victim had been accused of disrespecting one of the Mexicans by insisting on using a bathroom while the Mexican guy was cleaning it. There were other bathrooms he could have used, but he had supposedly made a point of doing his business straight after the toilet had been cleaned. It was all a show of dominance – an animal-kingdom move to demonstrate that he could get away with doing whatever he liked. Only this time he didn't get away with it. The Mexican had rushed straight off to gather his friends and they had exacted their revenge at the first opportunity. Nobody intervened, although a small crowd did gather to watch the bloodbath. The context didn't justify the violence, of course, but it did show that the attack wasn't entirely unprovoked.

I heard someone from the same unit talking about the incident on the rec. I asked him if he knew the guy who had been hospitalised, and he laughed and nodded.

'Couldn't have happened to a nicer guy. He walks around the place disrespecting everybody. Dude had it coming.'

It was a harsh lesson that here, respect really was everything. And it was also a reminder that nobody would step in to save you if you were judged to have crossed the line into disrespect. I hoped Junior would learn that lesson before it was too late – or in due course he too would be a victim.

One morning not long after this, Junior appeared in the laundry with a wad of paperwork. He believed he deserved a retrial, and he had recently filed a motion asking for one. The government had responded with a thirty-page countering document, which he would have to address if he wanted his motion to get any further. Seeing him poring over all those pages reminded me of the many, many days we had spent fighting our own case.

When we were bonded in Houston, we agreed with our hot-shot legal team that even if we didn't go to trial, we would have to be ready as if we were. We didn't have anyone to give up to the government, other than each other – Michael Kopper had seen to that – but we had agreed to stick together, so we knew we would need to present a strong and united defence if we were to have any hope of a good outcome. Our strategy was to prepare to fight the case in court, if it came to it, by arguing that the prosecutors' theory of the case was all wrong. But we needed to come from a position of strength, and we needed to find the evidence to get us there.

We were presented with thousands of pages of evidence, and we spent late 2006 and early 2007 working through this mound of paperwork, looking for areas where we could defend ourselves and introduce an element of doubt. In the US, any jury trial verdict has to be unanimous, so if even one person goes against the consensus, the result is a mistrial. So it was vital for us to introduce uncertainty into the case. Somehow, we had to show that we didn't know what Fastow had done with Swap Sub.

The indictment was in 2002 and the case was now over four years old. A handful of different prosecutors within the Enron Task Force had been in charge of it. But the indictment read so badly for us that successive prosecutors simply read it and thought we were slam-dunk guilty. We knew that our only chance was to demonstrate to the Feds that the case was much more complicated than they thought and that there were holes in their theory of the case.

One morning late in the summer of 2006, the chief prosecutor walked over to our attorneys in the courtroom and simply stated: 'We will be handing over the tapes in the next forty-eight hours or so.'

'What tapes?' Dan asked.

'Some recordings of your guys conducting their conspiracy.'

You could have knocked all three of us over with a single feather. Tapes? What tapes? When were they recorded? By whom? Who was on them? What was on them? Gary, especially, catastrophised about who had been recorded and what might have been said. It was impossible to remember phone calls from six or seven weeks ago, never mind six or seven years, but even so we spent hours theorising about the contents. It was excruciating. Would the tapes help us, or would they hurt us in the same way that the cut-and-pasted emails in the indictment had done?

When we finally got the tapes, we listened to them intently. It transpired that they were recordings made by the Canadian bank after we had learned of the criminality at Enron and reported our involvement in the deal with Fastow. The tapes covered numerous phone calls between the three of us over a three-day period following our disclosure. We didn't know we had been recorded and until then we had had no idea the tapes even existed.

It was immediately clear that the prosecutors hadn't listened to the tapes properly or even transcribed them, because they demonstrated unequivocally that we believed we were involved in a legitimate transaction with Fastow and had no knowledge of any criminality. They were the conversations of a trio of naïve bankers completely in the dark about what had been going on at Enron. There was nothing incriminating about them at all and yet they were being presented as evidence against us. We were certain that if the tapes were played to a jury, we would have a great chance of being exonerated – at least from that part of the conspiracy.

There were some fifty taped conversations in all and, as I have said, we had no idea we were being recorded. In one conversation between Gary and me about Fastow, it was patently obvious that we believed the entire Enron operation was above board during our dealings with the company. 'I'll tell you something,' Gary said in another of the tapes, 'I'm absolutely convinced that Fastow won't be guilty of anything other than, you know, he went along with the accounting treatment, maybe he bullied and pushed people, but Andersen's [Arthur Andersen were Enron's auditors at the time] are supposed to be big enough to be able to deal with that.'

In another taped exchange between Gary and me: 'I just don't think these guys did any fraud at all, they had all the fucking [accounting and compliance] structure in place to protect them.'

I responded: 'Oh, mate, I'm sure of it.'

Gary again, in mid-conversation: 'There's a number of things … one principally, the most important one, is we didn't do anything wrong.'

These tapes were recorded in November 2001. Clearly we were wrong about Fastow but, because of the context in which they were recorded, and what they revealed about our mindset, they provided the break we needed. The prosecutors would now have to think twice about their theories concerning the case.

Gary, on a tape again: 'If we thought for one second that we did something wrong, do you think we'd be sitting here now without a lawyer, do you think we'd be writing all this down?' This is a reference to the disclosure statements we were making to the bank and to the FSA. At this point, stupidly as it turned out, we didn't have any legal representation. What was that I said about us being amateurs?

From the tapes, it was evident that we didn't understand what Fastow had done to make the money with which we had been paid out from the deal we had invested in. The prosecution theory was that we had knowingly undersold the Swap Sub asset, but nowhere on the hours of tapes that had been given to us is either Swap Sub or its value even mentioned. At no point did we ever focus on our actions at GNW – all of the discussion was about what Fastow and his team had done, and from the tapes it was clear we had no idea.

Of course, when the activities of Fastow, Kopper and others eventually became known, our involvement was presented in a very different light and we were made to pay dearly for our naïvety.

We were convinced that if we played these tapes at trial, at best we would get a not-guilty verdict and at worst a mistrial. However, there was another strand to our defence. We knew that on the date we agreed to sell the asset, $1 million was a great price for the sale of Swap Sub and that NatWest had received fair value for the sale of its share … but how to prove it? David's book again goes into great detail on this but, in summary, we decided to commission an expert witness to help our case – an eminent professor of mathematics at a Texan university, who independently calculated the value of the asset we had been accused of knowingly mis-selling to Fastow. The professor provided a series of calculations showing that GNW got a fair price for the asset at the time of the sale, completely undermining the notion that we had deliberately defrauded our employers. Together, the report and the tapes introduced the doubt in the prosecution theory that we had been searching for: our legal team agreed.

We put together the paperwork and sent it to the prosecuting authorities in the midsummer of 2007. Around the same time we submitted a motion to the Judge requesting the assistance of the Court under the Mutual Legal Assistance Treaty between the US and UK. Essentially we wanted access to some 15 to 20 witnesses and former colleagues in the UK with knowledge of the case and surrounding events. We were aware from supportive former colleagues that RBS had arranged legal representation for anyone that we had named or asked to speak with. The lawyers had then told them not to talk to us unless instructed to by either the Feds or the Court. Our motion named everyone that we wanted to speak to and call as witnesses and detailed why. The motion asked the Court to instruct them to co-operate under the Treaty.

A few days later, Dan was summoned to the Judge's chambers in the Courthouse. During the course of a very brief meeting, the Judge informed Dan that he had seen our recent motions about the tapes and the Swapsub value and that he would NOT be signing our new motion about witnesses. Dan enquired why ?

'Because Mr Cogdell you tell those boys that they need to find a way to do a deal and bring this case to an end'.

He went on to say that if we insisted on going all the way to trial and lost that he would lock us up and throw away the key, ensuring that we would serve all our sentence in the US. When Dan returned to the Office to tell us about the meeting, the mood was extremely sombre. It was absolutely not what we had expected.

A short while later in early September 2007, Matt Hennessey, my attorney phoned me asking me to go and see him as he had heard from the DOJ.

I made my way apprehensively downtown. It was now six years since this mess had begun and no interaction with the DOJ had been good. Matt explained that the prosecutors had an offer for me: agree to testify against David and Gary and I could go straight back home, all charges dropped, never do any jail time, not pay any fine – in other words, be completely exonerated.

I was stunned. 'What about Gary and David?'

'Well, if you testify against them, they will have no defence. They will probably get seven to ten years each.'

'Well then, that's an easy answer, Matt. I have two words for the DOJ, and the second one is "off". There is no chance I will ever testify against either of those two.'

My feelings were both clear and intense. How could I ever look at myself in the mirror again if I turned on the other two, the men who were my close friends and who were now enduring this ordeal with me, and put them inside for years? It wasn't only about David and Gary, it was about our wives and our families; and indeed all our friends and supporters who had been with us from the very start. Even our legal teams were in my mind, for they had been working so hard for us. I simply could not betray all those people, even if it meant that I could go home fully exonerated.

'Giles, it's a great offer and as your attorney and also your friend, I have to advise you to think very carefully about your answer,' said Matt. 'If you accept, it will all be over for you.'

'No, it won't be,' I said. 'How could I do this to my friends? How could I live with myself? I accept we made a bad decision about the option, but they don't deserve to go away for years because of that and I'm not doing that to them.'

'Okay. I want you to go away for two weeks. Discuss the offer with your wife and family, your friends. If you still feel the same, then we will turn it down. Your decision.'

Naturally, I told Gary and David and their respective legal teams what was going on.

When I met with Matt again, he reiterated that it was a good offer and that he wouldn't be doing his job if he didn't advise me to accept it. I thanked him, but told him my answer was the same as it had been two weeks previously.

Perhaps the prosecutors targeted me first because, as one of the attorneys said, there was no evidence against me apart from my share of the profit from the deal appearing in my bank account. Also, I had the biggest family, and they must have known I would be missing them all terribly. Whatever their reasoning, they got me wrong. They took the offer to David next, offering him the same 'get out of jail free' card. He also refused, telling the prosecutors that he wanted to go to trial and prove his innocence in front of a jury. Subsequently, Gary took the same position. I imagine they were stunned that we had kept up our united front, even when the prospect of going home was dangled in front of each of us. Their frustration was obvious at the next case meeting with our legal team.

'What is it that these guys want?' asked the chief prosecutor, throwing his hands in the air in exasperation.

'A deal for all three, and to go home quickly,' Dan replied.

'They've got to plead guilty to *something*,' said the prosecutor. 'This thing has gone on too long. They need to do some jail time. If we can't agree a deal and we go to trial, if we get "guilty" we will make damned sure they get a long sentence – and they will do it all in the US.' The US part was important as we were all aware that a UK repatriation would halve the time inside, but in the US there is no such allowance, so being repatriated was vital.

David was set against pleading and keen to go trial, but we had agreed to do whatever the majority wanted. We certainly were missing home terribly and even though we had now strongly countered the case against us, Gary and I were both terrified of either losing at trial or a mistrial. That would have meant having to stay in Texas even longer and going to trial all over again. The trial had already been delayed four times from late 2006 into 2008, for what we regarded as spurious prosecution reasons to increase the pressure on us. We were living off savings, with no income to speak of. The costs of the case, living in Texas and keeping families in the UK, was putting serious financial pressure on each of us. A mistrial would have taken us into 2009-10 and a whole new set of trial fees and assorted costs. The pressure of all this had been hanging over us since 2001: Gary and I simply wanted it over.

The next challenge was to agree a crime to which we could plead guilty. This was eventually settled by drawing up a Statement of Facts, which was part of the agreement. We pleaded guilty to stealing the investment opportunity from our employers. Crucially, from my point of view, the statement confirmed we had no knowledge of Fastow's fraud against Enron.

We proposed that we would serve twelve months, so long as we were sent back to the UK quickly, meaning we would plead to twenty-four months. The prosecutor said that given the effort to get us to the US, twenty-four months was simply too low a headline figure. We finally agreed to thirty-seven months – including the all-important promise that we would be transferred back to the UK as soon as possible and likely serve around eighteen months. That's how we arrived at that magic, life-defining number: a prosecutor somewhere in Washington needed a politically acceptable figure and we agreed to it, just to get it over with. We had been living in limbo for far too long and I for one wanted to be free of the whole ordeal before I was fifty.

We had to persuade David to give up the dream of his day in court, but by now even he could see the writing on the wall. A three-man plea deal was as good as it was ever going to get, no matter how good our defence looked. Going to trial and losing would have meant a life-ending sentence, which was simply too terrible a penalty to contemplate. We entered the plea at the end of November 2007 and self-reported in May 2008. At long last, the end was in sight.

CHAPTER 12

THE MAFIOSI

One afternoon, I heard shouting from the cell next door. There was a real slanging match going on – guys were calling each other every name imaginable, swearing and screaming. El and T were still at the factory, so I had our cell to myself. I settled myself on my bunk and hoped the argument would die down on its own. I didn't know what the guys next door had fallen out over, but it appeared to be something really bad.

After around ten minutes, during which time the shouting continued, one of the young guys poked his head around the cubicle entrance. He was known as Face and even from across the cell, I could see that he was seriously agitated.

'Yo, dude,' he said, by way of a greeting. He leaned back out of sight and shouted over his shoulder to his own cell: 'Let's ask Darby over here. Let's see what the English dude has to say.' I heard a muffled 'Okay, man' from next door.

Face reappeared in my cell. 'Hey, man, what do you say: a silverback or a lion?'

'Sorry?'

'You know, a silverback gorilla or a lion. Who would you back if they was to fight?'

'How would I know?'

Face looked angry, more so than before. 'Well, you must have some motherfucking idea, bro.'

I thought about it for a moment. Was this really what they had been arguing about next door? 'Well,' I said, 'it depends, I guess. Is the gorilla in the trees? Are they the same age? What are the circumstances?'

Face slapped his hand against the white breeze blocks that made up the cell wall. 'I don't fucking know, dude. Just tell me who is the fucking strongest. Which one wins in a fight?'

I'd worked out by now that logic wasn't part of this discussion. I gave Face an answer to make him go away. 'The gorilla,' I said.

I heard a shout from next door. 'What the fuck are you talking about?'

'Well, there's the size,' I said. 'Then brain capacity—'

Face interrupted me before I could continue. 'See!' he shouted, practically dancing with glee. 'You fucking see!' he shouted to his cellmate. 'I was right. I'm always fucking right!'

Another angry shout from next door. 'Sure you fucking ain't, man! This dude don't have no clue. He's like you, man. He don't know shit, either.'

It was embarrassing to listen to, real playground stuff. But in prison it never took much to set someone off.

Thankfully, the moronic argument died down not long after that, leaving me with enough peace to read and write for a few hours. El and T eventually came back from their shift and I told them about the argument they had missed. T shot a contemptuous look in the direction of the dividing wall.

'Meaningless shit, man,' he said. 'People in this place get so fucking worked up about the most meaningless shit.' I could only agree.

I bumped into Ralph the next day as he was coming out of his cell. It was early afternoon – the ideal time to spend a few hours on the rec. Ralph told me he was heading for the rec too, and said he wanted me to meet someone out there. After a brief wait for the next move, we walked out into the sunshine and made our way over to the cluster of picnic-style tables, the sort where I spent many afternoons writing my letters and listening to the radio. Sitting at one of the tables was the little old man whom I had seen Ralph talking to before.

'I think you'll find him very interesting,' Ralph said, under his breath.

He steered me over and introduced us. The man's name was Frank and the first thing he told me was that he was eighty-one years old. He was lucid, sharp, witty – all the things I would never have expected from an incarcerated pensioner. In fact, you'd never have guessed he was so old if it wasn't for his hunched figure and slow, shuffling gait. I didn't even have to ask – he told me his story straight up, perhaps because he wanted to see how I would react.

In his steady, bridge-club voice, seasoned with an Italian-American accent, he told me that he was here because he had 'popped' two guys and then gone on the run for a couple of years afterwards. He had already served seven years by then, and had eight more to go. Eight more years to go at the age of eighty-one.

'I gotta make sure I beat this shit,' he said. 'I gotta get out. There's more work to do.'

I was left wondering exactly what this work was that was left to do, but before I could ask, he had moved on to his next topic.

'You work for the laundry lady – Miss Anderson, right? That fucking woman. She made me walk up and down to the laundry six times to get my clothes because she kept giving me the wrong size. "I know who you are," she said. "I know all about you." What right does she have to know about me?'

'She has a habit of looking people up,' I said. 'I wouldn't take it too personally.'

'Yeah, well she's got a terrible attitude. I hate that woman.'

Over time, Ralph introduced me to more of his colourful friends, including a guy called Jimmy, although I was fairly certain that wasn't his real name. He was another Italian-American and he told me he was in for drug smuggling. Jimmy was a bit of a joker and he used to make me laugh. The funniest thing about him was his commitment to wasting the BOP's money and resources. His philosophy was that if the government was going to keep him in prison against his will, he would make it as expensive for them as possible. He always used to leave showers and taps running and if he walked past a light switch, he would make a point of ensuring the bulb was on. In the canteen, he would grab huge fistfuls of disposable cutlery and dump it all in the bin.

'I'd say it's cost them around four hundred thousand dollars so far to keep me in here, Darby, including my trial,' he told me, swelling with pride. 'It's probably costing them around thirty thousand to keep me in here every year. I just hope they run out of fucking money and have to let us all go.' It was unlikely, of course, but I admired his spirit.

Jimmy was older than me, in his early fifties, but he looked and acted like a far younger man. He had been wealthy before everything came crashing down and he told me that he had owned boats, planes and a ranch in Texas back in the good old days. He ran a building company alongside his drug venture and lavished most of the money on his three daughters. He and I were both doting dads, at least similar in that regard.

I had a regular table I would sit at to read and write during my weekday afternoons on the rec, and Jimmy would often join me. He liked to talk about his life, and we would laugh at his endless stories. Our conversations wouldn't have been out of place in my local at home, and he reminded me of one of my closest friends there, Simmo.

Jimmy's chat was a breath of fresh air and he was a pleasure to be around, but he had a problem: he was a serial womaniser. His wife of thirty years knew about this, but she had put up with Jimmy's philandering ways, for reasons known only to her – until now. He had arrived at Allenwood a few months before me and now he was learning that his wife was having second thoughts about their marriage. Plainly, all that time alone had left her questioning whether Jimmy's indiscretions deserved to be forgiven, and she was starting to reckon perhaps not. The topic of Jimmy's past infidelities cropped up repeatedly on the phone, and was causing a great deal of stress for them both. Jimmy spoke about his marriage quite often, and each time the subject was brought up, things sounded worse than before. I sensed that something was about to give.

Then, one shining August day, he came and found me at our usual table. He was brandishing a letter, which he dropped dejectedly onto the table in front of me.

'Read that, Darb.'

It was a long and very sad letter from his wife, outlining the pain he had caused her over the years, the pain he had caused consistently despite the fact that she had only ever had eyes for him, only ever supported him, and only ever wanted him. She went on to say that their separation had given her a surplus of thinking time, and that she had reached a decision about what to do with their marriage. She said she was willing to stand by him and wait for him, but not if he was going to behave again in the way he always had. I could sense the pain behind every word. I imagined that the letter must have been as hard for her to write as it would have been for him to read.

'What are you going to do, mate?' I asked, as I set the letter back down on the table.

'What the fuck can I do? I'm stuck here for the next four years. I'm trying to get my sentence reduced, get on the drugs programme – that's giving me enough grief without all this.' He gestured to the letter. 'I don't fucking need it.'

Jimmy was already locked in an unpleasant tussle with the prosecutors over his plea. He wanted to revise it, so he admitted to holding a smaller volume of drugs, a move that would result in a ten-month sentence reduction if it was accepted. He was also desperately trying to secure a coveted place on the drug rehabilitation programme, which in itself would make him eligible for another twelve-month reduction (as I have explained previously), and also qualify him for a move to a camp, an open prison. That would be infinitely better for him than being stuck behind the fences at Allenwood.

He shook his head sadly. 'We talked about it last night, but it was no good. It's impossible to have a serious conversation on those damn phones with the time limited to fifteen minutes. Of course, we had a row about it.'

'Jim, mate,' I said, 'you know her letter was totally reasonable. She just wants to be happy. I mean, what would you do if the roles were reversed?'

'I know, I know. Four years is a long time, though. I don't know what I'll be like when I get out of here. I don't know who I'll be. I want to be good to her, but I don't know what's going to happen. What should I say?'

'Maybe you should let her go,' I said. 'In the circumstances she's got a right to get on with her life, and it would save you both worrying about things. Don't you think?'

His shoulders dropped. He looked like a broken man. 'I'm not sure I can do that, Darb. I know I hurt her, but she means too much to me.' Poor old Jimmy.

As for Ralph, he too had his share of issues, but he was also a fascinating and often funny character to talk to. As I got to know him better, he gradually revealed more about his own story. I was in my cell one afternoon, passing the time while El and T were working, when he came in to see me.

'Hey, Darby,' he said. 'Did I ever tell you about the time I was going to cut a guy's hands off?'

What a greeting, I was thinking – only in Allenwood! 'No, Ralph,' I said. 'Funnily enough, you didn't tell me that one.'

He smiled at the look on my face. 'Both of them,' he said. 'Both hands. Well, anyway, that's a story I got to tell you about.' At this he smiled coyly and backed out of my cell, leaving me to ruminate on such a nightmarish anecdote. I heard him laughing all the way down the wing.

Later that day I caught up with Jimmy. His wife had been to visit and he was in pieces. Many of the guys struggled after a visit – the next few days afterwards were always difficult. One guy I knew used to go to bed straight after every visit, so he didn't have to be awake thinking about everything. Another guy used to stand in the shower – the only place where you can let your emotions overflow without anyone else seeing – for half an hour after saying goodbye.

Evidently, the tough part was watching the other person walk away and then having to return to the prison on your own. Jimmy was always going to struggle after seeing his wife, but the precariousness of their marriage served only to heap even more emotional strain on him.

'My head's all over the place,' he told me. 'I still don't know where we're at or what we're doing. I can't think straight at the moment.'

'Do you feel more confused or sad?' I asked.

'Sad. You know, there's a psychological state called a cognitive deficit. Normally people suffer it after a bereavement. It's essentially a gap in your mental awareness, brought on by extreme stress or grief. I see guys in here with symptoms of it every day and I swear visits make it worse.'

'What sort of symptoms?'

'People withdraw into themselves, they get these blank expressions and want to be alone all the time. It makes it hard to have conversations. Seeing her made me wonder whether I have it. You know, I was pleased to see her, but now she's gone it's unbearable.'

I knew what he meant about feeling that way. With my family stuck on the other side of the Atlantic, I didn't have to contend with the hardships of visits, but I still struggled with the separation, and I recognised many of the same symptoms in myself and my friends. It wasn't so bad for me, both because I knew my transfer application was gradually being processed and because my sentence was so short in comparison to most. Even if I was feeling really dreadful, I knew that Jimmy would be feeling far worse. Sure, he had made his share of bad mistakes, but I still felt for him. I thought he deserved better than to be here. Then again, I thought most of us did.

I wasn't the only one fascinated by Ralph and his mob friends: even stony old Miss Anderson took an active interest in the comings and goings of Allenwood's sizeable Mafia population. Incidentally, it was Miss Anderson who told me the wildest story about one of them, a real hoodlum who had been incarcerated at Allenwood some time before I arrived. She reckoned that this senior Mafioso had connections with some of the guards, and was therefore allowed to get away with pretty well everything, short of murder. 'It's not what you know, but who you know' was certainly an accurate adage in business, but nowhere was it more true than in prison.

According to Miss Anderson, this man had been going around the prison with a picture of a baby he said was his. But that wasn't physically possible, as he had been inside for a number of years. The prison authorities decided to investigate and it turned out that he had been under pressure from his lady on the outside who desperately wanted a child. I'm still not sure whether I believe it or not, but Miss Anderson told me – with a straight face – that the mob worked out a way for this Mafioso to impregnate his girlfriend without leaving the prison. Apparently one of the guards procured a squash ball and cut a slit in it. The ball – and some time alone

– was given to Mr Mafia, and then one of the guards rushed out with it to the girlfriend, who was waiting in her car at the front of the prison. She then used a syringe to impregnate herself. Miss Anderson assured me that this story was true, and she wasn't the kind for jokes.

In its own grubby way, the story was an indication of the privilege that surrounded the serious gangsters – a privileged position that many underserving, small-fry inmates tried to emulate. In fact, it seemed as if for every genuine gangster at Allenwood, there was at least one desperate pretender who wanted to be one. Such people as these, more so than the real killers, caused the most trouble and showed the least respect for their fellow inmates.

Steve – the guitarist who spent his days writing songs for his long-lost girlfriend – had the misfortune of sharing a cell with one of these pretenders. He was in the process of moving cells, he told me, owing to the increasing volatility of his notorious roommate. Mizik was a Russian-American with a mean streak, who really belonged in a penitentiary, not a low-security facility like Allenwood. He had somehow got it into his head that he was a shot-caller for all the white guys and a prominent and powerful figure within the prison. This was despite the fact that he was almost universally disliked and in reality a small-time criminal – whereas any real shot-caller would have needed to be a serious gangster to command the kind of respect that Mizik fantasised about.

Steve said that his cellmate only ever talked about gangs. The man had even started going so far as to round up a couple of wannabe Aryan-Brotherhood types and telling them to secure a block of white-only seats in the TV room.

In fact we were fortunate to be in a prison where racial tensions didn't dominate. Unlike many American prisons, Allenwood rarely needed its ethnic shot-callers to step in, precisely because inmates of all races tended to mingle freely and without any serious friction. Yet here was an idiot who was trying to spoil the delicate balance of racial harmony – the very thing that made Allenwood fairly safe – by declaring himself the leader of all the whites. The only saving grace was that very few people in the compound were willing to go along with Mizik's stupid fantasies. The most glaring sign that he wasn't really a white shot-caller was the fact that his and Steve's third cellie was a black guy, called Pray. Pray was a real lump of a man, possibly the fattest guy on the compound. He must have weighed about twenty-five stone, and I couldn't imagine Mizik giving him any trouble to his face.

Mizik had never approached me, thankfully, and after talking to Steve I had no intention of ever speaking to him. 'He's totally delusional,' Steve warned. 'Stay well away from him, Darby.' It was people like Mizik who kept shanks hidden in their cells, praying for the day when they would be able to use them. They were a danger to themselves and everyone around them, and I was glad to hear my friend was going to move: I know that I'd have done the same.

Thankfully, my associations with the real gangsters proved to be far more enjoyable. Ironically, it was much safer to hang out with actual big-time criminals than it was to mix with the wannabes. Most of the serious gangsters had already learned from their mistakes by the time they made it to Allenwood. It was more like a retirement home for the Mafiosi, the old boys having already lived out their gangster days. Now they were paying the price.

However, of all the serious criminals in Allenwood, there was one who really did terrify me. Sergei (as I will refer to him here) was a Russian mob leader. He was an interesting, forthright but downright fearsome a man as you could ever wish to meet. He had served eighteen years in the prisons of five different countries by the time I met him, and he was still in his early fifties. The most serious charges on his rap sheet included multiple attempted murders and the setting up of a sprawling heroin distribution business in the States, sparking a turf war that brought bloodshed to the streets of a major American city.

Strangely, he found himself in Allenwood for one of the most innocuous crimes of all: violating the terms of his probation. In the States, inmates can spend years after the end of their sentence on probation. They are allowed to live at home, but are subject to a litany of rules that make it impossible to live any semblance of a normal life. The terms could vary, but generally they included: no drugs, no intoxication, no being in the presence of firearms or other felons, no run-ins with the police, regular reporting to your probation officer, always being available for contact by the probation officer (yet not being allowed a mobile phone), and strict accounting of every dollar earned and every dollar spent.

These numerous and, in places, contradictory rules meant that newly-released inmates had no choice but to live like eunuchs, or risk being picked up for a parole violation and shipped straight back to prison. I suspected that if parole terms were relaxed a little bit, the reoffending rate for American prisoners would not be anywhere near as high. When you're dealing with men who have already paid the price of serving a long prison sentence, a little leniency could go a long way.

I asked Ralph what he knew about Sergei while we were in the queue for chow and he shrugged. I guessed that he had seen and heard it all before.

'All right then, Ralph,' I said. 'Have you ever seen anything that has really shaken you?'

He sighed. 'Look, Darb, I killed a man. What the fuck do you think?'

'Okay, okay. I get it.'

'Actually, since you ask, I'll tell you one thing that did surprise me.' He licked his lips and fixed me with one of his serious stares. 'How easy it was to do it. Afterwards, I just walked away. I thought: is that it?'

He looked at me like he always did when he had shocked me and he knew it, then he burst into hysterical laughter. What a character.

We shuffled up to the counter with our trays and watched as the server ladled out our dinner – wet beef tacos and a measly portion of undercooked rice. I nodded a half-hearted thanks and joined Ralph at his usual table. He pointed to the table next to us, which was populated by a group of lollipops.

'Look at that lot,' he said. He didn't care who heard him. 'Fucking scum. They wouldn't be safe anywhere else.'

'Do you get them in the pen?' I asked.

'Sure, but they're all held in protective custody. Occasionally, one of them thinks he can make it to the general population by making up a cover story, but they always get found out. Anyone who is suspicious gets asked to show their papers. If you don't produce, you're in big trouble.' He spooned some beef sauce into his mouth. 'I got asked to produce mine once. I said to the guy, "Okay, I'll get them, but when I get back, you'd better have your boots on." He backed down after that!' Ralph said, laughing again.

I laughed along with him, but there was still a part of me that was pretty wary. I genuinely enjoyed Ralph's company, but he was the real deal: a full-blown Mafioso who had lived and breathed that culture since the day he was born. I had never met anyone like him before and probably never would again. He certainly had an uncompromising attitude. If I was feeling a little down, he would say to me, 'How long you got till you're out?' And regardless of the figure, he would reply, 'Well, I've spent longer on the can than that, so shut the fuck up with your moaning!'

Back in the chow hall, I decided to change the subject. Allenwood had a fairly large religious community and all the amenities to go with it, including our very own man of the cloth to watch over us. I wasn't interested in any of this – I blamed myself for my situation and didn't need to attribute any of the credit to a divine plan – but a lot of the guys were. However, one inmate, a tall guy with a greasy ponytail, had recently asked whether Satanism could be practised in the chapel. I could only imagine the look on the chaplain's face. I asked Ralph if he had heard about this.

Ralph scoffed and nodded. 'I did hear about that. I also heard someone asked him why he wanted to switch to devil worship, and he said praying to Jesus hadn't done him any good, so he thought he'd try the other lot.'

I burst out laughing. It was hard to fault the man's logic.

CHAPTER 13

PRISON GAMES

I knew that surviving my sentence would be easier if I could stay busy and, as far as possible, keep active. In that regard, I was lucky. The gorgeous summer weather meant it was almost always an option to spend the long evenings out on the rec, and there were plenty of things to do out there. Softball, basketball, American football, soccer – all the popular sports were played on the sprawling grounds, and whenever I didn't fancy playing, I could always find myself a decent seat to watch the proceedings and enjoy the beautiful views of the valley we were living in.

Having always been a big football fan, and a lifelong supporter of Bristol City, I took a keen interest in the 'soccer' games played on the rec most nights. The standard of football at Allenwood was impressive, and I'll admit that I was a little intimidated when I watched my first game among the inmates. But it takes a lot for anything to come between an Englishman and his football, so right from the start I made sure to join in. My knees weren't what they used to be, but I was still in good enough shape to keep up with the skilful Latinos. And what I lacked in flair, I made up for with good old-fashioned English grit.

My first ever game of prison football came a few days after arriving at Allenwood. I was the only white guy who wanted to play, so I think I must have been viewed as something of a novelty. Still, nobody objected to me trying out, and I took my position on the pitch along with a handful of South Americans and a large contingent of Jamaicans. Imagine my delight when I scored, only to turn around and see a whole team of hardened, tattoo-covered prisoners cheering for me.

'Beckham!' one of them shouted. 'David Beckham.' We all burst out laughing and from that moment Beckham became my nickname on the pitch. The guys mostly spoke Spanish, but they tried their hardest to include me, and for that I was grateful and pleasantly surprised.

What shocked me the most, though, was how seriously some of the players were taking it. We often played against other units, and many of the guys were willing to dig deep to defend Gregg Unit's pride. Friendly games were anything but, and late challenges would regularly go flying in. More than once, I found myself inches away from being caught by a leg-breaking tackle, although I tried to give as good as I got. The atmosphere was often febrile, and it was impossible not to get sucked in.

As such, I looked forward to those evenings on the rec. The football pitch was one of those places where it was possible to forget where I was. For ninety minutes at a time, I wasn't a convicted fraudster alone in a horrible American prison – I was a normal guy playing football in the sun with my mates. Those games helped to keep me sane, and I quickly developed close and firm bonds with my regular teammates. They would call out to me at chow: 'Hey, Beckham – you playing tonight?' As if I had options to be elsewhere!

I had been in Allenwood for a couple of months when the guards announced that they were setting up a prison league. I was well known by the football crowd at this point, and I was pleased to be asked to play for Gregg Unit's side. In no time, the unit teams were decided, with coaches and proper football kits. People took it very seriously and I didn't blame them. You snatch at any distractions in a place like Allenwood.

Unfortunately for Gregg Unit, it turned out that five of the unit's best footballers happened to be five of the Colombians who had been sent to solitary over the beating in the TV room. We ended up scrabbling around to find replacements for them and registered our side just in time. It didn't bode well for us – our cobbled-together team was missing its entire spine. I bet they don't have to deal with stuff like that at Bristol City.

Thankfully, there was still some footballing talent left on the unit. There was a guy called Cuba (guess why?) who often played with us, and he signed up just before the deadline. He and I had been chatting about the situation with the Colombians when the conversation turned to our personal lives. Like so many people I met, Cuba was friendly and chatty, and he had no qualms about sharing his story. I asked him how he ended up in America.

'Me and my friend, we floated across the ocean.'

I thought that something might have been lost in translation. 'On a boat?'

He laughed. 'No, no. We floated for five days in a huge tyre. Then we hit land.'

'A tyre? What kind of tyre?'

He made a circular gesture with his hands. 'A tyre from a tractor.'

'What? It kept afloat for five days, across the Gulf of Mexico? Through waters filled with sharks?'

He nodded. 'It was very frightening.'

'So what happened then? Did you get picked up when you hit land?'

'No, no. I got here okay and I was here for two years with no troubles. Then I was arrested for drug conspiracy. I got twenty years. Seventeen to go.' He rolled his eyes. 'I wish I had never come here, to this place. Should have stayed.'

Remarkable. I was collecting these incredible tales and relaying them in my letters home. I couldn't believe the length of the sentences, and the often low-key crimes that warranted them. But Cuba's story was something else. To survive that journey across the ocean only to be picked up short years later for drugs is beyond ridiculous. What a world.

When we weren't playing sport, most of us spent our free time watching it. I was in the microwave room one morning when I saw Oleg, the little Russian guy I knew from our unit. I had seen him glued to Fox Soccer in the TV room on many occasions, and we had watched a fair few games together. The 2008 European Championships weren't far off and I assumed that they would be right up his street.

'Hey, Oleg, do you know when the Euros start?'

'Hey, Darby.' He pulled a notebook from his pocket and flipped it open. 'I've got it all written down here. I'll show you.'

I walked over and saw that he had written, by hand, everything you could possibly need to know about the Euros. He had the stats, the fixtures, the groups. He flicked back a few pages and I saw he had done the same for Champions Leagues, World Cups, Super Bowls and Olympics. Every sporting event of note had been jotted down in his notepad, with the results of every game recorded in meticulous detail.

'Wow,' I said. 'How long have you been keeping this?'

He flicked back some more pages and I saw another few years' worth of sporting events recorded in his neat handwriting. 'Since I was inside,' he said.

I noticed he had all the details of Euro 2000. 'Bloody hell, how long have you been in?'

Oleg smiled wistfully. 'Nine years.'

'Nine years?'

'I have four more Olympic Games to go, including the one this summer.'

I looked from the notebook to Oleg's face. 'That's another twelve years,' I said.

He nodded. 'I get out after twenty-one years. That is, if you include the good time.'

I looked at little Oleg in a whole new light. 'Can I ask what you're inside for?'

He shrugged. 'You know. Customs and excise stuff. Smuggling.' A microwave dinged, signalling the end of our conversation. He went off to retrieve his breakfast, slipping his notebook back into his pocket as he went. I stood there in shock. Again. Twenty-one years. Five Olympic Games. These people threw months and years around like confetti.

Eventually the highly anticipated first game of the Allenwood season rolled around. I had been inside for almost two months by that point, and was a regular at the evening kickabouts. The first day of the season was a strange one – a fog had descended on our valley, and it had come down so thick that you could barely see your hand in front of your face. As a result, the day's work duty was cancelled and all inmates were ordered to stay in the units.

The guards were worried that some people might view the fog as a good opportunity to escape, although I couldn't imagine how that would be possible, with armed guards in the numerous watchtowers and double-banked, fifteen-foot-high barbed wire fences. Attempting to escape would automatically add five years to your sentence, so I figured you'd have to be insane even to try.

We spent the morning cooped up in the unit, but by lunchtime the fog had lifted and business as usual had resumed. All talk turned to the night's football match – the inaugural game of the Allenwood league.

There were five teams, each of which would play each other twice. At our team meeting called by our Mexican coach, Lozano, we laughingly said that we would have overachieved if we could manage to win a single game. We were rank outsiders, so we all agreed to enjoy the matches and, as a minimum, not argue among ourselves, which was easier said than done with the temperamental Latinos on board.

Our starting line-up was wonderfully diverse: I was the token Englishman alongside three West Indians, two Mexicans, three Colombians, one Cuban and two very fit, young white Americans, who could run forever but had no idea how to play. Our coach, meanwhile, was a Mexican who barely spoke any English, so I suspected right from the off that we might have some difficulties with communication. As the oldest player in the team, the guys had developed a new nickname for me – 'Papa'. It wasn't quite as insulting as it sounds; in fact, I understood that it was a Latin American term of endearment and respect.

In the end, against all odds, we managed to scrape a point out of our first game, snatching a 0-0 draw. It was probably the most tense ninety minutes of football I had ever played, and I was ecstatic when the final whistle blew. Our team of reserves and misfits had managed to get a result without the help of the Colombian maestros in the SHU. It was a miracle!

With so little for us inmates to look forward to, and very little to live for on a day-to-day basis, it made sense that we took the match so seriously. Before kick-off, every player had to hand in their ID card to prove they were representing their own unit, and each side was provided with a brand-new kit. Those of us playing for the mighty Gregg Unit were given bright green shirts with yellow stripes down the side – a fetching cross between Brazil and Norwich City. All of us were kitted out with shin guards as well and, for the first time since I'd been there, goal nets were set up at either end of the pitch. The refs were even given their own black-and-white kits – that's how legitimate it was, and we all treated the games with the requisite seriousness.

A few days later the next game rolled around. Imagine our delight when we not only kept another clean sheet, but actually won the match 1-0. A handful of decent players had been released from the SHU the night before and they were slung straight into the starting line-up, powering us to our first unlikely victory.

We lost the third game, but won the fourth. Admittedly, this was largely thanks to the opposition team suffering from some selection issues of their own. There was an unfortunate fight earlier that week which resulted in many of their best players being sent to the SHU, rendering them ineligible for the match.

For a while, it looked as if they would be without a goalkeeper, too, following a separate incident in the visiting room earlier that day. The keeper had supposedly French-kissed his wife at the end of her visit, breaching the strict rules about the contact inmates and visitors are allowed to have. I had heard on the grapevine that he was sent to the SHU for the infraction, but to my surprise he appeared on the pitch that evening. Obviously, that was bad news for our team, but I was still pleased to see he hadn't been punished too harshly for the crime of kissing his wife. He was a Colombian who had been caught smuggling drugs into the US via the Gulf of Mexico and we had chatted a few times before.

'Good to see you,' I said. 'I heard you were in the SHU.'

'Hey,' he said. We bumped fists. 'Nearly. The guard wrote me up, but I just about escaped the hole. Lost my commissary privileges for the rest of the month though.'

'Well, at least you won't lose your good time, right?'

He shook his head. 'Dude, I'm doing twenty-seven years. Do you think I care?'

As the games went on, bigger and bigger crowds started appearing on the rec. I learned that lots of the inmates had been betting on our last game, most of them backing the other side. More than one person on the unit told me that our upset had cost a lot of people a great deal of money. Of course, nobody was betting with real money, but we had certainly cost many inmates a lot of dried fish and stamps. I had no idea how the bookies were keeping track of it all, but the black market for gambling was obviously more sophisticated than it appeared.

We lost the next game 3–2, but not before I found myself right where I didn't want to be: at the centre of attention. A small scuffle had started after I was tackled in their penalty area and duly took a theatrical dive. I skinned my arms as I went flying into the baked ground, but the sight of the ref pointing to the penalty spot was enough to make all my pain disappear. I couldn't believe my luck – and nor could the other team. One of their players, a guy known as Ice because of his staggeringly blue eyes, squared up to the ref and started screaming in his face, all the while fixing him with a trademark terrifying stare.

'I know where you live, you fucker, I'll get you!' he shouted. 'I swear, I know where you live.'

I couldn't help laughing – I was simply chuffed that I had won a penalty. I made a flapping mouth gesture with my hands and told him to calm down. 'All you do is talk, Ice. Start fucking playing.'

He fixed his cold stare in my direction and started walking over. 'You wanna do something about me?'

He was only a few steps away when the rest of his team caught up with him, dragging him away and telling him to calm down. After that, he spent the entire duration of the game trying to kick me, lashing out with his boots whenever I came close. Thankfully, I was too quick for him, and I made it through the game in one piece. At full time, I thought it would be wise to extend Ice an olive branch, so I congratulated him on his victory and said he played well. He seemed okay with me after that, which was good news, because as far as I could tell he was legitimately crazy. Not the kind of guy you want to bump into on the outside.

I was walking back to the unit when I heard a commotion from over on the basketball courts. I thought I recognised one of the voices and, sure enough, as I made my way over, I could see El embroiled in an argument with two younger black guys. El was yelling at them and the other guys were shouting back, and from a distance it looked heated and potentially serious.

Despite the pain in my knees, I walked over as quickly as I could and asked El what was going on. The two younger guys were players in the unit basketball team, which El had been coaching. But after a controversial decision to drop one of the most popular players, the team had mutinied and removed El from his coaching position. El was genuinely upset, and I had to steer him away from the other guys to prevent anything from getting out of hand.

El was raging about the younger guys, saying they had no respect for him. 'They were fucking dead when I took that team over, Darby. Fucking ingrates. Fuck them.'

'El, mate, it's not worth a row. You're meant to be getting out of here soon, and you're really going to start something over a game of prison basketball?'

It was playground stuff, but El's anger proved a serious point. These men had so little to care about, and so little to live for, that the smallest, most petty things could blow up into major issues. Even at Allenwood, there simply wasn't enough to keep the inmates occupied. The result? Grown men would have screaming matches over who got picked for the basketball team, without even realising how childish they looked. And to them, it wasn't silly at all. If all you had to live for was a game of basketball once or twice a week, then you would want that game to go your way as well.

Unfortunately, we caught some of El's bad luck and lost our next couple of games. By now, the exertion of the tournament was catching up on me; my knees were shot to bits and after ninety minutes I could barely walk any more, let alone run. After the third loss in a row I was relieved to hear the final whistle and even more thankful that there were only a few more fixtures left in the prison tournament. Plainly, I was getting too old to be running around with the kids.

I found El back in the cell and eased myself onto my bunk, taking care not to put too much weight on my legs. I probably reeked of sweat, but he was too kind to say anything. There had been a lockdown the previous day, owing to a series of thunderstorms, and we had been forced to spend eighteen consecutive hours in the unit. I had been delighted that the yard was reopened in time for our match, but now, aching and still winded, I wasn't sure what I had been so excited about. We got chatting about the lockdown and I said it had been one of the worst times for me since I'd arrived at Allenwood. I found the boredom and claustrophobia of being trapped in the unit too much to bear.

El shook his head. 'Darby, you're ridiculous. In the pen, I was once on a three-week lockdown. That means you're stuck in your cell twenty-four hours a day with your cellie. They let us go for a fifteen-minute shower every three days, but otherwise that was it, man. It was a regular event.'

'Why, though?' I asked. 'How come it happened so often?'

'Violence, man. It was how they punished us whenever something went down in the prison. I used to keep myself stocked up from the commissary just in case. I'd hoard things – four packets of batteries for the radio, plenty of food and snacks. They used to feed us through the door.'

T had quietly slipped in while El was talking. He smirked and looked from me to El. 'You talking about lockdowns? In the pen, my worst was two months. Two months in my cell. They just pushed baloney through the door for us to eat. It got so bad, I forgot what fresh air even tasted like.'

'Too right,' El said. 'One time, when I was under investigation, I spent nine months in the hole. I lost all commissary and I wasn't allowed to use the phone for three years. Three fucking years, Darby. So, you with your eighteen hours, what are you moaning about?'

I felt rightly embarrassed after that and we all laughed at my ridiculous whining. I apologised and slunk off for a shower.

Before I knew it, there was only one group match left for us to play. On balance, we had done surprisingly well in the league, and we were in with a chance of progressing to the next stage of the tournament. Unfortunately, our last group game was against one of the better teams on the compound. On their day, we knew they could beat anyone. Our strategy? Hope that it wasn't their day.

Knowing that a win would earn us a place in the play-offs, Gregg Unit delivered a consummate performance. Within fifteen minutes we were 3–0 up. When the third goal thundered in – a blistering volley by Cuba – their two best players walked off the pitch. This provoked an exodus of their other players and before we knew it, the match was abandoned, chalked up as a swift win for us.

We had started as rank outsiders, and now the prison championship title was within our reach. The next stop was the semi-final, and I was loving it.

I looked forward to the semi-final, knowing it could be my last match at Allenwood. By now my transfer application was well on its way to being approved, and I knew I wouldn't be spending another football season in the US. In fact, once I was transferred, I'd never set foot in the country again. There was no chance of me getting another US visa. So, in the knowledge that it could be my last ever game on American soil, I vowed to play on through whatever pain I felt and make a real match of it.

We were up against one of the teams we had already beaten, but the match turned out to be a stalemate. It was 2–2 after extra time – meaning the game would be decided by penalties.

It was a blisteringly hot and humid summer's evening – the sun had been beating down all afternoon and by then the temperature was around thirty degrees. Every single man on that pitch was wiped out, barely able to stay upright. My entire body was slick with sweat and my knees were telling me to give up. But with a place in the final up for grabs, I ignored the pain and reluctantly put myself forward to take a penalty.

Lozano told me I would take the sixth, if the shootout went that far. I could feel the pressure and hoped desperately it wouldn't come to that. There was a large crowd, eighty or ninety football-mad inmates, all with bets on the game. I was well aware it was not only pride that was at stake.

We lost the toss and were told we would be kicking second. The opposition striker slotted the first penalty home – it was a beauty of a shot right into the top corner. Next up was Cuba, with a chance to level the score. He pelted it to the right, the keeper dived left, and the scores were level.

We took penalty after penalty with nothing between us. The game was in danger of going to sudden death – meaning I might have to take the shot that would decide our team's fate. But then they missed their fifth penalty, giving us a golden opportunity to win the match.

Our little Vietnamese striker was down to take the final spot kick before sudden death. If he scored, we would be through to the final. If he missed, all eyes would be on me. He took a short run-up and slotted the ball towards the right. The keeper guessed correctly, diving the same way, but the ball powered underneath him and into the net. The celebrations were wild – you'd have thought we had won the Champions League, the way everyone was jumping around and hugging each other. None of us had expected to reach the final and yet there we were, one game away from being crowned Allenwood champions.

I felt sweaty hands slapping my back and, moments later, I was in a pile-on with the rest of the team. I knew the sheer elation we all felt in that moment was out of proportion to what we had achieved, but in our sad and lonely world, even the most trivial joys demanded to be cherished. In those few minutes of celebration, we were able to forget who we were and why we were here. We were all friends, and we had achieved something brilliant – at the time, it more than made up for the fact that we were isolated from our families, far away from home, and separated from the real world by impassable fences. They don't call it 'The Beautiful Game' for nothing.

The following evening, we all gathered at the pitch to watch the other semi-final. The favourite side, Union, were playing the far less accomplished Brady Unit. We expected Brady to take a real hammering. Sure enough, Union scored within the first few minutes, but late in the game the underdogs scored two in quick succession, stunning the favourites and sending the crowd wild. We were delighted, too – it meant we would avoid Allenwood's best team in the final and play Brady instead. That was a match we could win and, as we celebrated that night's result, we all knew it.

I watched the match standing next to Stan, one of the Americans on our team. I had heard some wild rumours about what he was in for, but I didn't know whether I believed them. I thought the walk back to the unit, while spirits were high, would be a good time to find out whether the claims were true.

'So, Stan,' I said, 'I heard you're a bit of a terrorist.'

He laughed. 'Sort of. I put some pipe bombs in a few mailboxes and blew them up.'

'Bloody hell,' I said. 'Why?'

'Something to do, a bit of a laugh. My hometown is in the country and was a bit quiet and I wanted something interesting to happen. If I'd have known I was going to get seven years, I wouldn't have done that though.'

'What did you do exactly?'

'Well, we made four pipe bombs and put them in the mailboxes of a couple of people we didn't like. They all worked. The next morning the news was mad – people were saying someone had launched a terror campaign in our town.'

'Well, what did you expect?' I asked. He shrugged. 'And how did you get caught?'

'Someone recognised my car while I was dropping the bombs off. I got picked up the next day and haven't seen the outside world since. I've been in for two years already. You know, that's why I like the football so much. It takes my mind off what I did.'

I was stunned by Stan's confession, but I tried to put it out of my mind. We had a football tournament to win. I could be baffled by my teammate's idiocy after we had lifted the trophy. At the time, that was all that mattered.

On the day before the big game, a Friday, Lozano called a team meeting. He had coached us this far and now he was outlining his strategy to win us the title. He spoke only the most fragmentary English, so some of the others had to translate for him as he delivered his little speech, dipping in and out of Spanish when he was unsure of a word.

'Team. Tomorrow night, we will enjoy the game. I know it is the final and we all want to win, but let us all be happy. It won't matter if we lose, not really. So, let's not argue with each other. Let's not fall out. And friends – don't have a late night tonight – no drinking and, for sure, no sex!'

Funnily enough, I followed Lozano's orders to the letter. The day seemed to drag even slower than usual, but after a ponderous morning and a dull afternoon, it was finally time for kick-off. It was another hot and humid night and the crowd was the biggest yet, in excess of 200 inmates all gathered around the barren football pitch. There was time for a final team talk from Lozano and then the match started.

The first half was a cagey affair, with neither side willing to take any risks. When the half-time whistle blew, the score was still 0–0. By then the day was starting to cool, but it was still too warm to be running around. I was already exhausted – it must have been twenty-six degrees at that point, but it felt even hotter. Sweat was pouring from all of us and I could feel a headache coming on from the exertion – even though we still had at least forty-five minutes more to play.

Our big break came late in the game. After a promising attack by Cuba, there was a mad scramble among their defenders. We got a shot away, but it was blocked and then cleared, although only as far as Pauli – our Puerto Rican midfielder who was lurking just outside the box. Time seemed to slow down as I watched him wind up his right foot and lash the ball against the crossbar. It hit the underside of the bar and then bounced down into the goal, missing the gloves of their diving goalkeeper and smashing into the net. Cue pandemonium. The big Latino crowd went completely mad.

The big Latino crowd went completely mad, glad as they were to see one of their own doing well. Every player on our team sprinted over to Pauli and mobbed him, dragging him to the ground in a team pile-on. The sheer joy of that moment was incredible. This wasn't simply a prison kick-about – I was playing in a cup final and we were winning. Even our substitutes ran onto the pitch to join the celebrations, while Lozano jumped around like a madman on the touchline.

The whistle blew with the score at 1-0 and that was that – the boys of Gregg Unit were the champions. We were all ecstatic, jumping around as if we had won the World Cup and slapping each other on the back.

Someone upended a jug of water over Lozano while Cuba pulled me in for a sweaty hug. The tournament really meant that much to these guys and I was overjoyed to have been a part of it. Lozano, dripping wet but grinning like a lunatic, called us over and said he would throw a banquet for the whole team later that night, provided he and his Mexican friends could get hold of enough microwaves to cook all the food.

We weren't the only ones celebrating. After the game, a Latino guy walked over from the crowd and came to thank us. He said he had won 150 packets of fish betting on the game and he was going to reward us by giving us all two packets each. His jackpot was worth around $200 – a staggering amount of money in the context of a prison. It would no doubt keep him betting for the foreseeable future.

We all trooped back to the unit aching and tired, but as happy as we'd been in a long time. I suspected that this would be my best day in Allenwood – I knew I wouldn't feel this good again until the day I was sent back to the UK and, after that, the day I was eventually released. Until then it was all about killing time and what better way to do it than winning a football tournament with your fellow inmates? As El always used to tell me, 'Darby, you've got to do the time. Don't let the time do you.' Without football, I wasn't sure how I would have been able to do that. The Beautiful Game indeed.

After a football season comes a transfer window, and I was hoping that the same would be true for me. My application had bounced between the UK and US authorities a few times, but it had finally been rubber-stamped by all the right people. By now, I knew my transfer home couldn't be far away, and I was more than ready to be going. Every part of me was strained, and I was physically and mentally spent. Almost half a year had passed since I had last seen my family, and the snatched phone calls had done little to stop me missing them.

My body was also in anguish – sleeping on the thin prison mattresses did nothing for my back, and I was becoming stiffer and stiffer. My knees were also ruined after overdoing it on the football pitch and, for the first time in my life, I was starting to feel as if I wasn't a young man any more. To make matters worse, I had been eating poorly for months, and I was about as skinny as I had ever been. I needed a long course of home-cooked meals if I was to return to a healthy weight any time soon.

Of course, leaving Allenwood would not mean that my sentence was over. I would have to serve the rest of it in a UK prison, where I hoped I would be able to see my family and friends regularly. But crucially, being transferred to the UK meant that in an instant, whatever time I had left of the thirty-seven months would be cut in half.

The transfer process, like anything to do with the US justice system, was far more complicated than it needed to be. First, the prison counsellor had to send the rubber-stamped paperwork to the BOP, where it was passed up the ranks until someone senior enough could sign off on it. Then, the papers had to be sent to the UK, where the relevant authorities also needed to sign on the dotted line. It took months to reach even this point, and I spent many nights worrying about the slow passage of my approval documents on both sides of the Atlantic. Once the Brits were happy with the papers, they sent them back to the US government, where the documents needed more signatures and rubber stamps.

With the US government's approval, I then had to appear before a district judge to confirm that I wanted to be transferred and had requested the move of my own free will. Then the Brits needed to be notified of the district judge's ruling, at which point someone in the UK government had to make the arrangements to get me out of the US. The wheels of bureaucracy turn slowly, and few bureaucracies are as useless and inept as the respective governments and justice systems of the UK and the US. At least now the wheels *were* turning. With all the necessary approvals in place, I knew I would be going home soon.

Throughout my stay, I was always drawn to a little farmhouse up in the valley that we could see from the rec. It was nestled in a forest clearing on the far side, and I used to look at it during my evening walks around the running track and think about going back to Britain. It always reminded me of home – the scenery in the rural West Country and the cottage I kept in the New Forest, where we would go on family weekends and holidays.

Now, as my time at Allenwood was coming to an end, I found myself looking at the farmhouse and thinking about all I had to look forward to. That squat building, separated from me by a fence and watchtowers and armed guards, always served as a symbol of my freedom, of the outside. It made for a beautiful picture, and now I was so close to leaving and going back to the UK, it seemed to be even more picturesque.

Paul saw me looking at it one evening as we were ambling around the track. There was a fine mist about the valley, but not enough to obscure the farmhouse.

'Look at that,' I said. 'Isn't that beautiful? That's how I remember the outside.'

He smiled and stopped walking, so he could better appreciate the view. 'You know, I've never really stopped to take it in before. But you're right. It's lovely.'

Paul was also due to be transferred out of Allenwood soon, to a low-security prison that provided counselling for drug addicts. He wasn't a junkie, but his place on the drug rehabilitation programme meant he qualified for a move and, crucially, a sentence reduction. I asked him whether he would have done anything differently if he was indicted again.

'Of course I would,' he said. 'Now I know almost all federal cases plead out, I wouldn't have fought against it as hard as I did. I would have told my attorney on day one to go and get me the best deal possible, as quickly as possible. And once the deal was agreed, I would have worked to get in here much sooner. The longer you leave it before going to prison, the worse it is. For me, indictment to imprisonment was eighteen months. But the emotional stress and strain, the trauma, it caused me and my family was another punishment all in itself.'

I know now that ninety-seven per cent of federal cases end in a plea bargain, a consequence of the draconian sentences that are handed out to those who have the nerve to make it to trial and lose. I nodded my approval at Paul's sage advice.

'What about you, Darby?' he asked. 'Now you're nearly out of here, what would you have done differently?'

'I don't think I prepared myself properly for the separation issues,'

I said. 'You know, being apart from all your loved ones. I didn't realise that not being able to communicate freely, and at your whim, would hurt so much. I've always been used to talking to people whenever I wanted to, particularly my family. It's bloody hard when you lose that.'

'What about the case? Would you have fought that differently?'

'Yeah, definitely. I would have liked someone to have sat me down right at the start and explain that I never stood a chance of beating the US justice system. The dice are so heavily loaded in favour of the prosecution that it's almost impossible. But we were dealing with British lawyers, who were all well-meaning, but knew nothing about US justice.

'I needed someone to tell me that practically nobody ever wins, and that my only hope would be to get a good deal by giving somebody up. It's like you said. Instead, I wasted so much time labouring under the belief that the system was fair.

'And I wish I could have understood from the start that the Feds weren't really after us. Knowing what I know now, on day one, the three of us should have gotten ourselves a serious and respected US attorney. We should have gone to the DOJ and asked for immunity in return for giving them info about Enron. They only wanted us so they could get to the Enron guys. If I had properly understood that, I wouldn't have fought so hard, or for so long. Eventually we did get ourselves a really good legal team, but by then we were indicted and extradited and the die was cast.'

'Amen to that.' By this point we had completed a whole lap of the track. The farmhouse was looming in front of us once more. Paul laughed. 'There's your farmhouse again.' We walked in silence for a little while, both of us chewing over what we had put into words. 'How long did you spend fighting extradition?' he asked eventually.

'Four years. And then it took two more years in Texas before we pleaded out.'

'Six years of your life,' he said. 'Do you think those years were wasted?'

'The easy answer is yes, but in all honesty, no. At the start of this whole process I was this arrogant, money-obsessed investment banker. I was always away, focused on the next business, the next deal, never at home. And now I've become somebody I quite like. I moved back to my home town while we fought everything and spent more time with my family and friends. I'm a much better person for it.'

Paul smiled and nodded. 'I'm glad to hear it, my friend.'

I spent the rest of the evening reflecting on our conversation. I was still thinking about Paul's words, about the things we would both have done differently, as I was lying in bed that night. It was so clear to me that I didn't belong in this place. I needed to get back to Britain as soon as I could. I thought that by the time I was back on UK soil, the worst of my ordeal would be over.[1]

It was testament to how few British guys there were in Allenwood – and, by extension, how out of place I was – that most people thought I was Australian when they heard my accent for the first time. Some people even guessed that I was Mexican, although I took that as a compliment on my extreme tan. There was one guy who made me laugh, though. He was an African-American and I'd never spoken to him before, but when he heard me speak, his eyebrows shot up.

'You from Australia?' he asked.

'No, mate,' I said. 'I'm from England.'

He looked confused. 'Yeah, but that's near Australia, right?'

'Yeah, not far. Only about ten thousand miles.'

He nodded sagely and turned to his friend. 'I knew it,' he said.

My last handful of days passed in their usual slow, steady way, most of them without incident. Until, one afternoon, I was approached by a couple of hard-looking young guys. I had seen them around and understood that they were in for drugs. They looked like a couple of gangbangers, so I could believe it. I had been sitting at one of the tables, reading the latest *Telegraph*, when the pair came over to me. We hadn't spoken much

---

1 In fact, that wasn't the case. When I got back to the UK, I went via Wandsworth and Ford to Leyhill, Gloucester. It's one of only two open prisons in the UK that take sex offenders. Over half of the inmates there were lollipops. It was a dreadful place and the inmates were particularly awful. I absolutely hated being in there – having to mix with those people every day.

before – only the occasional nod and hello – so I was instantly on edge, wondering what they wanted to talk about. They sat either side of me and got straight to it.

'Darby, I've heard you're a good guy. People say you're a good guy. People like you.'

'Thanks,' I said, confused as to where this was going.

'But, look, do you know that some of the guys you hang out with are lollipops?'

'I do my best to steer clear of them. I didn't know I spent time with any of them, though. Who?'

'Here's a hint. If anyone is a non-violent white guy from the US, then they are either drug guys or sex offenders. Most white-collar guys would be in a camp. Most computer guys would be in a camp. You can tell a drug guy easy enough – all you need to do is ask how much they were indicted for. They'll tell you to the nearest gram.'

My mind started racing. 'What about Paul?'

They gave me a knowing look. I already knew the answer from the expressions on their faces. 'Shit,' I said. I hadn't ever suspected Paul, but as soon as the guys told me, I was able to join the dots. An internet gambler would be in a camp – an open prison. And I remembered the conversations we had in the wake of the revelation about Brian from the laundry. Paul was always defending him, imploring me to see the other side. Paul's friendliness had blinded me to the truth.

'Hey, man,' one of the guys said, noticing my expression. 'It ain't your fault. You don't know how prison works and we know that. This is the only compound in this part of the country where those motherfuckers get any kind of protection and that's why there's so many of them. In other prisons they'd get a shank. I've seen it happen.'

This revelation about Paul put me in a foul mood. It felt like another betrayal – a blow to my conviction that most of the guys in Allenwood were at least decent people. It hurt, although I couldn't bring myself to confront Paul about it yet. I needed time to process what I had been told and to work out how I felt about him now, knowing what I knew. But then, when I thought my opinion of the people around me couldn't get any lower, a couple of days later I suffered what seemed an even greater betrayal: I learned the truth about T.

We were in the cell, talking about his case. He had finally produced the paperwork I needed to send to my lawyer friend in Texas, in the hope that he would be able to help him in his plight. I had thought that T would hand over his case files right away, but it took him a long time to get them to me. I knew that if I were in his position, and someone had offered to help me, I would want to get the ball rolling as soon as possible. T, however, had been in no rush.

Even now that he finally had the papers in his hand, he seemed strangely reluctant to give them to me. I could tell that something was wrong.

'What's up, T?' I asked. 'Is there something you're not telling me?' He was silent, looking down at the scuffed floor. I gave it a few seconds before prompting him again. 'You are in for drugs, right?'

He took a deep breath and let out a low sigh. 'Darby,' he said, 'I've got to be honest with you now. I'm sorry for not telling the truth before, but I'm not in for drugs. I'm in for robbery.'

I mulled this over. The lawyer I knew was a specialist in drug cases, that's why I had thought about him being a good fit for T. Now he was telling me that he wasn't in for drugs at all. It blew my plan completely out of the water.

'Why didn't you tell me this before?' I asked. 'And bloody hell, T, how much did you steal to get over thirty years? It must have been millions – too much to carry, surely?'

'We didn't get anything,' he said. 'We didn't even get into the bank. It was armed robbery. That's why the sentence is so long.'

I was still confused. 'But T, that still sounds like an extreme sentence.' The cogs turned inside my head. 'Wait, you didn't kill anyone, did you?'

'No.' He sighed again. I could see shame in the way he sat, slouched forwards, never looking up from the floor. 'We kidnapped the bank manager and his wife. Here, you better read this.' He held out a sheet of paper with a transcription of the hearing where he was sentenced.

As I read the transcript, my heart sank. T hadn't acted alone. Along with an accomplice, T had held the two hostages captive for thirty-six hours and, during that time, had abused them both. The transcript specified very few details, but reading it was enough. I didn't want to help T any more – I couldn't bring myself to. I told him that I would still ask my friend what he thought about his case, but I had no intention of doing that. I decided to sit on the papers for a few weeks and then tell T there was nothing we could do for him.

I hated this place. I hated having to mix with these people and never knowing who was telling the truth about who they were. I hated having to be constantly on guard, worrying about who I was talking to and whether they were undesirable or not. I didn't belong here and I was desperate to leave. Thankfully, I didn't have much longer to wait.

CHAPTER 14

INFECTION

A rumour was going around the compound that a serious staphylococcus infection had taken hold in Brady, one of the other units. There was talk of one man being carted off to an outside hospital with over fifty sores on his body, while his cellies had allegedly reported to the sick bay as a precaution. The advice from the medical staff was to wash the cells daily, wash all clothing and bedding twice a week and disinfect everything. Depending on who you spoke to, around twenty people had already been diagnosed and were waiting it out in the sick bay.

With a hundred and seventy-five guys to a bathroom (three toilets and four urinals), it was no surprise that bacteria were thriving. Even though the bathroom was cleaned twice a day, I still hated going in there – and that was before I knew about the infection. After the rumour spread, most of the inmates became hysterical about hygiene: some people wouldn't even touch the handle on the TV room door, and you could forget about any of us going anywhere near the shower curtains. Despite the increased awareness, it wasn't long until someone I knew was diagnosed with the staph infection. He was called Bishop, an enormous weightlifter whom I knew vaguely through some of the Gregg guys. If he had it, then that meant that the infection was no longer isolated in Brady Unit.

I saw Bishop in the queue for chow and I could tell something was wrong from the way he hobbled over. He was a fit guy, in his physical prime, so it was alarming to see him struggling even to walk properly.

'What's wrong with you, mate?' I asked.

'I've caught that damn staph infection,' he said. 'I think I must have got it from the weights. Look at these boils.' He lifted his shirt to reveal two enormous sores on his side. I winced involuntarily. 'That's not even the worst of it,' he said. 'I've got more on my back and the doctors had to cut a big one out at the base of my spine. I'm still sore from that, which is why I'm walking like a gimp.'

'Bloody hell,' I said. The sight was more than enough to crush my appetite.

'They tell me there are about two hundred people in the compound who have some kind of infection. It's worrying, don't you think?'

'Very. Did they give you antibiotics?'

'Nope. They aren't giving them to anyone. They're worried that if they do, the infection might develop a resistance – you know, become one of those superbugs. Then everyone's in some serious shit. They say my body will be able to fight it off within a couple of weeks.'

Junior saw us loitering near the back of the queue and came over. 'Darby,' he said, nodding at me. 'Bishop.' He reached out his hand for a bump but neither of us met his fist.

'We've been talking about the staph infection,' I said, by way of explanation.

'Ah. It sounds real nasty, doesn't it?'

'It sure does.'

'You know that guy who went to hospital?' Junior asked. 'I heard he's died now.'

Poor Bishop turned white at this news. That was classic Junior – gobby and tactless to a fault – but his remark set my mind racing. I was very conscious that we were touching inmates' clothes every day in the laundry, and with my release so close, I couldn't countenance getting the infection myself.

The next day at work, I went straight over to Bob.

'Did you hear about the guy who died?' I asked.

He nodded gravely. 'Yeah. I spoke to one of the cops about it to see if they can do anything for us.'

'What did he say?' I asked.

'Well, he was one of the guys who's normally stationed in here. He tried brushing it off at first, but then I reminded him that he's as exposed as we are. He said he'd talk to Anderson about it.'

'Okay, good. I'm going to go and talk to her as well. Don't you think we should at least be given gloves if we're touching the clothes?'

'Yeah, of course. Good luck getting her to have any sympathy for us, though.'

I found Miss Anderson in her office. She was perched behind her computer, no doubt doing some more due diligence on her employees.

'Miss,' I said, 'Sorry to disturb you, but I have a problem.'

She looked up from her monitor. 'What is it?'

'Apparently some guy on the compound has died from that infection that's going around. Don't you think we should be taking steps to protect ourselves?'

She scoffed. 'Nobody has died, Darby. He's in the SHU, in quarantine.'

Admittedly, that made me feel a little better, but not by much. After all, I had seen Bishop's sores. 'I still think we should be protected,' I said. 'Can't you get us some gloves or something?'

A sigh from Miss Anderson. 'Okay, Darby, I'll see what I can do.'

At that, I left her to get on with whatever it was she did in her office. As if there wasn't enough for me to worry about already, with the assortment of nutters and predators on the compound, now I had to try to dodge a staph infection as well.

I was also worried about the next phase of my journey. After Allenwood, I knew I would be taken to the Metropolitan Correctional Centre (MCC) in Manhattan – a skyscraper prison that acted as a holding cell for both untried American prisoners and foreign inmates on the verge of a transfer back home.

I had heard nothing but bad things about the MCC. It was known as a claustrophobic place where inmates were confined to the windowless building almost 24/7. Supposedly, there was only a small rec yard on the roof of the skyscraper, where you could exercise for only an hour a day. The Centre was also noisy, dirty and dangerous: reputedly it had racial tensions, gang problems – the lot, from what I'd heard. Without a proper rec yard where the prisoners could let off steam, the place was like a pressure cooker. I knew that my transfer to the MCC represented another step on my journey back to the UK, but I was still dreading it. I was preparing myself for the worst, fully expecting to be more miserable there than in my first few days in the SHU at Allenwood.

I sought out Ralph, the most hardened criminal I could find, to ask for some advice about surviving the MCC.

'Look, Darby,' he said. 'I know you're in a comfort zone now, and you know a lot of people, but never forget where you are. Yeah, the MCC is bad, but in some ways so is Allenwood. You're in a prison right now, Darby. These places are all the same really. There's trouble everywhere – don't get caught out.'

It was as if Ralph had a sixth sense, because trouble came looking for me soon afterwards in the form of Sergei, the fearsome Mafia boss who had enough blood on his hands to clog a storm drain. He caught my eye from across the rec and sauntered over.

'I saw you at the basketball court the other night,' he said.

'Oh, right,' I said, wondering where this was going.

'You were with an Italian guy.' Probably Frankie, I thought. 'You pointed at me and said something to him. What did you say?'

Oh shit. I couldn't remember saying anything about Sergei, and I was sure that if I had, it wouldn't have been anything bad. But judging by his terrifying stare, he thought I had been bitching about him. There was something deeply unnerving in the way Sergei filled me with fear, simply with a look. I felt myself turning cold all over as he continued to stare at me.

'I really don't know, Sergei,' I said. 'I can't recall saying anything, but if I did it wouldn't have been bad.' I tried a smile, hoping that might defuse the situation.

'Why are you smiling?' He put the question in a disturbingly calm, even tone, but I could still tell that he was fuming. '*I said* – why are you fucking smiling? Is something funny? You better remember what you said and you better remember it right now.'

'Hold on, Sergei,' I said. 'I'm trying to remember what it could have been.'

'Try harder.'

'I think I was with Frankie. I probably said that you were a good guy and asked if he knew you.' I wasn't lying. As terrifying as he was, I didn't have anything against Sergei, so I really wouldn't have said anything bad about him.

Sergei still wasn't satisfied. 'Why would you say that to him? Why would you say I'm a good guy?'

'Because Frankie is a good guy. He's a nice fella and I just wondered if he knew you. Do you know him?'

'Not really.' He took a moment to think things through. 'Okay, Darby. Whatever. Careful who you talk to in here.'

With that, Sergei slunk off, probably to go and terrorise someone else. Our exchange was another reminder of where I was and who I was dealing with, and of the need to be vigilant at all times. I had failed to follow some of the most important rules of Allenwood: never let your guard down, mind your own business and keep your mouth shut – even if you happen to be saying something good. I had a feeling that these would be useful lessons to take to the MCC with me. There would be no second chances there, I knew, no benefit of the doubt. I had done well to get this far and I couldn't afford to slip up now.

If I thought I had it bad with Sergei, Steve had it worse with Mizik – his delusional cellmate, who, you will recall, thought he was a shot-caller for all the white inmates. I caught up with Steve on the rec and he told me that he had been allowed to move cells. I would have been overjoyed if I were him, but Steve didn't look so happy.

'Now Mizik is causing even more trouble,' he said. 'He took it personally that I asked for a move and now he's told everyone in his little crew to stop talking to me.'

'What are we, kids? That's kindergarten stuff!'

'Darby, it's all right for you. You don't have to have anything to do with it. But if it's kindergarten stuff today, then what will it escalate to tomorrow? Mizik is deranged, seriously. You don't want to go within a mile of him.'

Apparently Mizik had already done eighteen years and was working through another twelve-year sentence. Evidently, he was a lifelong criminal – pathologically incapable of keeping on the right side of the law. The rumour was that last time he had actually made it to a halfway house, a place where many inmates are sent when they have only six months left to serve. This is supposed to help integrate prisoners back into the real world, as they offer more freedoms than prison though fewer than being on parole.

While Mizik was at this halfway house, he assaulted a guard and went on the run with his wife and kids. He was able to escape justice for a couple of years, travelling around the States in a motorhome, hustling and defrauding for a living. This stint as a fugitive earned him a place on America's Most Wanted list for a while, something he now wore like a badge of honour. Steve explained that Mizik lived entirely by prison rules and prison ethics, having accepted already that he would be spending the rest of his life behind bars. Now Steve had crossed him, he was going to make a point of exacting revenge at some point.

'Steve,' I said, 'you're a smart, sensible guy. Why are you letting him get to you? You've got your whole life ahead of you, and he's going to be stuck in here forever. You've got a future – think of all the things you can do when you get out. Think of all the girls you can meet and all the fun you're going to have. None of this petty prison shit matters compared to that.'

He sighed. 'God, Darby, you're right. Thanks. I needed someone to say that. It's so easy to forget about the outside entirely, to be absorbed with life in here.'

'Good,' I said. 'I make myself think about the outside, about my future, every single day. I can't wait to get out and get back to my life.'

As I waited for news of the day of my departure, I became ever more aware of other people leaving. There was never much warning: one day, someone was there, the next, they were gone. That's how it happened with Paul – he was released early one morning before anyone even had a chance to say goodbye. He had been good to me when I first arrived, showing me a great deal of kindness and expecting nothing in return. But once I knew why he was really in prison, I couldn't think of him in the same way.

Another leaving story that has always stuck with me concerned one of El's crowd, a young black guy. He came into our cell one evening to tell

El that he had been given a place in a halfway house. While halfway houses are still very restrictive, being in one is nowhere near as bad as being in prison. This guy would be able to see his family, find employment and live with a greater degree of freedom than he was used to at Allenwood.

'I'm off, man,' he said, grinning at El. 'Shipping out tomorrow.'

El bumped his fist. 'Good luck, man.'

That should have been the last we saw of him, but three weeks later, the same guy was marched back down the corridor at count time by a couple of cops. Afterwards, he poked his head into our cell.

'Hey, El,' he said. 'I'm back.'

El was incredulous. 'Why? What the fuck? I thought you were at a halfway house?'

'I was. But I got sent back here. One of the guards was being a motherfucker.'

'What happened?'

'Well, I was just walking around, minding my own business, when this guard tells me to pull my pants up.' This guy had a habit of wearing his trousers really lowslung, around his thighs, exposing his boxers and backside to the world.

'Right,' El said, nodding along. 'So, what happened?'

'I said I didn't want to pull my pants up and the guard said that if I didn't do what he said then I'd get sent back here. It happened three times, and in the end I told him to go fuck himself if he thought he could tell me what to do. So now I'm back here.'

El was obliged to show some sympathy, because they both moved in the same circles, but I couldn't believe how stupid the guy was to blow his chance at a halfway house. It was bad enough that he had been sent back to prison at all, but to get sent back over an argument about how he wore his trousers was next-level stupid. I could only shake my head with disbelief as I listened to the conversation.

The next day, I was sitting with Ralph on the rec. A man I had never seen before was at the next table. He was tall but stocky, a well-built guy with a pockmarked face and shaven head. I was telling Ralph the story of the trousers. 'Have you ever heard anything more stupid?' I asked.

At that, the big guy at the table next to us turned around. 'Sorry to interrupt,' he said, 'but I overheard you and yes, I have.' He introduced himself as Glen and proceeded to tell us his story.

Glen was a minor criminal. He had served time on two separate felony convictions (crimes punishable by sentences of more than one year) before arriving at Allenwood – one for affray and one for GBH, both cases involving bar fights. After these two convictions, he had fallen foul of America's habitual offender rule – aka the three-strikes rule. Under this rule, if you are found guilty of committing three felonies then the automatic recommended sentence for the third conviction is a minimum fifteen years, regardless of the crime.

Glen was a free man, having served both his relatively short sentences, when he bought a gun. Contrary to the perceptions of many British people, there are a limited number of checks that have to be carried out before you can do so. He had to fill out a questionnaire and one of the questions asked whether he had any felony convictions. He lied and ticked 'No'. A couple of weeks later, he opened his front door to find around twenty armed policemen pointing their guns at him. A background check had exposed Glen's lie, and now they were going to throw the book at him. Without realising it, he had fallen foul of the three-strikes rule: he got the full fifteen years.

'Can you imagine how long that is?' he asked me, that day on the rec. 'I mean, how long will you serve?'

'Around eighteen months in total,' I said.

'Right,' said Glen. 'You can visualise that, can't you? You can actually see it. Eighteen months from now will just about be the year after next. Think about fifteen years. You can't think about or even see yourself in fifteen years' time.' Ralph nodded. He knew exactly what Glen meant.

Back to Glen's story: the next stop for him was the penitentiary. He quickly became institutionalised, and made a point of breaking every single rule he could. He gambled, he fought everybody and everything, and he developed a lucrative sideline by brewing hooch in his cell. He would mix sugar and fruit together and ferment the mixture into alcohol, which he then sold on the black market. He clashed constantly with the guards and with his fellow inmates, and spent months at a time in the SHU. One day, after this had been going on for some years, one of the cops sat Glen down and told him that if he didn't turn himself around, he was going to lose all his good time. He had already lost a chunk of it because of his behaviour.

'Good time?' Glen said to the cop. 'Go fuck yourself with your good time. As if I give a fuck. I'm here for fifteen fucking years – do you think I'll notice if you take away my fucking good time? You can fucking shove it.'

The cop looked at him grimly. 'Okay, I will, and one day I promise you, you'll regret saying that to me.'

Back on the rec, Glen had developed a wistful expression. 'That conversation was over ten years ago,' he said, 'but I've thought about it almost every day in the last couple of years. Guess what? I do regret it. I regret it more than I can say. I've grown up a lot since then, and I knuckled down. Gradually, that fifteen years shrank down and I was finally able to see the end. And, you know, if I'd have kept my good time, I wouldn't be here now. I'd have gotten out last year. You asked if I ever heard of something more stupid than that guy and his trousers. How about that?'

I had been told that on the day you were moved out of the prison, the guards woke you up early, without any warning. They didn't let anyone know in advance, because they were worried about prisoners' crews busting them out during transit. Every morning for weeks, I woke up hoping against hope, daring to anticipate that today would be the day when I would open my eyes to see guards at the foot of my bunk, waiting to escort me out of Allenwood forever. As I awoke each morning to the bright lights above our cell being turned on at 7 a.m., I was inevitably disappointed. This early morning crushing of hope became a staple of the routine of my last few days. I wanted out so much, and now I knew the time of my release was inching closer, each day felt more torturous than the last.

The only thing to break up the predictable drudgery was the occasional shakedown – a chance for the guards to clear us all out of the unit and undertake a thorough search for contraband. One morning, the loudspeakers in our unit crackled into life.

'All Gregg Unit inmates to work or the rec,' came the metallic voice. 'All Gregg Unit inmates to work or the rec.' Once we had vacated our cells, the guards could turn over every mattress and bust into every locker. Shakedowns were a fairly frequent occurrence, although I always got the impression that the guards did it to make a point more than anything else. Occasionally, a shank or some other improvised weapon would turn up, but more often than not it was an enormous fuss about nothing.

On this particular day I made my way to the laundry and got to work folding. Bob was anxious about the shakedown – I assumed because he had been hoarding commissary supplies again. After a while, Miss Anderson came over to stare out of the nearest window.

'Look out there,' she said.

A sniffer dog was being led into Gregg Unit at the head of a group of cops.

'Uh-oh,' I said, 'looks like someone's in trouble.' We watched as the dog was shepherded through the doors and out of sight. 'Are there drugs in there then, miss? Have you heard anything?'

She scoffed. 'How naïve are you, Darby?' Bob started laughing at me.

'Well, I don't know, do I?' I continued. 'I don't go around looking for that sort of thing. Anyway, I don't see how anyone would even get drugs in here.'

'If you use your imagination, there are ways,' Miss Anderson said. 'I used to work in the visiting room at a medium-security, and one time a little old lady – probably in her seventies – was caught with candy bars stuffed in her bra. It turned out that the candy bars really contained drugs, wrapped up in rolls of plastic. You can work out the rest. And anyway, sometimes guards work with inmates to bring drugs or cigarettes in.'

I couldn't believe she was telling us this stuff. I had always suspected it went on, despite pretending otherwise in our conversation, but it was strange to hear Miss Anderson talking so frankly.

When I went back to Gregg, I was expecting the worst. Sure enough, the cell looked like a war zone. The guards had been through each of our lockers and the beds had been stripped, with the bedding now strewn all over the floor. Over the months, I had accumulated a few extra sheets to make the hard metal bed a bit more comfortable, but now they had been confiscated and I was back to sleeping on the bare mattress.

A large portion of El's and T's wardrobes had been confiscated as well – including some hats and shoes that had been bought from the commissary. Understandably, El was fuming when he came back and found that legitimate possessions of his had been taken by the guards, probably on the assumption that they had been obtained on the black market. In the end, all I could do to calm him down was remind him that we would both be out of here soon. That helped to defuse some of his outrage.

'I can't fucking wait, Darby,' he said. 'I'm sick of this place.'

'Me too, mate. Me too.' I was hoping and praying that it wouldn't be long now.

CHAPTER 15

PACKING UP

The weather turned at the end of September, and the glorious sunshine that had made the evenings tolerable was replaced by an overcast sky and leaden rainclouds. Forced to spend more hours in the unit, I began to feel my confinement even more acutely. The effect on my mood was pronounced as I became increasingly frustrated at the slow pace of the transfer process. I needed news, or I would have gone mad. Thankfully, on one of the most miserable evenings of the season, I was given a lifeline.

I was queuing for chow when the prison counsellor came to find me. She was the one directly responsible for handling my paperwork and ensuring that things kept moving on the transfer front. All of my papers had finally been approved she told me and, although she couldn't say exactly when, I would be on the move soon.

This was huge news! My exit day was definitely closer – but so was the dreaded MCC. Still, I knew I had to overcome that one final hurdle but then I would be home. I'd still be in prison, but at least I would be back in the UK.

By now I was counting down the days. I had been in Allenwood for over a hundred and fifty of them, and I had spent around seven years before that with the case hanging over me. The mental strain had taken its toll, and all I could think about was going back to my family and working towards starting a new life as a free man.

The weekend passed in its usual slow way, and on Monday I reported as usual to the laundry, where I told Bob about my good news. 'I'm glad to hear it, son,' he said. 'And I've got some good news of my own. They've put me in for a transfer back down south – to a camp, as well! I'll be able to see my wife and kids and grandkids again.'

It felt to me like our fortunes were changing with the season. I walked to the rec during my coffee break and once more admired the view of the valley, knowing I wouldn't be here much longer. The leaves had already melted into autumnal oranges, reds and yellows, yet that morning there was still a lingering summer warmth in the air.

I returned to the laundry and saw a cluster of new inmates queuing at the desk. It was almost half a year since that had been me, and I found myself thinking how lucky I was that the experience was in the past. The trauma of arriving here, surrendering myself at the prison, going into the SHU and then coming out into the bustle of the compound – I was beyond glad all of that was behind me.

I spent most of the afternoon collecting the few possessions I had accumulated since arriving at Allenwood. I was going to give everything away to the people who had made my time here bearable. It wasn't much – my prison radio, my prison watch, some relatively new clothes – but for some of the guys who were living on their prison wages and nothing else, I knew I could make their lives a little easier.

As I was sorting through my possessions, El came into the cell. I was surprised to see him during his usual working hours, but apparently he had been told he could leave early. That could mean only one thing: he was on his way out, too. It was all happening at once.

He was smiling as he bumped my fist. In his other hand he held a single sheet of paper – a sentencing print-out with his updated release date, now only a few months away. A judge's signature was scrawled at the bottom of the sheet.

'Got all my papers through, man,' he said. 'It's official.'

'El, that's wonderful!'

'We're both leaving, man.' He sounded like he couldn't believe it himself. 'They've put me in for an immediate place at a halfway house. As soon as a spot becomes available, I'm out of here. Could be any day now, same as you.'

'Have you called your family yet to tell them?'

'I called my ma just now. She screamed down the phone! I told my sister too – it's wonderful, man.'

'Have you told your daughters yet?' I asked.

'No, I'm gonna surprise them. I told my ma and my sis not to tell them. One day, soon, I'm gonna just walk in on them all.' He shook his head, unable to believe his own good fortune. 'It's over, man. Fifteen years and it's finally over.'

The world had changed so much since he was locked up, and now he would have to learn to navigate it all by himself. But El wasn't fazed. He was too happy to care at that point.

That evening he spent hours asking how much things cost outside prison – 'on the street', as he called it. We covered the cost of phones, rent, shirts, computers, bus tickets, basically all the essentials he would need to know about when he became a free man again.

'How about sneakers, Darb?' he was asking. 'How much are they?'

This had already been going on for most of the evening and although I was happy to help, I got the impression that we were starting to annoy T.

Sure enough, after this latest question, T slapped his hand against the frame of our bunk bed in agitation.

'Man, would you fucking stop it already?'

El looked sheepish. It was poor form to flaunt your impending freedom in front of someone who still had more than a decade to serve, and he knew it. He said sorry to T and we spent the rest of the evening in silence. I read the latest *Telegraph* for a while, El busied himself writing a letter, and T stewed on his bunk. I was glad when the lights went out and I went straight to sleep. There wouldn't be many more of these nights left to endure.

The following morning, a young inmate reported to the laundry, carrying a bundle of khaki in his arms. He made his way to the reception desk, where Miss Anderson was sitting, and set down a well-worn pair of trousers – the regulation kind we had to wear at visits.

'Excuse me, ma'am, but I'm getting married tomorrow,' he said. 'I was wondering if I could get a decent set of khakis that fit me properly? These ones are too big and they're really old.'

Miss Anderson sighed and got up from behind her desk. She disappeared into the bowels of the laundry for a few minutes and returned with another pair of trousers. Frayed at the bottom, scuffed and faded from being washed so many times, they looked even worse than the worn-out trousers the poor guy had brought with him in the first place. He told Miss Anderson, politely, that these substitutes looked terrible and that he didn't want to get married wearing them. Miss Anderson didn't seem to care about this, and she sent him away with the 'new' pair without any regard for his complaints. He looked like a broken man as he shuffled out of the laundry and around the corner.

I had seen the whole episode from the folding table. She saw me looking over at her in disbelief. 'Miss,' I said, 'why did you do that? It's hard enough in here already for these guys. If he's getting married, you could at least help him, couldn't you?'

I probably shouldn't have spoken to a prisoner officer so bluntly, but she really was awful to these guys, all the time. If Miss Anderson was offended by my outburst, she didn't show it. 'Darby, what stupid woman wants to marry a prisoner? In prison? Do you think that was ever going to be a nice, white wedding? These people must have screws loose.'

She may have had a point, but that didn't excuse her rudeness or her lack of compassion. I folded in silence, trying to get the image of the inmate being married in his ruined khakis out of my head. It was a depressing picture – the poor guy humiliated and degraded on what should have been the happiest day of his life, a perfect metaphor for the banal and petty cruelties of the justice system.

At around 9.30 a.m., a guard came into the laundry asking to speak to Inmate Darby. I looked up from the table and told him that was me.

'Darby, get your shit together and be at reception at twelve-thirty,' he said. 'We're going to get you packed up for your transfer.' It was the best thing I could have heard, as it meant I would be out in a day or so. I practically bounded out of the laundry and headed back to Gregg Unit, where I found El in our cell on his lunch break from the factory.

He was as pleased as I was and he gladly helped me pack a bag with my sweatshirt, a pair of shorts and my shoes, along with a few books and a bundle of letters. I had already given a lot of my stuff away, but I left the rest with El. He promised to make sure that everything went to the right people and bumped my fist as I made for reception with my 'out bag'.

News travels at lightning speed in prison and, as I walked through the unit, I was greeted by a chorus of shouts and a gauntlet of fists to bump.

'You going, Darby?'

'Finito?'

'You out of here?'

I had a great big smile on my face as I replied, 'Not yet. Soon though!'

At reception I was called into a side-room and met by a pair of guards.

'Darby, you only just got here,' one of them said. 'You leaving already?'

'Yes, sir.'

'You got yourself a good deal, then.'

'Well, I'm not out yet,' I said.

He laughed. 'Ain't that the truth!'

The other guard inspected the contents of my bag. He looked at my wrist. 'What about your watch? Is that going in the bag?'

'No. I'm giving it to a friend.'

'No, you're not.' He gestured to a box of reclaimed possessions, confiscated from inmates before they were allowed to leave. 'It's against the rules. No gifts. Now put it in the box.'

'I'll take it with me then.'

'No, you won't. In the box, Darby, I won't tell you again.'

I did as I was told. Thankfully, I had left my radio, my most valuable possession, with El. As soon as the watch had been sacrificed, I was cleared to go. That was me, packed and ready for the MCC.

The next morning I woke up disappointed. Nobody had come to fetch me, so that meant another day to get through before I began my journey to New York. I reported for work early and was greeted by Miss Anderson, in a cheerier mood than usual.

'What happened with the weddings yesterday?' she asked. Plainly, there had been a handful of ceremonies on the same day.

'I don't know, Miss,' I said.

'Ask around for me. Find out how many got stood up.'

'What? Why?'

'Normally about half the women don't turn up for the ceremony. They think better of it. Why would you marry a scumbag from this place anyway?' she said, endorsing her earlier view.

After a while, Bob appeared for his shift. He joined me at the folding table and we settled into our usual routine of folding and chatting.

'Do you know anything about the weddings yesterday?' I asked.

'I know that out of the sixteen guys getting married, eight women didn't show.'

I looked over at Miss Anderson. 'That's going to make her day.'

When the early morning rush of inmates collecting their hygiene packs had calmed down, Bob called Miss Anderson over to the table. He told her about the eight women who didn't turn up and she broke into a broad grin.

'Oh, I'm so glad those women saw sense,' she said.

'But what about the guys?' I asked. 'Don't you feel sorry for them?'

'Nope. Back when I was in the pen, I saw plenty of cases of men getting married and then going back to their cells to have sex with their boyfriends. Those men don't deserve any sympathy – it's the women I feel for.'

Sympathy wasn't Miss Anderson's strong suit at the best of times but, again, I could understand partly where she was coming from. I knew it must be hard to work in an environment like this and not become a misanthrope – or at least a cynic. I realised that in her own way, bitter old Miss Anderson was a victim of the system as much as the rest of us.

This was likely to be my last day in the laundry, so I made a point of saying a proper goodbye to Miss Anderson as I left. She wished me good luck and thanked me for my work. 'And stay out of trouble,' she added as I was leaving, for what I hoped to be the last time.

After work, I spent the rest of the day saying my various goodbyes. I felt a strange mix of emotions – on the one hand I was delighted to be going, but on the other I was saying goodbye to people who had been my lifeline over the past few months. I sought out what remained of the laundry crew, thanked everyone on the Gregg Unit football team, and had a final handshake with Ralph, Jimmy and their guys.

That night I said goodbye to El too. He had been a godsend of a cellmate, and I knew I would always be grateful for his company, guidance and friendship. Bonds are forged quickly when you share a cell with someone and I felt as if I had known El all my life as he pulled me in for a final hug.

T said his own muted goodbye later on. He had been good to me, but I still couldn't get over the facts of his case. Everything had changed between us since I had learned the truth about him.

'Well, cellie,' he said, 'it's been a pleasure to know you. Good luck out there.'

I managed to mutter something about how badly I felt for him and said it meant a lot for me to hear him say that. In truth, I wasn't too sad about the parting of our ways.

The next morning, it finally happened: I was woken early by a hand on my shoulder. As I came to my senses, I realised that it was a guard who was shaking me.

'Wake up, you're leaving.'

Those were the words I had been desperate to hear ever since I had stepped across the threshold of Allenwood and surrendered myself to the prison authorities all those weeks ago. I got dressed and was given a final chance to repeat last night's goodbyes with El and T, who had been woken up by the commotion. The sense of relief as I was escorted across the compound, knowing it would be for the final time, was enormous.

I had arrived in Allenwood in May, and it was now approaching the end of October. That's not a great length of time in the big scheme of things, but it was a hugely difficult time, nonetheless. Allenwood had proved to be the biggest challenge I had ever faced and I was grateful to be coming out on the other side in one piece. That was always my only goal.

It was a crisp morning and I drank in the cold air on the way to reception. There were four other guys waiting around, all of them due to be on the same bus out of Allenwood as me. We sat on benches around reception and were given our breakfast. I was next to a tall, well-built, but bespectacled and inoffensive-looking guy, whom I didn't recognise.

'Hey,' he said, 'you know Rob, right?' Rob was the English guy who always got my *Telegraph* once I was done with it.

'Yeah, I do.'

'Darby, isn't it? Rob talks very highly of you.'

It suddenly clicked who I was talking to. 'You're Rob's mate, aren't you? Wayne?'

'That's me.'

'Oh, man,' I said, 'I've heard a lot about you.'

He laughed. 'I bet you have.'

Wayne was something of a celebrity at Allenwood. Despite his innocuous appearance, he was a killer and a lifer, who was known to be utterly brutal to the people that upset or crossed him. Rob got on well with him, as did many other decent guys, but Wayne's exploits were the stuff of legend.

Wayne had a fearsome reputation for being spectacularly intolerant towards the lollipops. He was known to turn up routinely outside undesirables' cells and beat the hell out of them, or drag them into his own cell as they were passing and give them a pasting. He didn't even need an excuse – he just did it for fun, often leaving his victims in need of an extended stay in the sick bay and then an immediate transfer to protective custody. He was serving such a long sentence that he simply didn't care about whatever punishment he might get.

After breakfast, we were put in chains and leg irons and led out through the front gates. I felt slightly uneasy around Wayne, but our mutual connections gave us plenty to talk about. When we were led on to a waiting bus, it was Wayne who was escorted into the seat behind mine.

'Wayne,' I said. 'Is it true you killed your best friend?' I turned awkwardly in my chains to face him.

'Yes, sir.'

Wayne launched into his story – one I had previously heard only second-hand via gossip around the compound. Evidently, when Wayne was eighteen, he was something of a tearaway. He already had three children by three different women and the future looked bleak. He joined the military, hoping that discipline would be good for him and, at first, it was. By the time he turned nineteen, he had fallen in love with a local woman, got her pregnant and this time married her. It wasn't an ideal situation for a teenager, but at least he was settling down. That was until he came home early from exercises one day and found his wife in bed with his best friend.

Wayne filled me in on all of this as the bus pulled away from the prison, telling his story as the Pennsylvania countryside drifted past the window.

'My mind went blank,' he said. 'She hadn't expected me home. I walked in the door and could hear them. I ran up the stairs. I was filled with rage – nothing but rage – and I just went berserk. He was in the bed, my bed, with my wife. I grabbed him by his hair and held him down before he could even put his pants back on. I smashed him in the face a few times until he was gushing, then I started to work on his ribs. I broke a couple and one of the broken ribs was pushed into his body. It pierced his lungs and his heart – that's what killed him. I knew he was dead straight away, so I went downstairs, sat on the sofa and waited for the military police to arrive.'

I heard his chains rattling behind me as Wayne reached a lull in his story. We jerked around a corner and the sound of clanking came from all over the bus. We were heading south towards Lewisburg, according to the road signs.

'What happened next?' I asked. Wayne had piqued a morbid curiosity in me.

His voice came from over my shoulder. 'Well, because I was in the military, I got tried by the military. They offered me to plead out to seventy years. But I knew it was a crime of passion and I had some kind of defence, so I told them to stick it. I was tried by a military jury – the prosecution wanted the death penalty because I didn't plead out. Obviously, I was found guilty, but because it was a crime of passion, I was given only forty-five years.'

'*Only* forty-five years?'

I saw Wayne's shrug reflected in the window. 'Beats the seventy I was offered.'

'What about your wife?'

'What about her?'

'Did you see her again? Or hear from her?'

'Only when she testified against me. She wrote me a few years later to say she had remarried. I don't have any contact with her now.'

'How long have you been in?' This was now an interview, but I couldn't resist finding out the rest of Wayne's absorbing story.

'Twenty-four years now. Hoping to be out after thirty.'

The conversation lasted us until the bus pulled in at Lewisburg Penitentiary. We were here to collect more inmates on our way to New York and beyond, I assumed. The prison was a forbidding place, with high walls and gun towers spaced at intervals along the perimeter.

We waited outside the gates for a few minutes and then the driver killed the engine. A ripple of chatter passed through the bus. Wayne leaned closer to me and told me that Lewisburg was one of the worst prisons in the country. Supposedly, there had been so much violence there that the Feds were turning it into a Maximum Security Unit.

An MSU was even worse than a penitentiary – used to house only the most dangerous and violent offenders. MSU inmates were kept in one-man cells at all times, never to have contact with other human beings. All meals were passed through a gap in the door, and prisoners had to spend their one hour of recreation on their own in a cage. Visits, meanwhile, were conducted via a video screen. It sounded like a recipe for insanity.

The guard at the front of the bus stood up and told us that we were all going to be taken into Lewisburg Penitentiary to be processed, with outbound transit taking place the following day. My heart sank as I looked at the squat building, surrounded by walls and choked with wire. We were told to stand up and then marched in through the front gates to be processed. After an hour of milling about while our details were recorded and double-checked, we were sent to a large holding cell with about fifty other inmates, all of them in transit.

The noise in the cell was spectacularly loud and it was so crowded that it was difficult to pick a path across the floor without stepping on anyone. Three-man bunks lined the walls, while a single television blared out hip-hop music videos for a crowd of black inmates. Other than that, there was a water fountain and one toilet, and nothing else. I found an unoccupied bunk – a top bunk, right below a glaring yellow light – and climbed up.

Wayne took the adjacent bunk and we passed the rest of the day talking about his exploits. Over lunch – pizza from a slop tray – he told me how he had once taken a guard hostage over some minor dispute and earned himself two years in solitary confinement as a punishment.

After a while, people in the cell started talking about a midnight bus. According to one of the guards, a bus would be leaving for New York that night. I was desperate to be on it, if only to avoid spending a night here. People were stressing about who would be getting a seat, and after a while I started to worry that I might be forced to stay in Lewisburg a while longer. At around 10 p.m., there was a count and then a list was put up showing the names of everyone on the night bus. I scanned it desperately and saw with relief that I was on it. At midnight, a guard called out the names on the list. I said goodbye to Wayne and we were funnelled out of the main gates and onto another bus.

Next stop: New York.

CHAPTER 16

NEW YORK, NEW YORK

As we boarded our bus, I saw that the rear threequarters of it was caged off. About twenty of us were herded into the caged area, all of us in chains and leg irons, while five fully-armed officers sat in the front section, weapons at the ready. I was sitting next to a slim, middle-aged white guy with wild eyes, who told me he was being transported to Florida.

'Listen, dude,' he said. 'If I get the chance, I'm gonna try and escape this bus. You better be ready!'

'What the hell? How are you going to do that?' I was completely taken aback by this.

'If one of the guards comes back here, I'm gonna slip my chains round his neck and take his gun.'

'You're crazy!' I exclaimed. 'I'm not getting involved.'

'That's up to you.' His chains rattled as he shrugged. 'See if I try.'

That's all I need, I thought, some lunatic trying to take a gun off a guard, risking a shoot-out right here on the bus. Naturally I was terrified, but I couldn't say anything. Too nervous now to sleep, all I could do was look out of the window and hope that Wild Eyes wasn't presented with a chance to get us all killed.

Luckily, the ride turned out to be uneventful. None of the guards ventured into the back, but it was undoubtedly the most uncomfortable night I had ever spent. I was stiff and exhausted after seven sleepless hours curled up on a bus seat in chains and leg irons, but eventually we pulled up outside the MCC. It really was a skyscraper prison, about fifteen storeys tall, right there in downtown Manhattan overlooking Brooklyn Bridge. I would learn later that the prison was known to some in the media as 'The

Guantanamo of New York' – a name it earned because of the brutal living conditions and pressure-cooker environment.

My first stop inside the MCC was a solitary holding cell, furnished only with a bench and a toilet. I was passed a toilet roll as I made my way in and I was grateful for it – by turning the roll on its side, I could use it as a pillow and get a few hours' sleep. The one improvement over Allenwood was that the guards here seemed to be friendlier. One of them told me that I could expect to be here for around five weeks, and that Gary and David would be arriving soon as well.

After being left to simmer for a few hours, I was moved to the SHU. I had hated being in solitary confinement at Allenwood and I suspected that it would be even worse at the MCC. I was thrown in a cell with another inmate, a tall African-American called Mel. He was around forty-five years old, very friendly, and he knew the ropes. He kindly shared his watch and radio with me, so at least I could tell the time and pass a few hours listening to music until around 8 a.m., when the SHU became abuzz with shouting and chatter from other cells.

Mel and I had exchanged only a few words by this point, but I was desperate to learn more about the MCC. 'What's rec like?' I asked. 'I heard there's a yard on the roof – is that true?'

Mel nodded. 'Sure is.' He glanced at his watch. 'We go at nine, so you'll be able to find out soon enough.'

Sure enough, at 9 a.m. we were taken up to the top floor. The rec yard consisted of a big basketball court and a few benches to sit on round the edge. Huge walls closed off the view of the skyline on all sides, and a wire mesh was strung above our heads. It was a surreal and depressing place, especially in the cold of that brisk October morning.

Judging by the number of cells on the wing and the size of the prison, I suspected that as many as a hundred inmates could be in the SHU at any given time, but on that morning Mel and I were joined by only one other person. Everyone else had decided that, without coats, it was too cold to venture up to the rec yard. I found myself pulling my arms into the short sleeves of my orange jumpsuit, standing under the air vent and stomping from foot to foot to try to keep warm. After a while, and freezing cold, I didn't blame the others for forgoing their allocated hour of exercise and fresh air per day.

The other guy who had come up for rec was a well-built African-American known as Big Dog. In his company, Mel opened up a bit, introducing us and telling me some more about his own circumstances. Born not too far away in the Bronx, Mel had spent his entire life in and out of prison. All his stays behind bars were, in his own words, for 'bullshit' offences – drugs, bank robbery and, in this case, cheque fraud. However, he wasn't someone to mess with, being spectacularly muscular and around six foot three – a real unit.

'Have you shown him your party trick yet?' Big Dog asked, looking from Mel to me.

Mel laughed. 'Not yet, man.' He held up a finger to me. 'Watch this.' He sat himself down on the nearest bench and put a hand into his jumpsuit at the ankle. To my amazement, he pulled at his right foot and his entire leg followed through the opening at the bottom of his trousers. Having fully removed it, and with the trainer still attached at the foot, he waved his artificial limb around triumphantly.

Big Dog saw the look of disbelief on my face and burst into laughter, as did Mel. Seemingly he liked to surprise people with his fake limb. 'Deep vein thrombosis,' he said, nodding at the empty fabric of his trouser leg. 'Had to have it taken off at the knee.'

I watched, very impressed, as he inserted the prosthesis back into his trousers, reaching in through a hole in his jumpsuit to reattach it, while Big Dog guffawed as if he hadn't seen this act a hundred times over.

Back in the cell, Mel told me more about himself. Perhaps he had been lonely in the SHU and was glad of the company. He had been sent here a few days ago for insulting a counsellor, he revealed.

'I'd usually be more talkative,' he said, 'but I had some bad news and I'm still not over it. I'm not quite myself, you get me?'

'Sure,' I said, 'don't worry about it. What happened?'

'My wife had a stillborn baby only a coupla weeks ago. She wrote but she hasn't been able to see me since, because my visiting days changed and I lost phone privileges after I got sent to the SHU. We only get an hour at a time for visits anyway, once a week, so I don't even know what I can say to her when we do eventually get to see each other. I'm out of stamps as well, to make it even worse. We're both devastated, man, and it's so much harder with me being unable to reach her.'

I could feel Mel's frustration. I didn't have a personal tragedy to contend with, but even then it was bad enough for me being unable to call or write to my family. I didn't have any stamps with me and I hadn't been granted phone privileges at the MCC yet. To make matters worse, I would have to wait a week for commissary, because the guards messed up my shopping order when I first arrived. I was in total anguish not being able to contact anyone to let them know that I had arrived safely in New York. I couldn't imagine how Mel felt, being unable to comfort his poor wife after what they had been through.

We tried to distract ourselves for the rest of the day by playing checkers. I made an improvised board out of a sheet of paper and we tore up another piece to make the counters. We played for hours and then, when we were bored, we both tried to get an early night. I found myself lying awake though, looking through the narrow window in our cell. Through the grimy, barred glass, I could just make out the Chrysler Building up in mid-town, lighting up the darkening sky. I was in one of the greatest cities in the world and yet stuck in this horrendous place. It was a view that reminded me of better days, when I had been in New York on business or on holiday, and it was disheartening to think that I would never be allowed back to the States once this ordeal was over.

When I was finally able to drift off, I had a fitful sleep. I woke up in the middle of the night feeling intensely claustrophobic – not something I had ever experienced in Allenwood. Lying on the top bunk, I was only a couple of feet away from the ceiling and seeing the concrete right in front of my face made me feel boxed in, enclosed, as if I was in a coffin. I could feel the walls getting closer and my chest became tighter and tighter until it was hard to breathe. It took a great effort to calm myself down after that. I had barely slept for more than a few hours when morning started to break through the window.

We were called for rec at around 9 a.m. again, and we gladly made our way up to the roof. Unlike the day before, it was a glorious morning – pleasantly crisp yet still sunny. There would be no rec time over the weekend, so we each spent our hour jogging around the basketball court, trying to make the most of our final few mouthfuls of fresh air until Monday. I was already dreading the prospect of a whole weekend cooped up in the SHU.

Surprisingly, but thankfully, I was given a huge lift that afternoon. Mel and I had just had lunch – cheese and salami sandwiches made from some commissary supplies Mel had been hoarding – when a guard sidled up to our cell door.

'Is there an English guy in here?' he asked.

'Yes, sir!' I shouted.

'Hey, Darby, I'm Officer Butler. I'm handling your transfer. How are you doing?'

'You are? That's great.' I was practically pressed against the bars. 'Can you get me some stamps so I can send some letters? I have no phone time and I can't contact my family at the moment. I know they'll be worrying about me.'

'Don't worry about that. I'll get you out of the SHU early next week, Wednesday at the latest. And we'll have you back in England by the end of November.'

'Sir, that's great news. Thank you.'

Officer Butler smiled. 'Leave it with me.' At that moment, he was my hero. The news about a November transfer meant I would only be doing some six weeks in the MCC. I did some quick mental arithmetic: I did seven months at Allenwood ... plus six weeks, is eight and a half months. Take that off thirty-seven months and you're left with twenty-eight and a half months to do in the UK. That gets cut in half for good behaviour, so let's say fifteen months, and if I get released on tag and curfew, that's another four months off . . . All in all, this could mean being out towards the end of the next year – around November if all went well. The DOJ had stuck to its word. We would end up serving the eighteen months that we had agreed. It was the best news I had received for a very long time.

That afternoon there was more good news: I was allowed to take my first shower since leaving Pennsylvania three days ago! I couldn't remember the last time I had gone that long without washing. I was so glad to be clean that I wasn't even annoyed when the guards told me there were no more towels, so I would have to dry myself with my sweaty shirt. It was good to feel fresh and to get out of the cell, even if only for a few minutes.

However, not everyone on the wing was having such a good day. When I got back, there was a deafening noise coming from a nearby cell. Someone was laughing – hysterically, not happily – while another inmate kept making animal noises at the top of his voice and pounding on the cell walls. This was not a good place to be and I knew it. At least the prospect of the UK was close now – nearer than it had been at any point since I was extradited. I could see the end of the nightmare for the first time since that day in 2001 when we three were the headline on the breakfast news. That was seven and a half long years ago.

After dinner, things improved again. A guard came to our cell and called my name.

'Yes, sir?' I was hoping he would have the stamps for me to send a letter back to the UK. But he had something even better.

'Get your stuff, Darby. You're going to the general population.'

'What, now? Tonight?'

'Yeah. Get moving.'

What a gift! Mel was a nice guy, but it was a relief to be leaving our cramped little cell. After the relative openness of Allenwood, I was finding the confined conditions of the MCC hard to bear.

It took less than a minute to strip my bed and bundle up my sheets with the rest of my meagre possessions. Then I was out of there. I said a hurried goodbye and thank you to Mel and was taken in a lift to the fifth floor. There, I was handed over to the duty officer, who led me to my cell. On the way, we passed through a communal area with televisions and a pool table and eventually reached a cell roughly the same size as the one I had just left.

The difference here was that the cell door wasn't locked, so I was free to move about as I wished. It meant I could exercise, walk around, watch television, interact with other people and, most importantly, make phone calls. I could finally let my family know I was okay. The relief came crashing over me in a wave, almost overwhelming me. I was so glad to be out of the SHU that I could have cried.

A new cell meant a new cellie – a guy called Johnny, a tall and muscular African-American in his late twenties. He was in for drugs, he said. Other than that, he didn't say much, but he did give me a pair of khaki trousers and a T-shirt so I could change out of my jumpsuit, which I much appreciated.

I was making my bed – top bunk for the new guy, as usual – when someone walked into my cell. 'Welcome, stranger!'

I turned around and saw with surprise that it was David Bermingham – my co-defendant and old friend, the man with whom I had spent countless hours obsessing over the intricacies of our case. I was stunned.

'Wha-a-at? What are you doing here?' I stuttered. 'I never thought they'd put us on the same unit!'

'Nice to see you too, mate,' he said, laughing. 'No, I didn't think so either, but here we are.'

'Bloody hell, David, it's been a while. How are you holding up?'

'I've been better, but about as well as can be expected. How about you?'

'Much the same, to be honest. Wait, where's Gary? Is he here too?'

'Don't know. I heard he's stuck in a county jail somewhere in Florida. Apparently, they've lost his paperwork.'

'Shit,' I said. 'Still, I guess he'll turn up soon. We're flying home in five weeks or so.'

'Well, that's something. How was your journey here?'

'No fun, but I imagine it was better than yours?' David had come all the way from California.

'It took me two weeks of BOP travelling to get here. Penitentiaries, holding cells, Oklahoma, Atlanta, county jails, all-night bus rides in chains. Awful. Still, at least we're both here now.'

We spent the next couple of hours catching up. I had been apprehensive about seeing David again. The stress of everything that had happened to us had strained all of our relationships, but now we were in the same room I felt better than I thought I would. I told him I was pleased to see him, more so than I had expected to be, and he laughed.

'Why's that?' he asked.

'Well, we had our share of issues, didn't we? I wasn't sure how I'd feel when I saw you again.'

'Well, thanks very much!' he laughed. 'It's good to see a familiar face, isn't it?'

'It is. Don't take it personally, mate. I haven't found any part of this process easy and I'm not exactly thrilled to be here.'

'No, me neither.'

As miserable as the MCC was, it helped to have an old friend there. We swapped stories about our experiences for a while and then David showed me to his cell. Between David and his cellie, a Colombian guy called Torro, I was given a handful of supplies to get me through until the next commissary day. Before then, however, I had to make it through a weekend of being cooped up with nothing to do: I didn't have a radio, so I couldn't listen to the television, and there was nothing to read apart from a Bible.

There was only so much talking David and I could do. As good as it was to see him, everything we had been through made it difficult for us to be together for long periods of time. I started to withdraw into myself a bit more each day, spending my time walking around the basketball court on the rooftop rec yard, or watching American football without any sound. Even the meals were more boring than at Allenwood, as we were given our food on trays and ate it in our cells, or in the communal areas on the unit. There was no chow hall to go to, which meant one less way to kill time.

The MCC really was a miserable place. It was predictably claustrophobic being locked up at the top of a high-rise, and it was much harder to pass the days without a decent rec yard or any of the other amenities I had become used to. The only material improvement over my former home was that the MCC, or my wing at least, was cleaner and kept in a far more hygienic condition than Allenwood ever was. It meant that I didn't have to worry so much about picking up an infection that could delay my transfer home – or worse.

Within a few days I had been kitted out with my full clothing issue. I was also able to buy a radio and a smattering of other supplies at commissary. That certainly helped to take the edge off being stuck in the MCC, but I was still struggling to adjust to my new circumstances. For one, sharing a cell with someone new served to remind me how lucky I had been with El and, to an extent, T. Both of my old cellies were roughly the same age as me and very chilled out. The three of us slotted together nicely – we were respectful of each other and made a point of making sure that everyone had their own space and plenty of alone time.

My new roommate, Johnny, was much younger and still awaiting his sentence (expected to be around the twenty-year mark), so it wasn't as if he'd had the time to mellow out and relax about being in prison, in the same way that El and T had. Everything was still fairly unfamiliar to Johnny, and he was incredibly stressed out about everything to do with this new way of life. To make matters worse, he didn't have a job, so he spent days on end moping in the cell, bored out of his mind.

I knew first-hand that trouble starts when boredom kicks in, and I didn't want to be anywhere near Johnny when he boiled over. Judging by his body language and the aura of tension that he exuded, I suspected it would be a matter of when, not if. So I tried my best to avoid him as much as I could, spending time in the TV room or on the rec yard whenever possible. At first, I looked to David for company, but after a couple more days I found myself trying to avoid him as well. It was just too hard to be around him – it reminded me of all that had happened. I was still angry, devastated really, about how my life had been completely wrecked. For that reason too, I was already dreading the inevitable day when Gary would show up.

Thankfully, David's cellie, Torro, proved to be very good company. I found myself sitting with him most afternoons, enjoying his relaxed and positive mental outlook, a complete contrast to Johnny's moaning. One afternoon as we were eating dinner, Torro told me that he worked in the prison's watch, a job that, to my knowledge, didn't exist at Allenwood.

'What does that entail, then?' I asked.

'Well, the MCC is a high-security institution, because it's used as a pre-trial detention centre. That means there are all sorts of types scattered around all the units. I mean, I heard one guy here got sentenced to death last week. Anyway, you get lots of people with psychological problems and if any of them show signs of it, then they go into suicide watch. It's like the SHU but worse. You get dressed in a smock and put in a room with only a bunk, a toilet and a washbasin. That's it.'

'What do people do all day?' I asked. 'What about writing and reading or anything like that?'

Torro shook his head. 'They don't do nothing. Sleep. Exercise. That's about it. There's no books, no writing implements. Not even bedsheets in case they try to hang themselves. The idea is to take everything away from them and just observe their psychological state. There's a one-way mirror on the side of the room and that's where we watch them from. Every fifteen minutes we have to write down what the inmate has been doing and generally observe their behaviour.'

'But what do they actually do?'

'When they're not sleeping, a lot just stare into space. Some talk a lot to themselves about their cases, or about their families. They keep the lights on all the time, though, so it's hard for them to sleep properly. Some of the guys in there are in real trouble – they cry, try to harm themselves, slam their heads against the wall. Others just shout. The worst is when they take their own waste and either cover themselves in it or smear it on the walls. After a few days we're supposed to have a proper psychological picture of them. Then the doctors decide how to treat them, what medication to put them on. The truth is that some people simply can't cope with what is happening to them. They can't cope with their sentences, with being here.'

In the oppressive environment of the MCC, I could understand how some inmates snapped. The low ceilings seemed to be creeping closer by the day, such was the sense of confinement, and I had been here for less than a week. I couldn't imagine a worse place to spend an entire sentence – as some unfortunate inmates did.

Distractions were few and far between, but a couple of days after my chat with Torro, one presented itself. Our wing was arranged with eight cells sharing a small common area and a toilet, and all sixteen of us who used that space went to great pains to keep it clean and hygienic. We would all wipe and disinfect tables after eating, mop the floor in the bathroom, and generally keep a close eye on the state of our area.

You can imagine, then, that there was considerable concern one morning when I noticed the shower wasn't draining properly. I called a couple of the guys in to look at it and they agreed that things didn't look right. When one of the guys flushed the toilet, it started to fill with water and showed no signs of stopping. We watched in total horror as a well of water rose in the bowl and then started to pour over the sides, splashing all over the floor.

'Shit!' someone shouted. Literally, I thought, as I watched the water level in the shower start to rise as well, the water leaking back into our bathroom through the drain. 'Someone in the SHU must have flushed an overall or something,' someone else said. However, there was very little we could do about it – after all, we were criminals, not plumbers – so we went to chow and then came back to check on the bathroom later that morning.

We had hoped that the flood would have been fixed by then, but the situation had only grown worse. The shower tray was almost overflowing with water – dirty water, not the clean stuff we had been dealing with earlier – and the toilet was in a similar state. The smell was disgusting and the colour of the standing water didn't bear thinking about. We had arrived just in time, because filthy water started to spill out of the toilet bowl a moment later, soaking the floor and splashing over our shoes.

We knew that if something wasn't done, the rancid spillage would seep into our living area and, far worse, our cells. A couple of guys reacted quickly, grabbing the nearest mop and bucket and attempting to clear up the mess. The rest of us stood like horrified statues until a shout of 'Come on then, you motherfuckers, get some buckets and start helping!' spurred us into action.

A couple of the younger guys – including Johnny – disappeared, refusing to help. Someone else ran back into the unit and emerged a few moments later with a pair of wellies. I had no idea where they came from, but I pulled them on gratefully and splashed over to the shower. The water level was rising ever closer to the ten-inch lip that protected us from the deluge. I knew that if the water rose above that point, we'd have shit everywhere and be well and truly scuppered.

One guy handed me some gloves and a bucket and I started bailing out the shower, gagging as I scooped the bucket through the brown-tinged water. There was a big open drain in the laundry room and we figured out quickly that this would be our salvation. Chain-gang style, I bailed water and passed the full bucket to someone, who ran to the laundry to empty it. Meanwhile a fresh bucket was put into my hand and the process would be repeated once more. We had soon filled and emptied around ten buckets, but still the water kept coming, leaking endlessly from the shower drain so that we were never more than minutes away from being flooded.

All the while I kept retching, having to force myself not to vomit at the smell. It took two arduous hours before we had the situation under control, by which time we were all exhausted and reeking. Fortunately, someone elsewhere in the prison had fixed the plumbing issue, so the danger had passed: but there was still the not insignificant matter of the filthy state of the bathroom, which had been soaked with shitty water. It took another two hours, and a whole barrel of detergent, before the space was in a clean and sanitary condition again, by which time I was about ready to pass out from a combination of disgust and exhaustion.

Thankfully, a long-serving inmate on the unit insisted that I should get one of the first showers as soon as the bathroom was clean. I ended up scrubbing myself so hard and so thoroughly that it was amazing I had any skin left by the time I was done. The most perverse thing of all, though, was that I wasn't even mad about what had happened; if anything, I was pleased that I had been able to kill a few more hours dealing with the mess. Talk about a shitstorm.

CHAPTER 17

THE NATWEST THREE

Every night of incarceration brought me another day closer to the UK, to being able to see my family, have my sentence cut in half and my eventual release. I was desperate to 'lose' a few hours here or thirty minutes there in any way I could, always on the lookout for things to keep me occupied or to make the time pass that little bit faster.

Here in New York, I found a welcome distraction in the 2008 presidential election. I had been following the coverage whilst I was in Allenwood, watching the debates between Barack Obama and John McCain and between their vice-presidential nominees, Joe Biden and Sarah Palin. When the results of the election came in I knew that I would always remember the moment when America elected its first black president. Where were you when Barack Obama became President of the United States? I was in a high-rise prison in downtown Manhattan, witnessing the wild celebrations of the majority of the inmates.

I, too, had hoped that Obama would win. After the tenure of George W. Bush – a man who had played a significant role in my imprisonment – it seemed that change would be a good thing and that is precisely what Obama was offering. The mood in the predominantly African-American MCC was jubilant and indeed most of the prisoners were delighted. Many of them believed he would address the tricky subject of prison reform, and maybe even free some guys who shouldn't have been behind bars in the first place.

As CNN called the result, there was clapping, whooping and cheering throughout every wing, the sounds of delight echoing through the halls. It was an amazing moment and I could feel my hair standing on end. The atmosphere was that electric. A couple of days later, as the euphoria of Obama's victory began to fade, dull reality resumed. David and I were taken to a nearby courthouse to confirm that we had applied for a transfer of our own free will, and that we both voluntarily wanted to go back to the UK. We knew Gary would be at the hearing as well, the first time I had seen him since leaving Texas all those months ago. David and I were put in a holding cell at the courthouse and after a while Gary joined us. It was a strange reunion, by any measure.

Gary told us that he had been at the MCC for over a week, but had been forced to stay in the SHU the whole time. Not only that, it had taken him three weeks to get from his Texas prison to the MCC and he was still feeling run-down from the ordeal. He had been subjected to what inmates called 'diesel therapy'. When the BOP wanted to punish an inmate who was being transferred between institutions, the prison authorities would often cook up the most convoluted, protracted and unpleasant route across the country, stopping off needlessly at unpleasant facilities on the way.

It seemed that Gary was thought to be the ringleader of our little group, so the BOP had subjected him to a considerably worse cross-country journey than either David or me. He looked awful for it – haggard, thin, unshaven, unwashed and exhausted. Not that this was surprising, given the circumstances.

'Well, Gary,' David began. 'You look good.' He had a way of being gratingly, excessively optimistic at times, often in the face of bleak reality.

'No, you don't,' I said, meeting Gary's eyes for the first time. 'You look bloody awful, mate.' Even he laughed at that.

The good news was that Gary, like David and I, had in general kept his health and sanity intact, at least up until his miserable transfer. Despite our circumstances, this meant that we were soon laughing together like the old friends we once were, sharing stories about the ridiculous goings-on inside our respective prisons and now our shared home, the MCC. The time passed quickly and, before long, after a brief but joyful reunion with our legal teams, we were in front of the judge for our fifteen-minute hearing. Then it was back to the MCC, another day ticked off, another day closer to getting out of there. Now we were all together again, it felt as if we really were on the home straight.

Because the MCC was largely a pre-trial detention centre, most of the inmates were there for only a few months before being moved on. Knowing I would be there for just weeks, I didn't make much of an effort to get to know anybody. Compared to Allenwood, the inmates at the MCC were incredibly insular anyway, focused only on their own circumstances and unlikely to take much interest in anyone else. Very few of the people around me could be bothered with socialising, and I felt much the same. After a while, I even stopped going up to the yard at the daily 6 p.m. rec call – there was nothing to do on top of the skyscraper and nobody to do it with. It was such a contrast to the surprisingly vibrant and fulfilling social experience I had encountered at Allenwood. Here, there was no football to play, no basketball games to watch, no running track to walk around with fellow inmates. Mostly it was just me, and occasionally Gary and David.

Gary was released from the SHU shortly after our court appearance. He caught me by surprise as I was watching an old Bond film, on one of the rare occasions when nobody had laid claim to the television. I went to get a cup of tea and found him waiting for me in the living area when I returned. He had been given a chance to shower and shave now and as a result he looked considerably better than when I had last seen him at the courthouse.

With our stay in America likely to last only a few more days, we found ourselves reflecting on all our experiences. I had been thinking especially about the different pathways of our lives which had branched out in such unexpected directions. Some had led to success, some to failure – and this one path we had taken, which had led to criminality and then incarceration in the United States.

I recognised that, as dreadful as my ordeal had been, I was a better man because of it. I also saw that I was lucky. I still had my family and my friends, my sanity and my health.

All in all, I still had a future, and this nightmare experience would be over before I was fifty. It would always be painful, however, to reflect on the scores of men I had met in Allenwood who didn't have any of the things that I had.

Some might argue that men like them were just hopeless cases, but that wouldn't be true. Hope was the one thing I had encountered in abundance. Some of it was misplaced, but many of the guys I met were stoic in their outlook and so their current circumstances didn't even matter. Most of them believed that one day they would get out and have a chance to rebuild their lives, to start again.

Unfortunately, of course, that wasn't always how things worked out. When El and I were both back out on the street, we found each other on social media and stayed in regular contact. I wanted him to come to the UK, but he was never able to. Sadly like so many convicted ex-felons, he couldn't manage to stay out of trouble, and he got involved in drugs and firearms again. In August 2019, he received another twelve-year sentence and at the time of writing is incarcerated again. I wanted to weep when I found out.

Yet I still believe that people like El, who had been so kind to me and expected nothing in return, were not fundamentally bad people. They were victims of circumstance or, more simply, a broken system that they were unlucky enough to be born into: they were men who had made terrible mistakes once or twice in their lives but that didn't make them inherently and irredeemably criminal.

I sincerely hoped that everyone I had met would think about the pathways their own lives could have taken – and make the right choices next time. I knew that I would.

EPILOGUE

April 2021

No more than a couple of weeks after our final court appearance in America, first Gary and then David were repatriated to the UK. I was the last to go and was overjoyed when an officer from Wandsworth came to find me in the unit.

It was the day before Thanksgiving, in November 2008. I was handcuffed and secured with leg irons and chains before being bundled into a police car for the journey to the airport. We sped along in a three-car convoy under blue light, all the way through downtown Manhattan to JFK. That was the last time I saw – or will ever see – New York. The chances of me being granted a US visa again are precisely zero.

We raced along the airport road system directly onto the tarmac and I was whisked straight up the steps of the waiting 747. There was no customs or passport control for me – VIP treatment indeed. As on the way out, officers, this time from Wandsworth, sat either side of me at the back of the plane.

Once we had taken off, an air hostess came down the aisle towards us.

'Does he want a drink?' she asked. She had glanced at me before directing her question to one of the officers.

'Do you want a drink?' he asked me.

'Can I get a beer?'

'No,' he said. 'You can have a soft drink or water.'

'Okay.' The beer would have to wait. 'I'll have a Coke then, please.'

'Coke, please,' said the officer.

A few minutes later, the air hostess came back with my drink.

'Do you want a meal?' she asked him. 'It's Thanksgiving, so we have roast turkey.'

'Yes, please.'

'And what about him?' She looked at me.

'He speaks,' said the warder.

I couldn't help but burst out laughing, and before I knew it, I was peeling the cellophane off my turkey dinner. It was so good compared to prison food that I asked for a second meal – and I got one.

Hours later, we landed back at Heathrow. Over the course of a few weeks, I went via Wandsworth (an awful Victorian prison, where I was locked in a cell twenty-three hours a day) to open prisons at Ford, in West Sussex, and then Leyhill, near Gloucester.

At the time, Leyhill was one of only two open prisons in the UK that housed sex offenders and some two-thirds of the inmates were lollipops. Being surrounded by them day and night made it very different and a much lonelier place than Allenwood, or even the MCC, had been. To say I hated it was an understatement, but I do realise that you're not supposed to enjoy being inside: and I didn't.

I arrived at Leyhill in January 2009 and qualified for day release in March that year. I was allocated an outside job under prison control at a warehouse in Gloucester in June and granted HDC (Home Detention Curfew) with a tag, as it is commonly known, in October 2009. I was on probation until April 2010. Over a decade has passed since I was released.

This book isn't about my personal life, but I am now very happily married to the most wonderful woman I have ever met – my wife, Lisa – and my five gorgeous daughters have all grown into very happy and healthy women. In addition, they have to date produced nine beautiful grandchildren. My marvellous mother, who was my greatest supporter throughout all these events, is now into her eighties and still thriving. I can never thank them enough for their unwavering love and support throughout some very dark times that affected us all.

After coming out of prison, and having paid my debt to society, some truly amazing friends have supported me in business, and along with my family have enabled me to rebuild my life. I won't embarrass any of them by naming them, but they know who they are, and I thank each of them from the bottom of my heart.

I consider myself lucky to have lived the life that I have done. You can't change the past. It is over. I regret nothing that happened and have no resentment towards anybody involved in the events described in this book. Life truly is for living and that is what I have tried to do.

As my great and lifelong friend, Gary Mulgrew, says: 'It wasn't the life we expected, but bloody hell, mate – what a life!'

ACKNOWLEDGEMENTS

Gary, David and their families, always strong and determined even in the dark times.

Dan, Dick, Matt, Reid, David and Kevin for their patience, advice and guidance.

My gorgeous girls who never wavered in their support and my indomitable Mother who never flinched.

Alun, Peter, Malcolm and Stephan who gave us all the help and support they could.

Melksham Rugby Club 2002–06 for the haven it provided.

John, Katherine, Mike, Bev, Simmo and Woolfy. Always there. Always brilliant.

Bob, Teresa, Troy and Jimmy for keeping us all in line.

Ernie and the pickup soccer gang – would love to do it again.

The Richmond Arms and the Wet Spot crew. You know who you are.

John Mounsey and all at Key Finance who showed faith in me and helped me get back on my feet.

Gary and Kate Burlison who got us started in the trade. Thank you.

Ali, Dan, Trev, Deb, Mad and all our friends and locals from the Marlborough in Ciren. First pub, great times.

RIP Robbo. Great guy. Sadly missed.

The Howes family who went through hell with me.

George, Tom and all at Quiller Publishing for getting the book done.

All my family, friends, former and current colleagues and all the locals that there isn't room to mention

And finally, my gorgeous wife Lisa who saved my life and then helped me rebuild it, I am truly grateful.